D1480477

AMERICA'S
CHRISTMAS
HERITAGE

AMERICA'S CHRISTMAS HERITAGE

Ruth Cole Kainen

FUNK & WAGNALLS

New York

TO

MY MOTHER,

who taught me the pleasures of eating
and preparing good food
and

MARY JANE FISHER,

without whose inspiration and help
this book would never have been written

Published by Funk & Wagnalls,
A Division of Reader's Digest Books, Inc.

Printed in the United States of America
DESIGNED BY VINCENT TORRE
2
All photographs by City News Bureau, Inc.

Contents

Introduction

THE GLORY AND BOUNTY OF AMERICA'S CHRISTMAS

Christmas is a time of nostalgia when we can slip momentarily out of reality and daily problems into a Never-Never Land of innocent childhood and dream unashamedly of a world where everything always worked out right, and there was shelter, gaiety, laughter, and affection—and exactly the right presents under a magical Christmas tree.

"Christmas cheer is to be six years old on a sunny December day," one adult observed recently, "and have a parent, grandparent, or teacher to take you out to see the Christmas sights."

He was watching a tiny girl dawdling along behind her mother on New York's Fifth Avenue. Suddenly, the child spied a sidewalk Santa Claus. In a flash, she darted ahead and threw her arms around him. Lovingly, she planted a big wet kiss on Santa's cheek, then ran back to her mother, all in a few seconds and without a word. "Just look at that!" he exclaimed. "And she didn't even ask for anything."

Christmas is a glamorous, joyous period which returns unfailingly each year at exactly the same time, imperceptibly establishing a rhythm in our complicated, busy lives. For the majority of Americans, it is the only celebration which remains from ancient times when man observed countless seasonal rituals that reassured him of his place in creation and renewed his ties with his ancestors and his children, with the past and with the future. For this reason alone, the holiday is especially valuable in a country where individuals tend to forget their origins before they establish firm roots in the present.

Since it began, Christmas has been a family observance, and one intimately connected with the ceremony of breaking bread together and feasting.

"Christmas just does not seem like Christmas to me," a Swedish-American friend said, "if I can't go back to the South Side of Chicago for the ceremony of *'Doppa y grytan,'* to 'dip in the pot' with my family's Swedish friends on Christmas Eve." The ritual he mentioned (described in detail in Chapter XI) is only one of many cherished Christmas customs preserved in this country. On the North Side of Chicago, for instance, another national group celebrates in an entirely different manner, as described by a member of the Mexican Civic Committee.

"I am only to happy to say that we still observe the old Mexican customs," he wrote. "This year we had *piñatas*—one clown, one chicken, one burro—and it was a pleasure to see the children enjoy them. [See Chapter IX for further explanation.] We prepare tamales, bunuelos, and some prepare what is known as *Ti Limon* [a Mexican drink unlike our tea]. And above all the midnight mass. When the Child is born, and one young woman is sponsour of the Child, that is when all the fiesta comes to live." His unintentional misspelling somehow made his description more vivid.

No matter how affluent he may become in later years, and how accustomed to *haute cuisine*, every man enjoys most the foods he ate when a child, and never so much as at Christmastime. Ask him about Christmas, and a faraway look will come into his eyes as he describes the Christmas cakes and breads his mother made.

"My mother began baking in November," one Army general from Virginia volunteered. "I'll never forget her warning when I came home from school. 'If you go in the kitchen,' she would say, 'walk on tiptoe. The fruit cake is in the oven!' "

In New Jersey, a young Ukrainian-American said that she always makes *kutya* for her husband, "because he has had it for every Christmas since he was a tiny boy in Russia."

Kutya, traditional from pre-Christian times, is described in detail in Chapter XII.

Perhaps the most poignant illustration of how men long for childhood favorites came from a Norwegian-American living in Washington, D.C. "In Minnesota, *lefse*, a special bread made with potatoes, begins to appear in the bakeries around Christmastime," she said, "but you can't find it anywhere in this city. Last year, I happened to call on my neighbors one December afternoon. The wife is French and a wonderful French cook, but her husband is Norwegian. There he was in the kitchen, cooking *lefse* for himself! They were pretty good, too."

So it is with virtually every nationality which has come to the United States. Contributions to our Christmas bounty are not limited to those from Christian nations. Among the people who have given our Christmas an exotic flavor are the first Americans, the Indians. Before the coming of the white man, they held feasts of their own in December, around the time of the winter solstice. Today, in the Yukon, Alaska, they continue to do so, having moved the big community feast or potlatch to Christmas.

Each family in the Yukon brings plates or bowls for all its members, and the leaders serve the food—usually moose stew and bear meat—from common containers. It is customary for a woman to bring a dish for a man of her family who cannot come. After the feast, there are Indian dances, performed in beautiful costumes and strange masks. Just before the old year ends, villagers gather to scrub the floors of all public buildings, in the same way that many of our European ancestors have always done.

In our American Southwest, there are also Indian feasts and dances during the Christmas holidays. In addition, Spanish descendants honor a Mexican saint, the Virgin of Guadalupe; Swedish Americans celebrate St. Lucy's Day; German descendants decorate a German Christmas tree with aromatic cookies; Mexican Americans hold *posadas;* and American Jews keep Chanukah, the Jewish Festival of Lights which has become an integral part of our American holiday celebrations. (All these observances are described later, as well as the traditional foods which go with them.)

Oriental Americans add still different exoticisms to our Christmas. In San Francisco a loquacious taxi driver, telling of his family celebration, vividly illustrated how our American Christmas pattern continues to evolve. "We go both ways for Christmas," he said. "My parents are from the West, and they like turkey, but my wife is Japanese, so she makes some Japanese dishes to go with it. In the living room we have a regular Christmas tree; but she makes a Japanese-style centerpiece for the dining table with a huge boned fish that looks as though it were still whole."

Christmas, it has been said, has its own laws. By building on what it found, it formed a distinct pattern in each country where it took hold. In the United States, the pattern is myriad. As in a turning kaleidoscope, we see first one design, then another, but never the whole and seldom the same thing. It would be impossible to list every tiny facet of the complete American Christmas picture. So we shall try instead to display something of its infinite variety, and perhaps reveal the holiday in a new and different light.

NOTE OF EXPLANATION

An effort has been made in this book not to include recipes requiring ingredients not readily available. In a few instances, however, unusual items (bitter almonds, for instance, and Hungarian paprika) are given. These can be obtained directly or by mail from Paprika Weiss, 1546 Second Avenue, New York, N.Y. 10028. Any flour, including hard wheat flour, may be ordered from the Great Valley Mills, Quakertown, Pennsylvania 18951. Potash can be purchased from a druggist.

Pan sizes are not always listed for fruit cakes and breads if the size is not mandatory, so that the cook may use the pans she has. We find an 8½-inch tube pan with a removable tube and a 9⅝ x 5½ x 2¾ loaf pan particularly convenient for making cakes; a 9-inch tube pan and the loaf pan are especially good for breads. When bread is made in braids or flat loaves it may be placed on any flat baking tin that will hold it.

Directions for mixing bread with an electric mixer are frequently given, as this is an easier method than mixing by hand. When a mixer is used, the dough will thicken before all the flour is completely added, and it will crawl up the mixer blades. Obviously, at this point the operation should be completed by hand. Though directions may seem obscure on first reading, in actual operation they should be quite clear and self-explanatory.

An American Christmas Holiday
CALENDAR

Four Sundays before Christmas, Advent begins. On the first Sunday, some people light one candle, then add one more each succeeding Sunday.

December

5   Eve of the Feast of St. Nicholas
6   Feast of St. Nicholas
10 Beginning of Tortugas Indian celebration of Feast of Our Lady of Guadalupe in New Mexico
11 Continuance of Tortugas observance
12 Feast of Our Lady of Guadalupe, Patroness of the Americas
13 Feast of St. Lucia or St. Lucy
16 Beginning of *Las Posadas* in areas where the ceremony is conducted in its original form, as novena
24 Christmas Eve
25 Christmas
31 Eve of the Feast of St. Basil
    New Year's Eve

January

1   Feast of St. Basil
   New Year's Day
5   Eve of Epiphany
   Eve of Armenian Christmas
   Twelfth Night
   Beginning of Mardi Gras
6   Epiphany
   Date on which Armenians celebrate Christ's Birthday
   Christmas Eve, old calendar
7   Christmas, old calendar
18 Eve of Epiphany, old calendar
19 Epiphany, old calendar

February

2   Candlemas

AMERICA'S
CHRISTMAS
HERITAGE

CHAPTER I

How Our Christmas Began

Christmas is a time of renewal. It ends the old year and begins the new on a positive note. Just when we begin to succumb to the depression that increasingly shorter days and early dark bring, we are swept up in preparations for the Christmas-New Year holidays. By the time they are past, the days have begun to grow perceptibly longer once more and spring seems imminent, even though winter has just begun.

If there were no Merry Christmas and Happy New Year, we would have to invent an equivalent, just as our ancestors did some twenty-five centuries or more ago. Long before the time of Christ, many of our most treasured Christmas customs were part of pagan year-end festivities in the Near East, Rome, and Northern Europe. At a later time, but prior to Columbus' discovery of America, similar activities developed on this continent.

Primitive man directed all his energies to maintaining enough food to live. Consequently, he set his calendar according to the period of fertility and plenty. Where he depended upon a harvest of crops, as in Egypt and Rome, the year

3

revolved around the summer months of vegetation. Farther north, where herds were his mainstay, the year's pattern was controlled by the cycle of animal life.

At the end of his calendar year, when fertility ceased and starvation threatened, early man performed ritual ceremonies aimed at reinvigorating the soil, the sun, or his animals. At the same time, he began to weave myths of creation and existence to explain the natural phenomena of the seasons and the annual revitalization of nature.

In Egypt, the year began with the overflow of the Nile in mid-July. Early in the fifth century B.C. some astronomer must have noticed that the Dog Star always rose in the sky just before the annual flood and realized that time repeats its pattern. Taking this fixed date, he devised a calendar of twelve months with thirty days each.

The five remaining days were intercalary days and belonged neither to the year nor to the months. The Egyptians explained them by saying that Keb, the earth god, once laid a curse on the sky goddess, Nut, so that she could not bear a child in any month or in any year, and that the wily goddess outsmarted him by giving birth during the intercalary days to five important Egyptian deities.

In Mexico, the Aztecs also had a calendar with twelve thirty-day months, and the remaining period was known as the *nemontemi*, or five empty days. They were so dreaded and feared that all fires were extinguished and artistry and business ceased. As in Egypt, feasting was general.

The Egyptians considered the five days extraordinary and devoted them to honoring their gods, feasting, and predicting the future. It has been speculated, but never proved, that the sacred Twelve Days of Christmas originated as intercalary days and that their peculiar customs and superstitions derived from this background. The current favorite song, "The Twelve Days of Christmas," may be based on notions connected with the leftover period. The song apparently began as part of pagan year-end mummery.

The Romans inherited agrarian festivals from their ances-

4

tors. Their forebears had been concerned with a multitude of spirits representing the forces of nature, with which they sought to preserve harmony so the gods would work for the family's benefit.

For five centuries before Christ, the family unit or clan was supreme in Rome. It was a rather large organization comprised of the mother and father, their house and property, their children, their married sons and their wives, their sons' children, their slaves, and their clients. This miniature society was a rigid patriarchy in which the father ruled with absolute authority until death.

The Roman family was also an association of persons and property with gods. It was the center and source of religion, a religion that gave divine sanctions and support to the family. The father believed his spirit would suffer endless misery if no son succeeded him to tend his grave, so religion promoted fertility and accorded mothers profound love and respect. Public opinion condemned childlessness.

The home was thought to be protected by the god Janus, represented as having two faces, one watching over the entry, and the other facing the opposite direction to guard the exit. New Year superstitions involving front and back doors to a house are still prevalent today.

The Roman calendar was adjusted periodically in an attempt to make it jibe with nature. The calendar centered around festivals honoring the gods, a group constantly expanded through trade and conquest. Every December, Roman citizens held a joyful feast in worship of the spirits of the soil. The following month they laid out rich gifts for the goddess of fertility, in hope of a bountiful harvest.

The Romans believed greatest devotion was due *Terra Mater*, Mother Earth, magic tender of sprouting seed, source and sustainer of life, and home of the dead. Their innate reverence toward motherhood was further evidenced by the adoption in the second century B.C. of two new goddesses of fertility. From Greece they took Cybele, and from Egypt, Isis.

Cybele was honored by a spring festival, during which her

5

image was triumphantly carried through the streets and joyfully hailed by Roman crowds as *Nostra Domina*, Our Lady. Isis, referred to in divine litanies as the "Queen of Heaven" and "Mother of God," was even more popular. Her worship spread throughout Europe via the important waterways, and icons in her honor have been found on the Danube, the Rhine, and the Seine. A temple to her was unearthed in London.

Just prior to the period of Christian ascendancy in Rome, three major festivals were celebrated. Beginning December 17, there was an eight-day festival honoring Saturn; on December 24, a feast for the Oriental God of Light, Mithras; and at the beginning of the new year, the Kalends. In addition, the Jews kept what was then a minor observance, the Feast of Lights or Rededication of the Temple.

According to Roman legend, Saturn was the greatest god of all, the father of gods then worshiped. It was believed that as a prehistoric king he had taught the tribes the secrets of agriculture and brought law and order, peace and equality. His reign was fondly recalled as the Golden Age and imitated during *Saturnalia*, the festival in his honor.

Saturnalia began with public sacrifice of a young pig, a token of fertility, prosperity, and good luck. There were fairs and games, and banquets at which master and slave exchanged places in memory of the time when all men were equal. No punishment of criminals was allowed; grudges and quarrels were forgotten; schools and courts were closed. All work, and even war, ceased, as it usually has for Christmas in modern times.

Mithraism was introduced in Rome sometime during the first century A.D. and immediately gained great popularity. Mithras was a virile young hero, a god of light, purity, truth, and honor, who yearly overpowered the forces of darkness threatening to engulf the earth. Because of a miscalculation in the time of the winter solstice, the great feast in his honor was held on December 24. The fact that the days always grew longer afterward seemed ample proof of his invincibility.

The festival honoring Mithras was known as *Natalis Solis*

Invicti, the Birthday of the Unconquered Sun. When the celebration of Christmas was established, the word *Natalis* was incorporated into the formal Latin title, probably by design.

The Kalends in the first days of January, named for the double-faced Janus, were remarkable as a period of unusual generosity. Mutual wishes of health and prosperity were exchanged by all; presents were given to friends and children, and generous donations made to the poor. In the beginning the presents are said to have been boughs of greenery brought from the groves of the goddess Strenia. *Strenae*, the Roman word for the presents, found its way into the French language as *étrennes*, a word still used in France to denote the presents brought by St. Nicholas on New Year's Day. In Acadian Louisiana the term was commonplace for Christmas gifts until recent years, and is still heard occasionally. In Rome, *strenae* served as good-luck charms.

During the Roman festival period, mummers dressed in grotesque animal-skin costumes roamed and capered in the streets. In the home, candles and lamps were kept burning to frighten away the threatening spirits of darkness. Boughs of laurel and green trees were hung with trinkets, toys, and small masks of Bacchus. The followers of Mithras sometimes fastened an image of the sun god to the very tip of the tree and placed candles on the boughs. In America, this custom came full circle when golden sunburst discs were hung profusely on a White House tree as tokens of good luck. Probably elaborate tinsel-decorated ornaments with a tiny image of the sun god, a bridegroom's headdress imported from India, have also been used as tree-toppers. (See illustration, plate 3.)

As time went on, Roman New Year gifts became more elaborate—candles and lamps, precious stones, gold and silver coins, sweet pastry in the shape of animals and men, dolls, and imitation wax fruits. The pastry and dolls appear to have been symbols of former living sacrifices, and wax fruits were undoubtedly connected with ancient fertility rites.

THE BEGINNING OF CHRISTMAS
AS A HOLY DAY

During the first years after Christ, He was expected to return at any moment, and all consideration was turned toward the Second Coming. For this reason, little thought was given the Nativity or its date. Furthermore, with the persecution in Rome and with Christians in hiding, celebration was hardly practical.

However, in the eastern part of the Empire—Constantinople and Antioch (Turkey), Cappadocia (Asia Minor), and Egypt —it became customary to observe Epiphany on January 6, the date of the winter solstice according to the Egyptian calendar. Epiphany, from the Greek word *epiphaneia*, commemorated the manifestation of God to the world in Jesus Christ as revealed in His birth and at the time of His baptism by John the Baptist.

Initially, commemorating the birth of Jesus did not honor the event itself, but gradually the practice arose of setting aside one day in memory of Christ's birth *date*. It first gained firm hold in the East, where it was most commonly honored on the same date as the festival of the Epiphany. Christmas became, then, a double commemoration.

The persecution ended in Rome in A.D. 313, and some time later the Church officially blessed three new festivals, one of them being Christ's birthday. The first document in which the festival is mentioned was written in A.D. 336, but some authorities believe that as early as A.D. 320 the Church assigned December 25 as the time for celebration.

Selection of the date was arbitrary, and appears to have been a deliberate ploy, as least in part, to deflect worship of the unconquered sun to adoration of Christ the Lord. "Who is indeed so unconquered as our Lord?" asked St. John Chrysostom in 407, arguing in defense of the choice. Another reason may have been for the convenience of Christians in Jerusalem. They assembled in Bethlehem early in the morning of January 6 to commemorate Christ's birth, then rushed across town to

8

the River Jordan, some twelve miles away, to celebrate the Baptism. The Christians in Judea are said to have appealed for a change in date to end the difficulty.

The new feast day was given the name *Festum Nativitatis Domini Nostri Jesu Christi*, the Feast of the Nativity of Our Lord Jesus Christ, or, in shorter form, *Dies Natalis Domini*, the Birthday of Our Lord. The first known usage of the word *Christmas* dates from 1038. It was coined by the English, who titled feast days as mass days, and thus called Christ's Birthday *Christes Maesse* or *Christes-Messe*.

Members of the Eastern Church at first fought against the date of December 25 for the Nativity; but in the fourth century they began to accept it, at the same time maintaining the earlier tradition of Epiphany on January 6.

Concurrently, Rome began to introduce the Feast of the Epiphany in the West, but as commemoration of the visit of the Three Magi rather than the Manifestation. It was not until the sixth century that the Nativity was completely detached from January 6 and that all except one branch of the Church accepted December 25 for celebration of Christ's birthday. The Armenians have never accepted the change from January 6. (Details of their belief are discussed in Chapter XII.)

Acceptance of December 25 for Christ's birthday by both the East and West brought only temporary halt to dissension regarding times for Christmas and Epiphany. Open opposition between the two branches revived when Pope Gregory XIII inaugurated a new calendar in 1582. Gregory corrected the Julian calendar, in use since 45 B.C. and then ten days behind, by eliminating ten days and instituting leap years.

The branches of the Eastern Orthodox Church refused to accept a change in the previously established holy days, and continued with the "old" calendar. To compound the confusion, not all European countries began using the calendar simultaneously. Not until 1752, well after America was settled, did England adopt the Gregorian calendar, a fact that may account for the way some of our Christmas customs developed. In some areas of the South, it is said that old-timers still

angrily maintain that "December 25 just ain't Christmas."
In A.D. 542, Emperor Justinian designated February 2—formerly date of a pagan festival of lights—for official commemoration of the Presentation of Jesus in the Temple to His Heavenly Father and Purification of the Virgin. Jewish teaching prescribed forty days as necessary for purification of a new mother and ordered that the first male child be taken to the temple at the end of this period. Once December 25 was accepted as the date of the birth of Christ, February 2 automatically and fortuitously became the date for His presentation. In Britain, candles were blessed and distributed to worshipers on that date, leading to its designation as Candlemas.

While the date for Christmas was being established, Advent fasting, to prepare the body and mind for Christmas, became habitual. The practice followed that of ancient religions, which taught that new-year celebrations should be preceded by a period of fasting and penitence. They were believed to purify and eliminate all evil, thus assuring a plentiful harvest. At one time, Advent, like Lent, lasted forty days; but in the sixth century, Gregory I shortened the season to four weeks. At about the same time, Epiphany and the Twelve Days of Christmas were declared to be sacred and festive.

Today Advent is considered more important as a celebration viewing the mystery of the Incarnation in the life and achievement of Christ than as preparation for Christmas and the Second Coming. In the Western Church, Advent begins four Sundays before Christmas. Its observance as a fast period has greatly diminished, especially in the United States. In the Eastern Church, depending upon the calendar followed, Advent begins around the middle of November, and continues to be much more a period of penitence and fast.

THE GERMANIC INFLUENCE

Ancient Germanic traditions substantially influence our Christmas, but no exact connections can be traced because there are no surviving records written before A.D. 500. Word of the Christian religion and its practices had reached the German area by that time, and influenced existing accounts.

In the north of Europe, there were only primitive tribes—Franks, Saxons, Thuringians, Slavs, Bavarians, Swabians, and Vikings—and ceremonial emphasis naturally centered on the family and its ties with the past. As none of the tribes had yet learned to calculate by the stars, celebrations were seasonal.

Around November 11, perhaps with the first snow, the Germanic peoples thinned their herds and sacrificed a boar or pig to their gods, Odin and/or Freyr. Afterward, they held a great feast for the purpose of honoring the dead and keeping peace with restless ancestral spirits. Gruesome mummery accompanied the ritual, and bonfires and a clatter of noise—all calculated to frighten away the evil beings that hovered around homes and stables at this time. The occasion was known variously as *Jiuleis*, *Giuli*, and *Yule*.

In Norse mythology, Odin (or Wotan, Woden, Wodin) was the greatest of all gods, and one with a dual personality. On the one hand, he reigned over bounty and fertility as the god of sun, rain, and fruit; on the other, he was god of war, wisdom, prophecy, and magic. Freyr had more or less the same attributes, and in time became identical with Odin.

Odin governed the end of the year. Wrapping himself in a magic blue cloak and donning a broad-brimmed hat, he sped round the world by night on Sleipnir, a great white horse, with eight legs for greater speed. (As god of the blue sky and moving air, Odin inevitably became known as protector of sailors.) At other times, he preferred to travel on foot. In this role, Odin is portrayed as a wise old man with a long white beard, carrying a wanderer's staff in one hand.

In Britain and Scandinavia, the Druids honored Wodin by tying gilded apples to tree branches and making offerings of cakes. And in honor of his son, Balder or Baldur, *their* sun god, they placed lighted candles on the boughs of trees. As part of their ceremonies, the Druids gathered mistletoe with a golden sickle and burned it on an altar as sacrifice to their gods.

11

Priests distributed small pieces to the people to take home and hang in their houses (as we do now) as a powerful charm against evil.

According to Norse legend, winter came into being when Baldur was slain by a dart whittled from a sprig of mistletoe. His mother, Frigga, shed so many tears over Baldur's death that they clustered on the sprig and turned into white berries. Determined that the parasite should never do evil again, Frigga declared that thereafter it should serve as a token of love rather than hate, and asked that all who passed beneath it kiss symbolically. This myth spread as far south as Rome, where enemies would lay down their weapons, kiss, and declare a day's truce whenever they happened to meet underneath the mistletoe. Kissing boughs and balls based on the legend later became part of secular Christmas, but mistletoe never was officially sanctioned for use in the church.

To promote bountiful crops and also to provide light and warmth for the dead, the Druids cut an oak tree, blessed it with great ceremony, then lit it with a faggot from the preceding year. The "ever-burning" Yule log was supposed to cleanse and revitalize with its fire, burning up all the evil and inertia of the past year.

CHRISTMAS IN THE MIDDLE AGES

With the invasion and sack of Rome in A.D. 410, the Nordic and Germanic peoples came into direct contact with Christianity, and vice versa. Undaunted by the differences in language, the Church boldly sent forth an army of missionaries, and so began an exchange that operated both ways in building tradition. The northern tribes were easily persuaded to change the time of the Yule celebration to the Christmas period. In turn, they sent south the Yule log and other year-end practices.

Once the German peoples were conscious of the solstice, the fire rituals increased. In addition to the Yule logs, fires were built on every summit, torches carried in parade, and burning wheels rolled down hills and through fields. Cows were wreathed with greenery and led across the ashes of the bonfires (the word is probably derived from bone-fires built to drive away witches) to insure immunity from disease and accident the following season. There were ring dances around the fire, and a great deal of leaping back and forth by couples to predict the future.

In A.D. 604, Pope Gregory I advised St. Augustine of Canterbury to permit, even to encourage, harmless popular custom that could be given Christian interpretation. Pagan fire customs tacitly became part of Christmas festivities, sanctified by an observation in Luke at the time of the presentation of Christ that the Infant would be "a light to lighten the Gentiles." Candles, formerly carried in parade at the end of the year as symbols of the vitalizing sun and protection against plague, pestilence, and famine, became symbols of Christ, the Light of the World. Lighting of the Yule log was given a variety of Christian interpretations, depending on the locale.

In a similar fashion, decorating both the house of God and the house of man with plants and flowers on the Feast of the Nativity was gradually condoned. Holly, formerly a guard against witches, thunder, and lightning, became a symbol of the victory and glory of Christ.

Legend has it that the pagan evergreen was Christianized by St. Boniface early in the eighth century, during one of his stays in Germany. At a certain time, it was announced, Boniface would attack the sacred oak in which the Thunder God, Donar or Odin, was believed to dwell. It has been speculated since that the saint must have been something of a woodsman, for almost upon his first blow the tree split into four parts and crashed to the ground. Perhaps the tree-worshiping Druids simply transferred their decorations from the boughs of the oak to the fir; but it seems more likely that evergreens were approved for Christmas because they could be so easily interpreted as representing eternal life, and that the Christmas tree came about in a somewhat different fashion. (See Chapter IV.)

During the Middle Ages all the high jinks of old continued at Christmastime. There was masquerading and mumming, fortunetelling, singing, dancing, and abundant noise. A favorite character in the mummers' shows was the King of Misrule, held over from Saturnalia. At the end of the Twelve Days of Christmas there was another mock ruler, the King of the Bean, selected by cutting a traditional Twelfth Night cake. (See Chapter VIII for continuation in America.)

Above all, Yuletide continued to be a period of feasting and drinking. As early as 389, Pope St. Gregory warned against excessive indulgence in gluttony at Christmas, and against dancing and mumming. Women continued to prepare sacrificial cakes and symbolic breads, and ceremonial foods for the dead.

All this may seem irreverent today, but it was perfectly natural for the times. Man's life was hard and threatening during the Middle Ages. One reason Christmas was so joyous and welcome must have been that it offered a boisterous escape from the daily struggle, just as it does today. Religious experience was part of everyday life. The church was the center of every village, and all action swirled in and out of it as though it were the most important square in town—which, indeed, it was. Medieval man would never have comprehended the contemporary plea to "Put Christ back in Christmas."

"What do you mean?" he would have asked, bewildered. "We have always celebrated this way at the end of the year."

CHURCH DRAMA—MYSTERY AND
MIRACLE PLAYS

Initially, Christmas and Easter hymns were stately verses dealing with theological rather than human aspects of the Incarnation and Resurrection. They were sung in Latin, a language few if any understood. In an effort to render the service more meaningful and personal, priests began to insert vernacular explanations of the text, known as "tropes."

Those clerics who instituted tropes must have found irresistible the urge to explain more and more of the text. The subdeacon would read the Latin phrases, then clerks responded with a loose explanation. Soon meter and rhythm were added, then music. It was only a step further to simple staging of the action.

Thus was drama born, in the form of mystery plays dealing with the mysteries of Christ's birth and life, and miracle plays, so called for the miracles depicted. Scenes multiplied rapidly in length and number, and as the action expanded, so did the number of characters, until it became customary to augment the clerical group with laymen, a move that proved fatal. Uneducated secular actors would improvise their own lines, and sometimes make such liberal changes in the text that a new character was created in performance, and one so interesting that the theme of the play was obscured.

The result was earthy, often bawdy drama, which the audience of students, monks, peasants, and noblemen gleefully recognized and cheered. They particularly relished the scene of the Virgin's flight to Egypt, for example, portrayed by a young girl riding a donkey down the aisles of the cathedral.

The plays were highly entertaining, but they were no longer sacred drama. In an attempt to halt secularization, the Church abolished tropes. Mystery plays were transferred out of the church, and finally banned, but performances continued in some remote areas, and are still given in America. (See Chapter IX.)

CHRISTMAS AND THE REFORMATION

Before the time of Christianity, rulers took for granted that their subjects would worship the god of the particular state in which they lived. Religion, then, became a kind of department of state. It was the Christians' refusal to worship the Roman state gods that led to persecution. But once Christianity was accepted, it, too, became the religion of the empire. Christmas was declared a legal holiday in Rome, and eventually became a

15

despised symbol for those opposed to the Roman Catholic Church.

In 1517, the coming of the Reformation brought open warfare against all religious feast days and feast-day customs. In Scotland, Christmas was forbidden as early as 1583, on threat of dire punishment. In England, there was little change so long as the Tudors remained in power, but as soon as the Puritans took control, they passed a series of measures aimed at abolishing Christmas celebrations completely.

CHRISTMAS IN AMERICA

American Christmas celebrations began with Columbus, searching for the Spice Islands. In 1492, his flagship ran aground on a coral reef and was wrecked off the island of Santo Domingo on Chirstmas Eve. Columbus and his crew were saved by Indian natives, and the following day he feasted with their chief. Later, he built a small fortress nearby and named it La Navidad or the Nativity, in honor of Christmas and in thanksgiving for rescue.

When the Spanish explorers and missionaries who followed him reached Mexico, they discovered that the Indians held an annual year-end festival at the time of the December solstice. Not only were some of the Aztec terms surprisingly similar to those taught by Christian tradition, but, to the horror of the conquistadors, so were the rituals. Part of Aztec religious observances included a ceremony strikingly like the Eucharist, performed with wine and wafers. For the year-end festivities the Indians worked a candy-like paste, Tzoally, into shapes of men and animals and gave them to friends and relatives. Like the Roman cakes and dolls, Tzoally may have substituted for earlier living sacrifices. The same Tzoally is made in Mexico today, and called *alegria* or gaiety, but it is no longer part of Christmas.

The Indians in the Pacific Northwest and in Alaska had a well-established feast or potlatch at the time of the winter

16

solstice, when gifts were given. And a tribe in North Dakota had long observed a custom of hanging gifts on a cedar tree in expectation of special blessings and absolution of all guilt.

Europeans in America divided sharply into pro- and anti-Christmas groups, according to their attitude during the Reformation. Those who had cherished Christmas in their homeland did so even more in the strange country because Christmas traditions afforded ties with their loved ones and with the past. Initially, these people were primarily English, Dutch, and German, members of the Lutheran, Moravian, Episcopalian, and Reformed Churches. They brought two bodies of custom: religious—sanctified by the liturgy and Church tradition—and secular—Christmas in the home and in the streets, the part of Christmas that dominates today.

The first settlers clung tenaciously to tradition, but with succeeding generations and later migrations, much of the old was lost in assimilation, as ethnic neighborhoods began to break up and nationalities intermarried. The children of immigrants were eager to cast off the old, and Christmas became one of the symbols of "Americanization." Today, fortunately, in third-generation homes and later, many young parents are reintroducing ancient traditions, realizing the importance of ties with the past and its rituals. It is hoped this book will be helpful to all so interested.

Every nationality that came to the United States—and every nationality did—added something to the bounty and wealth of our American Christmas. Nowhere else in the world could such variety exist. In the United States, Christmas has everything.

Since Christmas is a joyous occasion, new customs continue to evolve spontaneously in individual families. In Portland, Oregon, for instance, everyone present in a certain Greek home forms a chain on Christmas Day and dances through the house.

If we could go from one town to another, we would find hundreds of holiday customs, old and new. Almost every household could tell of something they cherish that is not quite like their neighbors'.

The greatest variety of all would be found in the Christmas feast, not only in the dishes comprising it, but in the way each is prepared. The same dish may vary widely from home to home, even though it originated in a certain region of one country. Cookbooks were exceedingly scarce when America was settled, and recipes were handed down from mother to daughter by word of mouth, often as a jealously guarded secret. In the original recipes succeeding generations of cooks have also made changes, sometimes simplifying them, sometimes making them more complex. The result is that there are dozens and dozens of recipes for most holiday specialties, all "correct."

To make an absolute choice of which are best would be quite impossible. Instead, from the wealth offered by friends and interested correspondents, and uncovered by research, we offer a few of our preferences. Not surprisingly, the greater number of recipes are for cakes, cookies, and holiday breads. Man still regards them as special for the year's end, just as he did in the time of the Aztecs, the Druids, and *Saturnalia*.

CHAPTER II

SECTION A

New Amsterdam and New York City

THE CUSTOMS AND FOOD OF NEW AMSTERDAM

"St. Nicholas! thrice jolly St. Nicholas! Bacchus of Christian Dutchmen, king of good fellows, patron of holiday fare, inspirer of simple frolic and unsophisticated happiness, saint of all saints that deck the glorious calendar! Thou that first awakenest the hopes of the prattling infant; dawnest happiness on the school boy; and brightenest the wintry hours of manhood. If I forget thee whatever betide, or whatever fantastic heartless follies may usurp the place of thy simple celebration, may I lose the recollection of past pleasures, the anticipation of pleasures to come, yawn at a tea party, petrify at a soiree, and perish, finally overwhelmed in a deluge of whip syllabub and floating island! Thrice, and three times thrice, jolly St. Nicholas! on this, the first day of the new year 1826, with an honest reverence and a full bumper of cherry bounce, I salute thee! To St. Nicholas! *Esto perpetua!*

"To whoever fails in due honour and allegiance, be this his fate: Never to sip the dew from the lips of the lass he loveth best on New Year's Eve . . . never to taste of hot spiced Santa Cruz; and never to know the delights of mince pies and sausages, swimming in the sauce of honest mirth and homefelt jollity."

—James K. Paulding, *Scribner's,* 1867

St. Nicholas arrived in New York with the first boatload of Dutch settlers on Christmas Day. For many years the holiday was doubly celebrated, being commemorated also as "Landing Day."

The good saint came to the New World as the figurehead on the Dutch ship, *Goede Vrouw*. One of the first buildings erected was a church in his honor, and he naturally became patron saint of the new colony, just as he was in the homeland. Just as naturally the weeks following his name day became the most important Holyday period of a year liberally sprinkled with holidays.

Fortunately for the new city and state, the good Dutch were a tolerant, worldly people. Despite the determined effort of the Reformation to wipe out all saints and saints' days as remnants of popery, the Dutch had steadfastly clung to their cherished St. Nicholas. It is easy to see why. St. Nicholas was protector of the sea and sailors (like his predecessor Woden), and the Dutch were a seafaring people whose very livelihood depended upon safe conduct over the waters. What harm could it do boys and girls to believe that St. Nicholas would bring rewards to good children and punishment for the naughty ones?

Indeed, the whole idea of Puritanism and the Reformation was alien to the people from Holland. They were a hearty, fun-loving lot who enjoyed life to its fullest. Their famous Director-General, Peter Stuyvesant, took full advantage of their tendency toward pleasure. Upon the slightest pretext, and especially when there was trouble, he would declare a public holiday of prayer and thanksgiving. Once the solemn prayers were out of the way, the Dutch colonists proceeded to celebrate as they pleased, with beer, liquor, bonfires, dancing, games, and rough sport. By the time the English took over in 1664, the practice of setting aside a day of thanksgiving when war, famine, or disease had threatened and been averted was well established.

In the first years of New Amsterdam, St. Nicholas was supposed to come each year from Holland to the new land (somewhat as Dutch children today believe that he comes to the Netherlands from Spain). On his name day or thereabouts, the eagerly awaited Dutch ship would arrive in the New York port. Probably a description given of the late eighteenth-century Christmas ship would have been equally applicable to the St. Nicholas ship. She was "freighted down deep as she could swim with all sorts of toys, cakes, fruits, and books," wrote John Pintard (*ca.* 1830) in his diaries, "for St. Claas to bestow his annual presents to the good children of the ancient city of New Amsterdam."

Children believed that when St. Nicholas landed, he mounted a white horse that carried him from home to home. The question of how he and the horse got together after the long ocean voyage seems never to have troubled any of the children he visited.

On December 5, St. Nicholas Eve, a white sheet was spread on the floor, and children gathered around it. As they sang songs of welcome to "St. Nicholaes, Goed Heilig man," the front door flew open and a shower of sweets was scattered on the floor.

While boys and girls scrambled after them, St. Nicholas strode in, dressed in full clerical vestments—white robe, crimson cassock, white gloves, and a tall red miter. He was attended by a servant, Knecht Ruprecht, who held in one hand an open sack into which he could throw particularly bad boys, and in the other, a menacing bunch of rods which he shook expressively from time to time.

The good saint distributed small parcels to the children, and when these had been opened and sufficiently admired, the young ones were trundled off to bed. Then the dust sheets and wrappings were cleared away, and the adults gathered round for chocolate punch and a steaming dish of hot chestnuts. Afterward, the head of the house took out his Dutch pipe ornamented with a head of St. Nicholas, and the evening ended with singing and dancing.

The Dutch ship bearing gifts plowed up the Hudson to Albany, and all along the way excited children prepared for the saint's visit. They put out hay for his horse, and in some homes tokens of his most famous good deeds were hung on the walls: a wet, salty sailor's suit, seven green branches, or three oranges.

21

The wet garment symbolized St. Nicholas' having saved a drowned mariner and brought him back to life, in accordance with his role as patron saint of the sea. Another time, he saved seven young boys, represented by the seven green branches. They had been slain by a wicked butcher, then chopped up and hidden in a barrel of brine. When St. Nicholas discovered the evil deed, he called out to the wooden barrel, and out the boys jumped, whole once more.

St. Nicholas' most famous acts were represented by the oranges, symbols for gifts of gold he surreptitiously gave as dowries for three poor but deserving sisters. According to the legend, each gift was made in a different way. The first was tossed through an open window; the other two thrown down the chimney because all entrances were barred. One bag landed on the fireplace hearth, but the other bounced into one of the stockings which the last unmarried girl had just washed and hung by the fire to dry.

St. Nicholas brought very simple gifts—candy, cookies, trinkets—and what may be best described as "April Fool" presents. Unimportant objects were wrapped in elaborate but unattractive disguise, often of many layers, and were accompanied by a scrap of taunting doggerel detailing the recipient's faults. The rhymes were supposedly written by St. Nicholas, who could make sharp comments that mere mortals dared not utter. It was all a big Dutch joke.

Children in the Hudson Valley still remember St. Nicholas by wrapping small gifts in several layers of gaily colored paper and presenting them with a funny verse on his name day, December 6. In Castroville, Texas, children of Alsatian descent hang up their stockings on December 5.

Christmas in seventeenth-century New York was known as a holy day reserved for churchgoing and quiet family feasting. However, contemporary authorities suspect that greater attention was given to the Christmas feast. Among foods known to have been served were game pies, oysters, and wild duck.

The week following Christmas was thought of as one of holidays. Until early in the twentieth century, friends would say, "Come see us during the Christmas." In many a New York State home the dining table was kept set until New Year's Day, in case a visitor might drop by unexpectedly.

During this week English friends and family members vied with each other to be the first to call out, "Merry Christmas!" upon meeting, as the first to do so was entitled to a present from the other. Christmas week came to a great climax on New Year's Day, when the cry "Happy New Year!" brought another gift.

In early Niew Amsterdam, Dutch wives donned their best dresses on New Year's Day and sat in their seldom-used living rooms to receive guests making New Year's Day calls. Nearby were mighty bowls of punch and cordials prepared from treasured family recipes, simple cookies, New Year's Cake (a rude cookie spiced with caraway seed), and *oleykoeks*, doughnuts fried in hog's fat.

The custom of open house on New Year's Day gained importance as society developed. Great rivalry developed between hostesses, who advertised the hours they would receive guests, just as commercial establishments had been doing. Any gentleman wishing to remain on a lady's social list dared not overlook her. In Baltimore, young men were out as early as 10 A.M., carrying lists of houses to visit and a previously prepared geographical route.

The modest fare of former times mutiplied into an array of "splendid ornamented and iced plum cakes, with almost numberless other cakes, confectionaries, and fruits, not forgetting the true New Year's Cakes, together with madeira and other wines, and cordials and liquers." (Gabriel Furman)

New Yorkers were by no means alone in making much of New Year's Day. Rather, their receptions were typical, if somewhat more sophisticated. Presidential receptions were also customary: In the new Federal City, it became accepted that the New Year's Day Presidential reception should be open to all citizens—a custom which perplexed European visitors. The crowd which gathered astonished them even more, for standing side by side in their normal dress might be seen a frontiersman, an ambassador, and an Indian chief.

In 1842 New York's Governor Seward substituted lemonade and cold water for punch and wine on New Year's Day, because of violent opposition to liquor by the Temperance League. "His action was considered a bold innovation upon long established custom," Furman noted, but "one the spirit of the times seemed to demand."

The custom of open house persisted, however. In Atlanta, crafty hostesses invited pretty young girls to assist in receiving guests. Probably more than one wedding resulted. Southern parties were staggered so that callers could proceed from one to another without apology, and so hostesses could join in once their receptions ended. In order to be received, callers presented highly elaborate personal cards similar to the first Christmas cards, with birds, baskets of roses, and cupids. Sentimental young men sometimes added small silk ribbons tied in love knots.

In Atlanta, any person had the right to present his card at the door and walk in without an invitation. Elsewhere, private invitations completely replaced public announcements by the end of the nineteenth century, and in New York City open house on New Year's Day was more firmly entrenched than ever.

In New York City today, the variety and spectacle of Christmas set the pace for the rest of the United States. In some areas like German Yorkville, a distinctly "old country" air is visible; but along Fifth Avenue, fresh new ideas sparkle as lines form before particularly effective store windows. The light, color, and imagination exhibited vividly embody this country's commercial spirit at its best.

On and off Broadway, theater has its best weeks of the year. Music is offered for every taste—in Radio City Music Hall, at Lincoln Center, in Carnegie Hall, and in every church.

The Messiah is probably the most universal musical tradition for Christmas in New York, as it is in other cities. But there are constant innovations which can very shortly develop into hallowed tradition. When George Balanchine re-created

The Nutcracker in 1954 for the New York City Ballet, he could not have foreseen its future popularity. It has now become mandatory at Christmas, not only in New York City, but throughout the United States. In some cities, such as Washington, D.C., several different companies present rival productions over a period of weeks.

The tradition of Pro Musica's annual musical-dramatic presentations began in 1958. Pro Musica is a group of skilled musicians brought together by a gifted director, the late Noah Greenberg, to give authentic performances of medieval and Renaissance music on ancient instruments. Greenberg conceived of reproducing *The Play of Daniel*, a French mystery play based on Chapters 5 and 6 of the Book of Daniel. It had been a great favorite with twelfth- and thirteenth-century audiences, but neglected since that time. The initial presentation was in the Romanesque Hall of the Cloisters, and a great hit.

Daniel's popularity led Greenberg to begin preparing a complete repertory of medieval music-dramas. In 1963 the play of *Herod* was re-created and produced in the old Spanish Fuentiduena Chapel of the Cloisters.

Since 1963, the two music plays have been given in conjunction at Christmastime in various places in New York City, and in nearby states and the District of Columbia. In 1965, the play of *Daniel* was put on television tape by the National Education Television Network and shown all over the United States on Christmas Eve.

In 1967, Greenberg's successor, Director John White, turned to something strictly of this century and produced an *Electric Christmas*. The Pro Musica group explored the possibilities of combining electronic music with exotic lighting effects popularized initially by LSD users. The *Electric Christmas* could be the beginning of a completely new kind of Christmas tradition that will sweep the country as completely as *The Nutcracker* has.

Few of the foods lovingly listed by James K. Paulding would have met with the approval of Temperance author Mrs.

Horace Mann (Mary Peabody of the famous Peabody sisters in Massachusetts). Her cookbook entitled *Christianity in the Kitchen*, published in 1861, began with the grim warning, "There's death in the pot." Mrs. Mann went on to condemn not only excessive drinking and eating, but also "unhealthful preparation," a category which included any dish of which she did not approve.

The New Year's drinks, Floating Island and Sillabub, would surely have fallen in one or all of her classifications for "Unchristian" foods.

The Floating Island he eulogized was not the custard dessert we know today, but a very rich beverage. Undoubtedly its delicate pink color added much to the pleasure of serving it. The following recipe is from Maria Randolph's cookbook titled *A New System of Domestic Cookery by a Lady*, published in 1816:

Floating Island

"Mix 3½ pts. of thin cream with a quarter of a pt. of raisin wine, a little lemon juice, orange-flower water and sugar. Put into a dish for the middle of the table, and put on the cream, a froth, which may be made of raspberry or currant jelly."

Raisin wine was made at home by steeping raisins in water. Sometimes brandy, oranges, and lemons were added for flavor. It served as a kind of substitute for sherry and Madeira.

Raspberry cream was raspberry jam or jelly mixed with cream.

The origin of the name "Sillabub" or "Syllabub" is obscure. The ending, "bub," was an old slang term for liquor. The prefix, "sylla" or "silla," could have been attached with the meaning of the adjective, silly. Another theory is that syllabub came from Sillery, France, which produces both champagne and fine still white wine. A third explanation attributes it to Anne Boleyn, who is said to have referred to the beverage as "Silly bubbles," which was later shortened to the present form.

In any case, it was very popular with the English, and came

in many varieties and flavors. Lemon juice and rind were often included in old recipes. The following syllabub recipe from Mary Randolph's 1831 cookbook, *The Virginia Housewife or Methodical Cook*, reinforces the notion of silly bubbles:

Recipe

"Put a pint and a half of port or white wine into a bowl, nutmeg grated, and a good deal of sugar, then milk into it near 2 quarts of milk, frothed up. If the wine be not rather sharp, it will require more for this quantity of milk. Clouted cream may be put on the top, and pounded cinnamon and sugar."

Clouted cream was produced by heating together beaten eggs, cream, milk, rose water and mace, then removing the top when the mixture had cooled overnight.

As Americans became more civilized, syllabub churns were invented to make the milk froth. The inventory for the Tryon Palace in New Bern, North Carolina, listed "Syllabub fluted bowls with covers of Ditto," indicating that the Royal Governor and Mrs. Tryon served syllabub during their residence (1765–1775). The Palace restoration is proud to display a set of six syllabub glasses and bowl which were made in England around 1750, and came to Edenton, N.C. shortly thereafter. The glasses are somewhat in the shape of a lily—tall with long thin stems. When the syllabub was poured into the glass, the wine-milk mixture settled to the bottom and the froth remained in the scalloped upper portion of the glass.

The most popular Dutch holiday confection was *oleykoeks*, which translates literally as "oily cakes."

Oleykoeks
(Dutch Doughnuts)

½ cup raisins
Brandy to cover
1 package of yeast
¼ cup lukewarm water
¾ cup milk
¼ cup sugar

1 tablespoon shortening
1 teaspoon salt
1 egg, well beaten
1½ cups sifted flour
2 cups additional sifted flour
Deep oil for frying

Sifted confectioner's sugar

Cover raisins with brandy and place in covered container to soak overnight. Dissolve yeast in warm water. Scald milk, then add sugar, shortening, and salt; stir until shortening is melted and sugar dissolved. Cool to lukewarm, then stir in dissolved yeast and beaten egg. Add 1½ cups sifted flour. Beat thoroughly. Add enough additional flour to make a soft dough. Turn out on floured surface and knead until smooth. Place dough in greased bowl, flip over, and cover with damp towel. Put in warm place to rise until double in bulk.

When dough has risen, take out and punch down. Cut off small pieces and shape into balls, enclosing a few brandied raisins in center of each ball. Place on greased tin, cover with greased cloth, and let rise again until double. Fry in hot fat (370°) until golden brown. Drain and, while still warm, roll in confectioner's sugar.

Yield: approximately 2 dozen

It is interesting to note that when New York came under the English rule, the Dutch word *koekje* was retained and came into our American language as "cookie." The English term would have been "biscuit," and there is no true equivalent in any other foreign language. We received a number of other terms for our American foods from the good Dutch. The two Dutch cookie recipes given here would be hard to surpass. The Hollanders could not be easier to make.

Jan Hagel

(*Hollanders*)

1 cup butter	*2 cups sifted flour*
1 cup sugar	*1 egg, beaten lightly*

½ cup chopped nuts, preferably pecans

Heat oven to 350° F. Cream butter and sugar together, then cream in flour gradually. Pat into two ungreased 13″ x 8½″ pans or one 15½″ x 10½″ pan. Brush with beaten egg, then sprinkle with nuts. Bake 15 to 25 minutes, until golden brown. Watch carefully during final baking period as cookies burn easily. Cool momentarily, just long enough to "set," then cut with a sharp knife into strips, squares, or diamonds.

Pitmoppen

(*Dutch Butter-Almond Cookies*)

1¾ cups unsifted flour	*1 tablespoon milk*
1½ teaspoons baking powder	*½ teaspoon almond extract*
⅔ cup sugar	*½ teaspoon vanilla extract*
¾ cup butter	*Additional milk*

Unblanched, sliced almonds

Heat oven to 400° F.

Sift together flour, baking powder, and sugar. Cut in butter, as for biscuits. Mix together 1 tablespoon milk and extracts. Stir into flour mixture. Work dough with hands until it will form a ball. (Add additional spoonful of milk if necessary.) Roll out to ¼″ thickness on floured board. Cut into 1½″ squares, or use cutters. Place on ungreased sheet. Brush lightly with milk. Form diamond on each cookie top with 4 almond slices. Bake 8 minutes, or until lightly brown.

Yield: approximately 5 dozen

CHAPTER II

SECTION B

New Amsterdam and New York City

SANTA CLAUS COMES ON CHRISTMAS

"St. Claas is too firmly rivetted in this city ever to be forgotten, or mince pies to be omitted on Christmas Day."
—Letter from JOHN PINTARD, (*ca.* 1830)

"In our land, we were so fortunate as to have not only a 'Mother Country,' but also a 'Fatherland,' or Vaderlandt, . . . the Dutch inhabitants used all their endeavours to prevent the language and customs of the good old Vaderlandt from going out of fashion . . . the Dutch and English, by living as neighbors, and by intermarriage became one people, and the Dutch talked English, and the English talked Dutch. They also ate sourkraut and smoked goose and Rolichees, and roast beef and plumb pudding with each other, and everything went on as comfortably as could be."
—GABRIEL FURMAN, 1844
The Customs, Amusements, Styles of Living, and Manners of the People of the United States from the First Settlement to the Present Time.

 Everyone knows that Santa Claus was once St. Nicholas, but how did he change from a stately clerical figure in white robes to a roly-poly elf dressed in red wool? Why did he give up

30

making his visit on his name day, December 6, and elect instead to bring gifts on December 25? And where did his eight reindeer come from? No one can say for sure, but Gabriel Furman furnishes the key to the mystery in his matter-of-fact description of how Dutch and English customs became inextricably entangled with each other.

Although St. Nicholas always visited Dutch children in New York in early December, he did not bring his prized *étrennes* for good French Huguenot youngsters until New Year's Day, almost a month later. The English, also, were accustomed to giving children gifts on New Year's Day, and continued to do so long after gifts for Christmas became standard. From the time of the English takeover of New York in 1664, both English and French influence grew increasingly important. A compromise in dates, then, was decidedly logical, especially if it had the added effect of cutting down the long period spent Holydaying. Information may also have sifted into New York from Pennsylvania Dutchland that the German Protestants gave gifts on Christmas.

A propitious change in the calendar made such a solution almost as painless as it was practical. In 1752, the English belatedly adopted the Gregorian calendar, nearly two centuries after it was instituted by Pope Gregory. To bring about the change, thirteen days were arbitrarily skipped over sometime that year. With the moving forward of dates, Christmas "new stile," in 1752, fell exactly one week later than St. Nicholas Day had come the year before, 1751.

American newspaper articles printed at the time reveal that there was great indecision on the part of devout churchgoing people as to whether they should accept the change. Some demanded that their ministers preach a Christmas sermon on January 7, Christmas "old stile." Others went on expeditions into the woods on December 25 to see if the trees had yet budded, for according to ancient superstition they should do so on Christmas Day. This situation continued for a period of some years.

Suppose that in this uncertain situation—we offer it purely

as conjecture—there was a storm at sea or rough weather that delayed the arrival of the annual ship bringing St. Nicholas and his load from Holland. A delay of only a day or two would have demonstrated the wisdom of consolidating on Christmas Day, and would also have established a precedent in a time of confusion.

St. Nicholas' transformation and the substitution of reindeer for his beautiful white horse are not as easily explained. Such changes could only have taken place in the New World, where a great mixture of peoples and traditions acted upon one another, and where communication was haphazard.

Santa Claus was given his name in New York City, where St. Nicholas was affectionately known as *Sinterklass* by the Dutch and St. Klaas or Sancta Claas by the English and French; but his personality must have been influenced by a different kind of Christmas figure in nearby Pennsylvania.

The people who celebrated Christmas in "Dutch" Pennsylvania were primarily from the Rhineland, where St. Nicholas was a different personage from the Dutch saint. In Germany, he was portrayed more often as a wanderer than as a bishop. Wrapped in a cloak and wearing a broad-brimmed hat, and carrying in his hand a staff rather than a crozier, he visibly displayed his kinship to the old wind god, Woden.

In Northern Europe when the Reformation began to exhort against Christmas, St. Nicholas went underground, so to speak. In his place, not one, but two figures emerged. One was a fur-clad *Pelznichol* (which translates literally as "Nicholas in fur"), and the other, a beaming childlike figure known as *Christkind*. The custom of gifts at Christmas, it must be added, was so well established that it held its own.

The fair-haired *Christkind*, often impersonated by a young girl with golden curls, was a kind of messenger from the Christ Child. German children spoke of him affectionately as the *Christkindlein*, and as the German language changed into Pennsylvania Dutch, so did his name. Curiously, so did his identity. *Christkindlein* shortened to *Christ Kindel* or *Kriss Kindle*, and finally *Kriss Kinkle*. At the same time this was going on, the idea of *Christkind* and *Belsnickle* (*Pelznichol* in Pennsylvania Dutch) began to be interchangeable; it may be that they always were. Another "r" crept into *Kriss Kingle*, for alliteration, and out came Kriss Kringle, looking very much like New York's St. Nicholas. Kriss made his first-known appearance in print in Philadelphia in 1842 in *Kriss Kringle's Book*. It may well be the publisher was the guilty party who changed the spelling.

Gabriel Furman described St. Nicholas as "a pleasant little old gentleman in a cocked hat and breeches, with a large bag full of sugar plums and toys." St. Klaas came down the chimney in a little red wagon, he wrote, "and evidence of his visit was afforded by the tracks of his wagon wheels upon the ashes of the hearth." Whether St. Nicholas had given up his white horse, or attached him to the wagon, the writer did not say.

Furman seems to have been unaware of a publication which gave the greatest impetus to a new idea of St. Nicholas, Clement C. Moore's famous poem, "A Visit from St. Nicholas," written for private entertainment in 1822 and published sometime later. Probably it was influenced by a small juvenile work of 1821, *The Children's Friend*, which had color prints of "Santeclaus" riding in a sleigh drawn by one reindeer. Moore completed the concept of St. Nicholas as a rotund, pipe-smoking, jolly New York Dutchman. (His name throughout the poem, incidentally, is St. Nicholas. Nowhere do the words Santa Claus appear.) Kriss Kringle in the Philadelphia book was similarly portrayed.

Thomas Nast, a well-known political cartoonist, gave the definitive appearance to Santa. Between 1863 and 1886 he drew a series for *Harper's Weekly*, which changed St. Nicholas into Santa Claus once and for all. When the New York *Sun* published Francis Church's famous "Letter to Virginia" in 1897, Santa's fame and immortality were assured forever.

Where the reindeer originated is still a mystery. Perhaps the Swedish brought them here as part of Norse folklore. Maybe Moore saw *The Children's Friend* and added seven more reindeer for good measure. He may have gotten the idea of names from Cracker and Gnasher, the two white goats that drove Thor's chariot. Certainly, the sound of the names corroborates this theory. But on the other hand, Moore may have drawn them from his own imagination to delight children.

One point that cannot be disputed is the popularity of Santa Claus. Primarily because of three wars in rapid succession, his fame has spread around the world. Everywhere the American soldier went, he took Santa with him. In faraway lands where Christianity never really took hold, homesick G.I.'s gave Christmas parties for the local children, with someone dressed as Santa to give out gifts. In Vietnam in 1967, a life-size dummy Santa was placed alongside fully armed compound guards, and his brightly painted sled and reindeer on rooftops nearby. The military has spread the word so effectively that the idea of bounty and plenty has become widely associated with that of "Christmas" and "American." It is not entirely inappropriate.

The Latin countries are the last Christian areas to hold out against Santa. South of the Border and in Latin countries abroad, the Feast of the Three Kings on Epiphany is still the day for receiving gifts. However, Santa is fast making inroads into that tradition. Two years ago he was seen peeping slyly out from among figures gathered on the fringes of a crèche set up in a church near a remote Indian market in Ecuador.

In recent years a rash of Christmas villages has sprung up over the United States. Decorations and appearances vary, but a live Santa is a constant feature. Probably the prototype was the Santa Claus Christmas Village set up in 1948 by the Recreation Department of Torrington, Connecticut. Planned originally for local children, its fame has spread so widely that visitors come from miles around.

Santa's Village in Torrington is strictly nonprofit. To provide a gift for every child, the townspeople hold a toy shower the day before the village opens. There is also a large manger scene on the grounds.

In this country, it is only natural that commercial Santa Claus ventures would spring up. There are several places deliberately named Santa Claus; and a Santa's Workshop in New York state lists its address as North Pole, New York. These developments are aimed at summer tourist trade.

In Torrington, special mailboxes are set up so small visitors can post their Christmas letters and lists. Santa Claus puts quite a burden on the overworked postal system during the holidays. In New York City alone, some 2,500 letters pile up in the dead-letter section.

Response by the postmaster is typically American. He sends out an appeal for volunteers, who rake through the sorted mail and make a selection for replies and gifts. In 1967, one hundred volunteers took care of 250 letters. Other individuals send in checks, which are augmented by an annual allocation of $1,500 from the New York Post Office Employees' Recreational and Welfare Fund. Two dozen staff members take care of those cases which are most touching and indicate greatest need. Probably it could not happen in any other country.

There will undoubtedly be new additions to the folklore surrounding Santa. Only recently, Rudolph, the red-nosed reindeer, joined the reindeer team and has now become a standard part of Christmas. Every Broadway tunesmith's dream is to knock out a seasonal piece which will yield dividends forever after, in the manner of "White Christmas." Rudolph and his song were commercial products, carefully based on human psychology. It is safe to say that when new additions are made to the legend of St. Nicholas, it will be via this avenue.

Plum pudding began as a medieval harvest dish, an unsweetened wheat-grain stew called frumenty, and seems to be related to the traditional *gröt* of the Scandinavians and the Polish-Russian wheat-grain *kutyas* discussed in later chapters. As the dish evolved, beef broth was added, and brown bread for thickening, then spices, gingerbread, raisins and currants. Some authorities believe that setting the pudding afire goes back to the fire rites of *Saturnalia*.

In Old England, plum pudding was called simply "Christmas" pudding. According to one English tradition, it should be made on "Stir-up" Sunday, the first Sunday of Advent. The nickname derives from the opening words of the collect for the day, "Stir up, we beseech Thee, O Lord. . . ."

Other traditionalists maintain that plum pudding should be prepared many months before serving so it will be well aged. According to these, unless "you . . . have a plum pudding grown rich and black and solid," you will lose a friend between this Christmas and next.

Plum pudding can be as complicated and fruity as imagination suggests, but an easily made pudding can be just as good, if not better. Here is one, adapted from Eliza Acton's 1845 recipe, which fills the latter specification. An added virtue is that it makes a small amount.

Plum Pudding

¾ cup suet, ground or chopped fine   ¼ teaspoon salt

½ cup minced, peeled apples   ¼ cup candied orange rind

½ cup fine bread crumbs   ¾ cup raisins

½ cup flour, sifted with   ¾ cup currants

⅛ teaspoon mace   ¾ cup light brown sugar

½ teaspoon nutmeg   ¼ cup brandy

3 eggs, well beaten

Mix all ingredients except eggs until well blended. Work with hands if necessary. Stir in eggs. Tie tightly in a thickly floured cloth or, preferably, pour into a lightly greased pudding mold or coffee can which can be covered tightly. Place on a rack in a pan with boiling water extending two thirds of the way up the side of container. Boil for 3 hours. To serve, reheat by steaming, or wrap pudding in foil paper and heat in oven.

For decoration, as well as extra flavor, follow an 1820 suggestion: Stick blanched, split almonds all over the pudding and set aflame before bringing to table.

Serves 8 to 10

Plum Pudding with Plums

Plum (or "plumb") pudding got its name from raisins, which were called plumbs long ago. Here is a delicious, light caramel-type pudding made with real plums (prunes). It will keep satisfactorily for a month or more refrigerated, but gains nothing with aging. It can be served immediately after cooking, or reheated in the same manner as the foregoing pudding.

1 cup prunes	*1 teaspoon cinnamon*
1 cup light brown sugar	*1 teaspoon nutmeg*
2 eggs, well beaten	*1 teaspoon cloves*
1 teaspoon baking soda	*1 cup sifted flour*
½ teaspoon baking powder	*1 cup buttermilk*
1 teaspoon salt	*2 cups minced suet*
1 teaspoon allspice	*1 cup seeded raisins*

Put prunes in hot water and soak at least ½ hour before stoning and measuring. Cut in quarters. Cream sugar and beaten eggs. Add baking soda, baking powder, salt and spices to flour and sift together. Stir into egg mixture, alternating with buttermilk. Add minced suet, quartered prunes and seeded raisins. Pour into greased mold and boil. For small molds, boil 2 to 2½ hours; for large mold, 4 hours. Serve hot with or without custard sauce. Good both ways.

Yield: 2 one-quart molds

Custard Sauce

4 egg yolks	*¼ teaspoon salt*
¼ cup sugar	*2 cups milk, scalded*
	1 teaspoon vanilla

Put egg yolks in top of double boiler and beat slightly. Add sugar and salt. Slowly stir in scalded milk. Cook over water which is kept just below boiling point. Stir constantly until thickened. Add vanilla and serve.

This sauce is delicious with any caramelized pudding.

Yield: About 2½ cups

37

The two following recipes produce what we would call ice cream. Both are so good, it is impossible to make a choice between them.

Frozen Plumb Pudding

(Old Recipe)

½ cup maraschino cherries
Brandy to cover cherries
1 quart milk
2 cups sugar
4 eggs, beaten
¼ teaspoon salt

2 cups raisins
1 cup chopped candied
   pineapple
1 cup chopped nuts
2 tablespoons orange
   marmalade

1 quart cream, whipped

Soak cherries in brandy overnight or longer (or use brandied cherries). In a double boiler, simmer milk, sugar, and eggs, stirring constantly until custard forms. Add salt. Cool. When chilled, fold in fruit, nuts, marmalade, and whipped cream. Freeze.

Yield: approximately 3 quarts

Frozen Plum Pudding

(Another Way)

In the South, pounded macaroons, called for in the following recipe, were a common ingredient when ice cream was made in hand-turned freezers. They add both texture and flavor.

3 cups milk
10 egg yolks, well beaten
1½ cups sugar
¼ teaspoon salt, or to taste
¾ cup chopped candied
   fruit

½ cup chopped blanched
   almonds
½ cup powdered macaroons
   (in blender)
1½ cups cream, whipped (or
   more, to taste)

½ cup sherry

In a double boiler cook together milk, egg yolks, salt, and sugar, stirring constantly until thick. Chill. When cool, fold in candied fruit, nuts, macaroons, whipped cream, and sherry. Freeze.

Yield: 3 quarts

"Minc'd," "minched," or "shrid" pie has been traced to the Crusaders, who brought back all sorts of Oriental spices when they returned from the Holy Land. A pie containing such spices was thought to be particularly appropriate for the Nativity. The spices represented the gift of the Magi, even though Frankincense and Myrrh were not spices, but incense.

This led to a curious custom of baking the pie in an oval tin in the shape of a manger. Sometimes a slight depression was made in the top of the pie, and a small figure of the Christ Child placed in it. When the pie was eaten, the baby was removed and the manger served. The Puritans naturally looked on it as an idolatrous horror and condemned eating mince pie as a popish observance. Contrarily, Anglicans and Catholics stoutly defended it and perhaps ate more than ever to prove their orthodoxy.

In contrast with the Puritan attitude there is an old superstition that refusing a piece of mince pie at Christmas means ill luck for the ensuing year.

Eighteenth-century Americans made much less work of mincemeat than most contemporary recipes demand. Instead of spending hours simmering all ingredients, they combined cooked meat with the spices, brandy and cider, fruits and suet, and put it in a crock in a cool place to stand until used. With today's added convenience of freezing, there is no reason to make mincemeat a great deal of work. The small amount of time involved in the two recipes following is amply rewarded by the remarkable results.

Mincemeat for Pie

(*Said to be from East Chester, New York, 1760*)

2⅓ pounds "nice beef,"
chopped or thinly sliced
(roasted or boiled)
1¼ pounds ground suet
3 cups brown sugar
3½ pounds tart apples, peeled
and chopped
3½ pounds mixed chopped
candied fruit, citron, raisins,
and currants

1 cup dark molasses
1½ teaspoons salt
1 cup good sherry
2 cups sweet cider
1 cup good brandy
¼ cup ground nutmeg
8 teaspoons ground cinnamon
5¼ teaspoons ground allspice
1⅓ tablespoons ground cloves
Lemon juice optional

Mix all ingredients well and pack in stone crock, sterilized jars, or coffee cans lined with plastic wrap. Store jars or crock in cool place and use within 10 days; or store in refrigerator for several weeks; in freezer, three months.

To make pies, add chopped nuts to taste, and 1 spoonful black pepper per quart of mincemeat. As *The Virginia House-wife* observed, "This greatly improves the flavor and can better be mixed with a small portion than with the whole mass." Lemon juice may be added if tarter pie is desired. (The original recipe called for 3½ pounds of sugar.)

Yield: 8 quarts mincemeat

Duke of Gloucester's Mincemeat

(*Old Virginia recipe*)

3 large lemons
1¼ pounds ground beef suet
½ pound brown sugar
¼ pound blanched almonds,
chopped fine
½ pound citron cut in thin
pieces or shredded
½ cup brandy

1 pound apples, peeled and
chopped
1 tablespoon cloves
1 tablespoon ginger
1 tablespoon mace
1 tablespoon nutmeg
1 teaspoon salt
½ cup sherry
3 cups cider

Extract juice from lemons and save. Boil rind and pulp in three waters to extract bitterness. Pound in a mortar or put in blender until smooth as butter. Add lemon juice and remaining ingredients. Mix well.

Store as suggested in previous recipe.

To make pie, add 1 teaspoon black pepper per quart of mincemeat, and 1 tablespoon flour per pie (for thickening). Pour thin layer of mincemeat on prepared pie crust, then add layer of thinly sliced roast beef or boiled beef (preferably the former), then cover with additional mincemeat and crust.

Yield: about 3 quarts

The lemon in the foregoing recipe gives an especially delightful flavor, not too cloying.

The amount of suet given in these old recipes can be reduced with no great loss and may be an improvement according to today's taste. With modern heating we do not need the amount of fat and sugar that our colonial ancestors preferred. With either of these mincemeat recipes, the traditional method can be altered and the apples omitted at mixing time. Adding apples when making the pies will allow the mincemeat to be kept on a cool shelf for several months.

CHAPTER III

New England

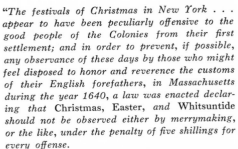

"*The festivals of Christmas in New York . . .
appear to have been peculiarly offensive to the
good people of the Colonies from their first
settlement; and in order to prevent, if possible,
any observance of these days by those who might
feel disposed to honor and reverence the customs
of their English forefathers, in Massachusetts
during the year 1640, a law was enacted declaring that* Christmas, Easter, *and* Whitsuntide
*should not be observed either by merrymaking,
or the like, under the penalty of five shillings for
every offense.*

"*In 1643 pastry, plum cakes, and 'sinful dalliance' were held in utter abomination by the
Puritanical Court of New Haven. In this year
they banished Goodman Hunt and his wife from
the Colony, 'for keeping the counsells of Wm.
Harding, baking him a pastry, and plum cakes,
and keeping company with him on the Lord's
Day, and she suffering Harding to kiss her.*"
—GABRIEL FURMAN

The first code of laws promulgated in Connecticut forbade any
colonist to "read the Common Prayer, keep Christmas or saint
days, make mince pie, dance, play cards, or play on any instru-
ment of music except the drum, trumpet, and Jews harp," and
succeeding laws in New Haven and Massachusetts were in-

creasingly stringent, encouraged by the accession of Cromwell in England.

The Puritans based their opposition to Christmas on doctrinal grounds. They read the Scriptures carefully—perhaps to find what they sought—and interpreted them literally. The Bible said that one day a week should be set aside for rest, but that the other six were for labor. Therefore, unless it happened to fall on the Sabbath, December 25 should be a work day.

In Puritanical New Haven, kissing was condemned as "sinful dalliance." It was not allowed on the Sabbath, even between man and wife or between parents and children. That must have astounded Gabriel Furman, for kissing games were an outstanding feature of Christmas Week parties in New York City.

English holiday revelry, which often interfered with the religious observances of the Puritans, offended them. Seasonal gaieties were intimately connected with the local churches. Christmastime music-making and games such as wrestling and cockfighting took place right on the church grounds in medieval times. Until after 1650, there were still dances in country churches in Northern England on Christmas Day, after the conclusion of the service.

However, the most important reason the Puritans hated Christmas undoubtedly was that it reminded them of the Tory establishment which had persecuted them. Unconsciously, they identified the Church of England with royal officials.

It has been speculated that their antagonism to Christmas was responsible for our Thanksgiving, and that it first began as a subtle substitute for the despised holiday. In any case, Puritan Thanksgivings must have been grim and cheerless occasions.

The first anti-Christmas laws in Massachusetts forbade *public* celebration. Anyone who felt compelled to observe Christmas "as a matter of conscience and devotion" could do so indoors. Perhaps the Puritans hoped the holiday would wither away. More probably, they were afraid to take stronger action; for, in 1659, soon after their percentage of the total population was increased—by a galaxy of ardent Puritan ministers—they passed a law ordering all men to work on Christmas Day. Anyone seen at play or caught loitering on the streets was subject to arrest and imprisonment, fine and whipping—a common punishment considered quite lenient. The people who had been bitter nonconformists in their homeland now became rigid conformists.

Ironically, the New York Dutch, who had once offered refuge to Pilgrims fleeing English persecution, now protected colonists driven out of Massachusetts by Puritanical wrath. Colonists who were expelled from Massachusetts or who left voluntarily founded Connecticut (except New Haven), New Hampshire, and Rhode Island.

The New England Pilgrims were not the only Americans who disapproved of Christmas. All religious sects that exalted the Sabbath to the exclusion of other days, and those professing an aversion to "waste," shared their distaste. These groups included the "Plain Dutch" (Mennonites, Amish, and Brethren), Presbyterians, Methodists, Baptists, and Congregationalists. But they tended to be minorities in areas where they settled, and did not attempt to impose their will on others. The Quakers, also, did not believe in celebrating Christmas because they considered all days to be holy and of equal importance.

In 1681, the anti-Christmas law was repealed in Massachusetts, but December 25 remained a working day and shops stayed open. Perhaps the first legally held Christmas service in the colony took place five years later when Governor Andros conducted one in the Boston Town Hall.

In 1791, separation of the Church and state were made secure by an amendment to the Constitution. Thereafter, members of the Puritanical churches were less inclined to oppose celebration of Christmas, since it no longer symbolized political domination by the Church of England. The arrival of new immigrant groups such as the Irish Catholic and German Protestants also reinforced Christmas. It should be noted, however, that Christmas became legal and remains so today only as a secular holiday, not a religious one.

Toward the latter half of the nineteenth century, Christmas

44

became increasingly popular in Massachusetts. Newspaper advertisements around 1840 for a variety of Christmas entertainment and for "rich and elegant goods, suitable for Christmas presents," indicate the great emphasis on secular pleasures. Indeed, a case could be made that commercialization of Christmas really began in New England. Gift exchange was not common elsewhere except in the homes of German immigrants.

The Christmas card, one of the holiday's most inescapable symbols, was first widely popularized in the Boston area, because of the presence there of Louis Prang. Although cards had been printed earler in Albany, New York, Prang was so skillful in designing and printing them that he became known as the "Father of American Christmas Cards."

The custom of exchanging illustrated greetings dates back to pre-Christian Egypt and Rome, where wishes for a happy new year were inscribed on year-end gifts. In the fifteenth century master engravers began producing prints carrying a religious motif along with the new year's message. An outstanding example is one by Master E. S., in which the Christ Child holds a scroll which reads, "A good and happy year."

Prang was a skilled lithographer who had been printing cards with scenes and floral designs for use as visiting cards, etc., for some years. In 1875 he added seasonal greetings. Some cards bore scenes of the Nativity; but others were more like valentines, with children, pretty girls, birds, and butterflies. Christmas cards grew rapidly in popularity, but cheap competition made them virtually a German monopoly by around 1900. Two world wars and increasing technology have changed this situation. The current trend, however, seems to be back to pre-Christian days, with simple messages and art work only vaguely related to Christmas, if at all. This is undoubtedly due in part to the mixture of races and religions in this country, and reluctance to offend anyone not devoted to Christmas.

Christmas in Boston today is a far cry from that of the seventeenth century. It is enough to make the anti-Christ's-Maesse Puritans turn over in their graves. Since 1949, the city has put on a spectacular Christmas display. Huge garlands of greenery are hung along the streets and over 70,000 lights and 24 miles of wire and cable are used to decorate trees on the Boston Common, where a life-size crèche scene is situated. There is also a Children's Playland featuring live reindeer, sheep, and donkeys. Choirs from all over New England furnish daily Christmas music.

And there is a huge Christmas feast, patterned after the early Thanksgiving feasts, with turkey as its mainstay. Mince pie is so commonplace and popular that often it is thought to have originated in New England.

A number of French Canadians migrated into New England, and especially to Rhode Island, the most tolerant state of all. A traditional Christmas dish they brought along was a pork pie, which was part of the midnight meal following Christmas Eve mass. In this country, the pie underwent some changes, the most notable being the addition of beef.

Rhode Island Tourtière

Double crust for one pie   *¼ teaspoon pepper*
1 pound ground lean pork   *⅛ teaspoon nutmeg*
⅔ pound ground lean beef   *1 teaspoon cinnamon*
1 small onion, chopped   *¼ teaspoon sage*
1 teaspoon salt   *Cracker crumbs*

Prepare double pie crust and refrigerate dough until ready to use. Put ground meat, chopped onion, salt, pepper, and nutmeg in stewing pan. Bring to boil and simmer 20 minutes. Add cinnamon and sage, and adjust seasoning.

Turn oven to 450° F. Roll out half of pie crust and arrange in pie pan. Add sufficient cracker crumbs to meat mixture to thicken. Pour into pie crust. Roll out second crust and lay on top, sealing edges. Bake for 15 minutes, then lower heat to 350° and bake until golden brown.

This pie rewarms very satisfactorily, or the meat mixture

may be prepared in advance and kept until ready to bake pie.

How the *tourtière* became a lumberjack pie is something of a mystery, since lumberjacks profess never to have heard of it! However, it, too, is traditional for Christmas Eve in some parts of Maine and Massachusetts, and would seem to have originated in hard times when it was necessary to extend the meat. It is just as delicious as the pie without potatoes, and rewarms very satisfactorily.

New England Lumberjack Pie

1 recipe tourtière *filling (omit   1 cup mashed potatoes*
cracker crumbs)

Dehydrated potatoes can be used very satisfactorily in this pie. In cooking potatoes, use only enough water to solidify them, and omit milk completely. Otherwise, follow instructions on package. Mix mashed potatoes with meat filling. If necessary, add a little broth or bouillon to give good consistency. Mixture should not be runny. Put together and bake as in *tourtière*.

Undoubtedly, New England's stellar contribution to the American Christmas feast is the cranberry. Cranberry pie looks Christmasy, and is a pleasant alternative to other traditional, rich desserts. It is delicious either as a deep-dish pie, or with a double crust.

Cranberry Pie

¾ cup raisins	*¼ teaspoon salt*
1 pound cranberries	*½ cup cold water*
1¾ cups sugar	*1 tablespoon grated orange rind*
¼ cup flour	*Pie crust*
3 tablespoons butter	

Pour hot water over raisins to plump, then drain. Grind cranberries, using coarsest knife of food chopper. Mix sugar with flour and salt. Add to ground berries, raisins, water, and orange rind. Mix well. For two-crust pie, turn oven to 450° F. Roll half the pastry to ⅛″ thickness. Line a 9″ pan with crust. Add cranberry mixture and dot with butter. Roll remaining pastry to ⅛″, cover pie and seal edges. Cut gashes for escape of steam. Bake 15 minutes, then lower heat to 375° F. and bake another 30 minutes, or until golden brown. Serve cold.

For deep dish pie, turn oven to 425° F., fill deep pan with cranberry mixture. Dot with butter. Roll out crust and cover cranberries, overlapping edges of pan with crust. Gash. Bake 30 to 40 minutes, until golden brown. Serve cold.

CHAPTER IV

SECTION A

Pennsylvania

THE PENNSYLVANIA DUTCH

> *"The most important thing the Pennsylvania Dutch do on Christmas day is visit the cemetery and leave flowers for the dead.*
> *"I try to preserve my husband's family traditions. . . . We begin the year by taking a silver coin in the left hand and eating a piece of fish from the right as the clock strikes twelve on New Year's Eve."*
> —Young wife of a Pennsylvania Dutchman

"Christmas is the most German of all German folk festivals," Theodore Dreiser once observed, properly placing emphasis on the secular aspect which predominates in German year-end celebrations.

Christmas in Germany is *Weihnachten* or "Watch Night," a night of magical revelation. Mountains open, it is whispered, to reveal hoards of precious stones; church bells ring out from cities at the bottom of the sea; trees burst into blossom and fruit; and the sun jumps thrice for joy. The twelve-day period centering around Christmas is *Die Zwölf Rauhnächte*, the "twelve rough nights," or the raging rout that formerly centered around the winter solstice on December 21. Depending

49

upon the area and local custom, it may fall either before or after Christmas.

A person born on Christmas Eve can understand the language of dumb beasts, the Pennsylvania Dutch say, for at that time animals receive the power of speech and can predict the future. Water momentarily turns to wine, and if only one guesses the exact moment, he can dip it up freely. Three different kinds of food should be placed on the windowsill and a portion of each eaten on Christmas Day to prevent fevers the remainder of the year. Witches are prevalent, so it is best not to clean the stables during Christmas week. And it is bad luck to bathe—anyone who does will catch cold! (Strangely, these last two superstitions go against those of other countries which call for thorough cleansing of house and body for the new year.) On Christmas Eve one can take advantage of the presence of evil spirits and rid himself of his most hated enemy: Simply find a spot where two roads cross, cast a bullet there, load it in a gun, and fire it. The shot will seek out its quarry, no matter where he may be.

So say the Pennsylvania or "Gay" Dutch, descendants of the first large group of German settlers to come to America. The confusing term "Dutch" is a literal appropriation of the German word *deutsch*, meaning German.

The Pennsylvania Dutch never merged with their neighbors as did the Holland Dutch in New York. Rather, they were criticized for their tendency to form cultural islands wherever they settled. They had such winning Christmas ways, however, that in time they succeeded in partially converting both the English Quakers and the less tolerant Scotch-Irish. Even the other Pennsylvania Germans, the "Plain People"—Amish, Mennonites, and Brethren—discovered it was possible to eat a cookie or two and take a glass of wine during the holiday season and not suffer ill effects afterward.

The German Gay Dutch were able to exert so much influence partly because there were so few Quakers. In 1750, Benjamin Franklin estimated that Penn's followers numbered only one third of the total Pennsylvania population. There were two reasons for this. The persecution of Quakers in England ceased soon after Pennsylvania was founded, thus destroying their chief incentive to leave the country. Secondly, Queen Anne, who ascended the throne in 1702, adopted a conscious policy of filling the American colonies with foreign Protestants hostile to France and Spain, while trying to keep her English subjects at home.

About that time Louis XIV inadvertently came to her aid. In a determined effort to annex the Rhineland to France, his troops overran the Palatinate again and again in a series of devastating raids. Thousands were driven from their homes in the dead of winter. Fields were burned to cinder, and vineyards chopped to the ground.

Queen Anne invited the victims of Louis' ruthlessness to settle in her American colonies. So many accepted her call that the Rhineland was soon threatened with complete depopulation. Before the migration ended, over 150,000 persons had left forever. Not all settled in Pennsylvania. A number went farther south to the Carolinas and Georgia.

The people who sought their fortune in Pennsylvania were so poverty-stricken, they came as redemptionists. That is, in order to secure passage abroad, they agreed to sell themselves to servitude for a period of three to five years upon arrival. For over a century they lived in isolation, without their own pastors or churches. During that period they either attended churches of other faiths, or gave up formal worship altogether. Most of the second generation, who grew up with little or no schooling, clung tenaciously to the basic German language and customs. When complaint was made about their refusal to learn English, they retorted that the Hanoverian kings in England spoke German better than English. The question as to whether the English rulers could readily have understood the rapidly evolving new language of Pennsylvania Dutch was apparently never posed.

Under the rude circumstances of their life, the Pennsylvania Dutch placed greater emphasis than ever on secular Christmas traditions. When they were able, they revived the customs they recalled from their childhood on the Rhine: Second Christmas; *Pelznichol;* mumming; good food and drink; and, most important of all, Christkindle and his decorated tree and gifts.

First Christmas was supposed to be a solemn and holy day, but Second Christmas was a day of relaxation, given more to fun and games. Until the turn of this century, Dutch Pennsylvania celebrated a second secular day for all traditional Church days, as is still customary today in most of Europe. They did so in a riotous way, with greased-pig races, shooting matches, fireworks, and free drinks.

In the 1850s, some ministers tried to sanctify Second Christmas in Pennsylvania by holding church consecrations and Sunday-school exercises on December 26. But to their dismay, the Pennsylvania Dutch appeared and turned the occasion into a kind of country fair by setting up stands to sell their cakes and wares.

To the transplanted Germans, accustomed to festive Christmas fairs from the time of the Middle Ages, their actions were perfectly normal. The Pennsylvania Dutch housewife must have longingly recalled the gaiety and conviviality of the fairs when she set about preparing for Christmas, especially when she took down and cleaned the carefully stored fancy cookie cutters brought to this country as part of her meager belongings.

First, she made lebkuchen, so they would have sufficient time to develop in flavor. From neighbors she borrowed additional cookie molds, for design was as important as taste in cookies, if not more so. And what an array of shapes were used in early Pennsylvania: fish, rabbits, elephants, men smoking Dutch pipes, men riding horseback, hatchet-bearing Indians, stars, dolls, stags, and hearts of all sizes. Some reindeer were over a foot long. Even doughnuts, seldom if ever served at any other time of year, were cut in elaborate designs.

The standard of measurement for baking in those days was "by the washbasketful," as it still is in many Pennsylvania Dutch homes. Washbasketfuls were needed. For one thing, several dozen were sent back with the borrowed cutters. Children chose the best specimens for lining the windows facing the roadway. A great many were needed for Belsnickles who came begging on Christmas Eve. And some were tucked in baskets for the poor.

Eventually, as the German population became more prosperous, other cookies came into vogue: Most common were sand tarts, sugar cookies, and something known variously as apies, appies, apiece, A. P.'s, etc. Their origin is unknown and still disputed, but a generally accepted story credits them to a young woman named Ann Page, who proudly cut her initials in the tops of the cookies before putting them in the oven to bake. Just why she would want to claim them so boldly is not altogether clear, if the following recipe is as authentic as it purports to be: "one pound of flour, half a pound of butter, a glass of wine, a tablespoonful of rose water, half a pound powdered white sugar, one grated nutmeg, a teaspoonful of beaten cinnamon and mace and three tablespoonsful of caraway seed." Miss Page, or whoever introduced the cookies to Pennsylvania, had evidently been in New York. The recipe's resemblance to the popular caraway-seeded New Year's Cake cannot be accidental.

Apies might not please the gourmet, but when gaily decorated with colored icing commas and question marks, they were ideal for decorating the Christmas tree set up on a table in the center of one room, and a great many were needed for it.

When and where the first evergreen tree was decorated for Christmas in America will probably never be known. One persistent legend has it that Hessian mercenaries who fought in the Revolutionary War were the first to have Christmas trees, but the story is largely supposition. The first written references indicate the custom had long been established in Pennsylvania. An 1821 diary mentions going out to get a tree, and in 1823 the York *Gazette* humorously told how a *Krischkintle Bauhm* (Pennsylvania Dutch for "Christ Child's Tree") was decorated.

For that matter, we do not know when or where the first Christmas tree was decorated in Europe. It is a curious fact that no records from the Middle Ages mention a Christmas tree. Is it because there were none, or because decorated trees were customary at many times of the year and taken for granted? Peasants decorated trees for Shrovetide, Palm Sunday, Easter, Ascension Day, St. Martin's, St. Nicholas', New Year's, et cetera; and for May Day they adorned a stripped tree, the maypole, with flowers and ribbons.

It is more likely that initially the Christmas tree went by some other name and that today's title came into usage in relatively recent times. In parts of Bavaria the Christmas tree is still referred to as the *Paradeis*. This confirms a theory that the Christmas tree was originally a "Paradise tree," of which there is a kind of history.

The Paradise tree was the most important stage property— in fact, the only one—in a popular mystery play about the fall of Adam and Eve. The drama re-enacted the creation, temptation, eating of the forbidden fruit, and expulsion from the Garden of Eden, or Paradise, and ended by foretelling Christ's coming and Incarnation. It thus led directly into the story of the Nativity, and was ideal for presentation during Advent.

Although the Roman Church never officially recognized Adam and Eve as saints, December 24 was commonly celebrated as their birthday in the Middle Ages. The play was frequently given as part of the celebration. A small fir tree was hung with apples to represent the tree of the forbidden fruit, and before the performance began, it was paraded around town by the actors, probably to drum up attendance. When a crowd gathered, the tree was placed in the center of the stage, and the play began. If the play was presented inside the church, burning candles were placed around the tree in a large circle and the scenes enacted within it.

When miracle plays were suppressed in the fifteenth century because of their growing secularity, the custom of a Christmas Eve feast in honor of Adam and Eve retreated to the home, where it was kept privately. The apple-hung Paradise tree was retained as part of the celebration, probably because of man's innate urge to liven his surroundings at this time of year.

54

Other uses of Christmas greenery and decoration co-existed with the Paradise tree. In the Northland, evergreens were hung in both house and barn in late December, often in the form of a treetop hung from the rafters, as protection against the devil.

In parts of Germany and Bohemia, a pyramid skeleton form was placed on a table and decorated with cookies, fruit, candles, and greenery. At first constructed of simple wooden strips brought together at the top to form triangular sides, they developed eventually into elaborate revolving structures with a series of platforms for baubles and decorations. The Moravians brought the custom of simple wooden pyramids to Pennsylvania and preserved it until the late nineteenth century. Such pyramids are still used in the United States today.

Decorating trees may have been partially inspired by the ancient custom of gathering branches of flowering trees in late autumn and bringing them indoors so they would be forced to bloom by Christmas. In parts of Germany and France today, cherry and hawthorne are cut on St. Barbara's Day, December 4, and the way the boughs blossom foretells the future. The flowers also fulfill the superstition that bushes blossom on *Weihnacht*.

The first known record of decorated trees is a 1603 fragment that refers to the Paradise tree. "At Christmas," it reads, "fir trees are set up in rooms at Strasbourg, and hung with roses cut from paper of many colors, apples, painted hosts [small white wafers used in Communion], sugar, etc." Sometime during the fifteenth century hosts were added to the apples hanging on the Paradise tree. In the eighteenth century, figures of Adam and Eve and the serpent suddenly appeared for sale in Hamburg, Germany. They were placed under the tree, and so seem to have been inspired by the Paradise tree.

Soon the urge to hang more decorations on the Paradise tree arose. Hosts were discarded and ornamental cookies took their place. Traditionally, brown dough was used for figures of men, animals, and birds; white for others such as stars, hearts, flowers, angels, et cetera.

The early Church frowned on gifts at Christmas, but the pagan custom of year-end gifts never really died out. By the twelfth century, it was accepted in Germany for Christmas Day or Christmas Eve. One explanation offered was that a Christmas gift was a "child's foot" for the Christ Child. When a new baby arrived in any German family, a gift was mandatory for each older child. The name given such gifts was "child's foot." Since the Christ Child was portrayed as the smaller brother of all children, a gift at Christmas could represent a "child's foot" for Him. The tree, too, was proclaimed as His gift, and christened "Christ's tree."

Such reasoning suggests how the Germanic people were able to escape the emotional violence let loose in England by the Reformation and Counter Reformation. Despite all strictures of the Roman and Protestant Churches against pagan custom, the Germans continued to keep honored tradition more or less as they had for centuries by making certain minor modifications. When St. Nicholas was denounced, he vanished temporarily. Then, as if by magic, a new gift bearer, the fair Christkind, appeared, pictured at times as bearing a small Christmas tree in one hand. He carried it with him all the way to Pennsylvania.

The custom of placing lighted candles on the Christmas tree came about sometime later in the wake of Lutheranism, but the time or place of the first candlelit tree is not known. According to one tradition, Martin Luther himself first thought of it. Late one December evening, the story goes, while trudging wearily homeward, Luther was greatly moved by the beauty of the clear, moonlit night. From time to time he could glimpse through the tall firs a skyful of stars so dazzling they seemed literally to dance on the patches of snow caught on the limbs overhead. At home, Luther tried to share the experience with his family, but words failed him. Suddenly he caught sight of a slender fir set up for Christmas on a table in the center of the room. Quickly, he took some small candles from a drawer, fastened them to the branches and lighted them. Then he snuffed out the only lamp in the room, and turned to his loved ones. "You see," he said, as the awestruck children gazed upon the glittering tree, "it was a little like this." It is pleasant to think it may be true.

It may be, as some people believe, that the candle-ornamented pyramids and decorated Christmas trees were combined. Pyramids attained their greatest popularity about the time candle-lighted trees became common and dwindled when Christmas trees too large for a table grew popular.

The conclusion is inescapable that when English-speaking people became acquainted with Christ's tree sometime in the nineteenth century, they renamed it Christmas tree, somewhat in the same way they changed Kriss Kingle into Santa Claus. In England, decorated trees were introduced in the 1820s by German merchants and court officials. (They really caught on overnight when Victoria married Prince Albert in 1840.) The first time we know that the term "Christmas tree" appeared in print in America was in 1830, in a newspaper story about a publicly exhibited tree in York, Pennsylvania.

The popularity of the Christmas tree spread throughout New England a few years later via the publication and wide circulation of a penny pamphlet. It was a reprint of an excerpt from a book of 1838 by Harriet Martineau, *Retrospect of Western Travel*, which described a "German Christmas tree" set up by a German professor at Harvard.

"The tree was the top of a young fir," she wrote, "planted in a tub . . . ornamented with moss." It was adorned liberally with cups fashioned from gilded egg shells and gaily colored paper cornucopias filled with "comfits, lozenges, and barley-sugar." Seven dozen wax tapers were fitted to the limbs, and "smart dolls and other whimsies glittered in the evergreen . . . there was not a twig which had not something sparkling upon it . . . the room seemed ablaze, and the ornaments were so well hung that no accident happened, except that one doll's petticoat caught fire."

Miss Martineau did such a good job of publicizing the Christmas tree in the Puritan homeland that by 1852 it was described as "One of the household gods of New England," a thought which would have driven the founding fathers into apoplectic rage.

The first American Christmas trees were in the German tradition, modest arrangements a few feet high, set on a table in the center of the living room. But in the new country, the tendency was then, as it is now, for everything to grow bigger and better with increasing prosperity. Sometime in the late 1800s table trees were abandoned, and a larger tree placed in the corner of the room against the wall—still an economical arrangement. A few years later, the tree became higher and wider, and moved from its corner nook. It touched the ceiling and spread out on all sides with decorations all around.

Today, figures show that Americans decorate over 40 million trees each year. In some homes each child has his own tree; in others, there is a different tree for every room. Indeed, the will to decorate and trim something at Christmastime often seems insatiable. In Florida, palm trees are decorated, while in Texas and California, oil wells, and so on.

It is believed that a farmer in the Catskills was the first to think of cutting trees for sale and taking them to New York City during the holidays of 1851. For years the custom in many families was to cut their own tree, as part of the holiday fun. Grandma Moses recorded this American experience for all time in a series of nostalgic, colorful paintings set in her own state of New York around the turn of the century.

Careful pruning and shaping is required to make trees full and bushy, a fact capitalized on by the first canny person to start a Christmas-tree farm. According to today's standards, less than 10 percent of naturally grown trees are considered satisfactory for use as Christmas trees. Not only does Christmas-tree farming provide a better product, it allows for a variety of species and greater choice.

Pruning is expensive, however. Skyrocketing prices have encouraged a return to sentiment and past practice. In some areas there are now Christmas-tree farms that encourage families to come pick out a tree, cut it, and haul it home. The farmer has less risk of unsold trees, the buyers a better tree.

The candlelit trees of olden days must have been a joy to behold, but the pleasure was necessarily a short-lived one because of the threat of fire. When bigger Christmas trees came in, the candles and the danger multiplied many times. For a 12-foot tree, some 400 candles were set aflame, while a home-grown fire brigade stood guard.

The necessity of finding a satisfactory replacement for lighted candles was obvious. In Pennsylvania around 1860, gas jets were sometimes used; and in the 1880s electric lighting was attempted, sometimes successfully, sometimes not. In Reading, Pennsylvania, in 1886, a 25-foot tree was illuminated by 220 two-candle-power electric lamps fired by a basement dynamo run by waterpower. It must have been an exciting moment, but the solution was hardly a practical one. Finally, in 1895, a New England telephone company employee conceived of stringing together the small signal bulbs used on telephone switchboards, and probably produced the first fixtures to resemble contemporary Christmas tree lights.

With the perfection of outdoor insulation, the possibilities for spectacular display multiplied. In Washington, D.C., approximately 4,000 bulbs are required for the national Christmas tree, and nearly 8,000 for the 53 smaller trees representing the states and territories. (The national Christmas tree should not be confused with the General Grant Sequoia in California which was officially dedicated in 1926 as the "Nation's Christmas Tree.")

The tree in the nation's capital averages from 65 to 70 feet in height, about the same as the one erected annually since 1933 in Rockefeller Center in New York City. Many consider the latter to be the most beautiful tree in the nation.

In a country as vast as the United States, with cities and states all seeking to outdo one another, it is manifestly impossible to name every unique or important Christmas-tree display. A random sampling would include the following as among the most outstanding: "The largest living Christmas tree," a 400-year-old live oak 75 feet high by 110 feet wide in Wilmington, North Carolina; 180 cone-shaped Himalayan or Deodar cedars over 80 feet high which line Christmas Tree Lane in Altadena (Pasadena), California; and the year-round Christmas tree maintained by the residents of Christmas, Florida.

Christmas, Florida, was not named for commercial purposes. Rather, its early settlers followed Columbus' example and named it because of an important event. In 1835, during the Seminole War, a log fort was occupied on Christmas Day. Consequently, it was christened Fort Christmas, and the town which later adjoined the fort named, simply, Christmas. Christmas got on the map in many other American spots in a similarly dramatic fashion.

The American Christmas tree has come a long way from the old German Weihnacht. It has become as symbolic of America as apple pie, as demonstrated in Vietnam, when a private wrote his governor and begged for one fir tree for Christmas. From the state of Washington he received a typically American reply: 1,000 trees. As a consequence, Christmas trees were dispatched all over the small country, and the Christmas tree joined Santa Claus as promoter of the Christmas faith in strange and faraway lands.

It might be said that the Americanization of the German Christmas tree began in Pennsylvania, where occasionally *schnitz* or dried apple quarters were hung on the tree, together with popcorn garlands and cranberries.

The first cookies Pennsylvania Dutch housewives hung on the tree were cut from brown lebkuchen dough. *Leb* (life) *kuchen* (cakes) are particularly suited to the Advent and Christmas season with its promise of new life.

However, some authorities suspect the use of brown dough stems from pre-Christian Rome, with cakes formed as men replacing human beings in year-end sacrifices. Similarly, figures of animals and birds might have been offered by people too poor to offer the customary living sacrifices at Yuletide. The figure of the pig, the most common sacrificial animal, is still pervasive with the Germanic and Norse peoples, and in Central Europe.

In olden days, before the time of artificial leavenings, the honey and flour part of the dough was mixed several months in advance and left to ferment. Such dough not only had excellent lifting power, but it developed the famous lebkuchen flavor.

Lebkuchen will keep indefinitely and improve with age, so long as they are not cooked in a pan greased with ordinary fat, which may turn rancid and spoil them. For baking cookies that are to be stored a long time, use either a silicone-treated pan or beeswaxed pans. To beeswax a pan, cover entire surface with beeswax. Dust lightly with flour and heat in hot oven. Allow wax to burn off completely, leaving only an insulating film on the metal. Cool before using. Pans treated in this manner may be used over and over. If using silicone-treated pans, experiment with heat, as such pans tend to faster and hotter cooking.

For the best lebkuchen, strong and flavorful honey is best. Do not boil the honey; it will destroy natural aromas.

Lebkuchen come in many varieties and shapes. The one important factor to keep in mind is that they must *age* at least three weeks before eating. A freshly made lebcake just will not do; but store it with a slice of apple or orange in a tightly closed container, and the flavor develops into something quite different.

Lebkuchen I

4 cups sifted flour	½ cup honey
¼ teaspoon baking soda	1 egg, slightly beaten
¾ teaspoon cinnamon	¾ cup candied orange peel,
⅛ teaspoon cloves	chopped fine
¼ teaspoon nutmeg	¾ cup candied citron, chopped
1 cup brown sugar	fine
2 tablespoons water	1 cup almonds, blanched and
	shredded or ground

Combine flour, soda, cinnamon, cloves, and nutmeg, and sift together three times. Boil sugar and water 5 minutes, add honey and heat almost to boil; then set aside to cool. When cool, add to flour mixture, together with egg, chopped candied fruit, and almonds. Work into a loaf (it will be sticky). Cover with plastic wrap and place in refrigerator to age several days. To bake: Turn oven to 300° F. Roll part of dough out on lightly floured board to ¼″ thickness. Cut in 1″ x 3″ strips, or as desired. Place on prepared cookie sheet and bake 15 minutes, or until lightly brown. Do not overbake. Ice cookie strips as they come from the oven.

Icing

1 cup confectioner's sugar   ¾ teaspoon vanilla
              1 tablespoon boiling water

To make icing, combine ingredients until smooth, adding more warm water if necessary, but taking care to add only as much as needed to liquefy icing. Brush onto cookies with pastry brush. The heat from the cookies will melt the icing and cause it to spread. Put lebkuchen in a tightly covered tin to age at least three weeks. If they begin to dry out, add a slice of apple or orange.

Yield: 3⅓ dozen

The following big round lebcakes come originally from Nuremberg. Many think they are the best of all the many varieties. They are certainly the most attractive.

Lebkuchen Rounds

1 cup honey	½ teaspoon cloves
¾ cup dark brown sugar	½ teaspoon nutmeg
1 egg, beaten	½ teaspoon salt
1 teaspoon grated lemon rind	½ teaspoon soda
1 tablespoon lemon juice	⅓ cup chopped citron
2½ cups sifted flour	⅓ cup blanched almonds,
½ teaspoon allspice	finely chopped
1 teaspoon cinnamon	Whole blanched almonds
Citron chunks	

Bring honey almost to boil, then cool. Add brown sugar, beaten egg, lemon rind, and juice. Sift flour with spices, salt, and soda. Stir into honey mixture. Add chopped citron and almonds. Store overnight or longer in refrigerator.

To bake, preheat oven to 375° F. Break off chunk of dough and keep remainder chilled until needed. Roll on well-floured board to ½" thickness. Cut with circular cutters of desired size. (Cookies will spread about 1 inch in baking.) Place on well-greased tin. Decorate with whole blanched almonds arranged like petals of a daisy. Put citron chunk in center. Bake approximately 15 minutes, or until just done. Watch carefully as cookies brown quickly.

Glazing Icing

1 cup confectioner's sugar   *Hot water*

Prepare glaze by adding just enough hot water to sugar to make a thin paste. Ice cookies immediately upon taking from oven. Let them set a few seconds, then remove and place on rack to cool.

Yield: approximately 4 dozen

My mother never tasted authentic lebkuchen, but in her words, "I like a spice cookie with coffee." Seeking a recipe to suit her needs, she came upon one for lebkuchen. She took out some ingredients, then added some of her own, and here is the result: a delicious cookie, but not one a Pennsylvania Dutchman would recognize. One advantage of these cookies is that they do not require aging. However, they do keep very well.

Teden's Lebkuchen

2 cups dark brown sugar	*2 teaspoons allspice*
3 eggs, beaten	*2 teaspoons cinnamon*
¼ cup honey or dark corn	*2 teaspoons cloves*
* syrup*	*3½ cups sifted flour*
1 teaspoon soda	*1 cup chopped walnuts or*
1 teaspoon salt	* almonds*

Cream brown sugar into beaten eggs, then add syrup or honey. Add soda, salt, and spices to flour and gradually stir into egg mixture, mixing carefully. Finally add nuts. Place dough in refrigerator to chill overnight. (It will keep there a week or longer.)

When ready to bake, remove dough from refrigerator and turn oven to 300° F. Grease baking tin with turned-up edges. Roll dough to ¼" thickness to fit baking tin and place in tin. Bake 15 minutes, or until lightly brown. Remove and let cool slightly before cutting into bars. These cookies keep well, but are equally delicious while warm.

To make a crisp cookie, omit nuts. When ready to bake, lightly flour board and sprinkle generously with shaved almonds or brazil nuts. Place dough on nuts, roll out very thin, and cut into desired shapes. Put on greased sheet and bake about 7 minutes in a 400° F. oven. Watch carefully and bake only until just done.

Mae Gerhard's colored Christmas-stocking cookies contain a hidden treasure, just like a real Santa Claus stocking. They are ideal for packing in boxes of Christmas cookies, because they fill in the corners so well.

Christmas Stocking Cookies

1 cup shortening	2¼ cups flour
½ cup confectioner's sugar	¼ teaspoon salt
1½ teaspoons almond extract	Red and green food coloring

Filling

½ cup chocolate morsels	½ cup chopped pecans

Cream shortening and sugar well. Mix in almond extract, flour, and salt, creaming thoroughly. Divide dough in half (or make two batches) and add red coloring to one, green to the other. Chill one hour or more.

To make cookies, preheat oven to 375°–400° F. Take spoonful of dough in palm of hand; flatten it; then place small amount of nuts and chocolate in it lengthwise. Fold dough over filling and seal edges. Shape filled dough into stocking. Bake 10 minutes. (The chocolate will not melt during this time.) Remove and lightly frost toes and cuffs while still warm. If stockings are to be hung, run through with darning needle while still warm to make a hole for the string.

Icing

½ teaspoon butter
½ cup confectioner's sugar

½ teaspoon vanilla
2 teaspoons or more hot milk

Cream butter with part of the sugar. Add vanilla. Add remaining sugar and milk alternately, using enough liquid to give a good spreading consistency. Beat until the icing stands in sharp peaks. Spread with knife or decorating tube. Decorator icing made with egg white may be substituted.

Pennsylvania Dutch cookies used to be big and thick for dunking. These days sand tarts are made thin and crisp. The following recipe produces a particularly delicious old-fashioned sugar cookie if rolled out thickly in the old way. The name Saints' Hearts was sometimes given this recipe.

Pennsylvania Dutch Sand Tarts

1 cup butter or margarine
2 cups sugar
3 eggs
3½ cups sifted flour
1 teaspoon salt
2 teaspoons baking powder
1 teaspoon vanilla or lemon
   extract

2 tablespoons milk
3 tablespoons sugar ⎫
1 teaspoon
   cinnamon   ⎬ optional
Nutmeg
Raisins   ⎭

Cream butter and sugar together, then add eggs one at a time, beating well after each addition. Sift and measure flour, then add salt and baking powder. Gradually add to creamed sugar mixture. Stir in extract. Chill dough overnight.

65

To bake, turn oven to 350° F. for small thin cookies, 325° F. for large, thicker ones. Roll dough on a floured pastry cloth. If dainty, crisp cookies are desired, roll dough very thin, then cut with fancy cutter. Follow directions given below. Bake approximately 8 minutes.

For an old-fashioned sugar cookie, slice dough as for ice-box cookies, or roll out ¼-inch thick and cut with large circular cutter. Place on greased sheet, at least 1½-inch apart as cookies spread. Brush tops with milk, then sprinkle with mixed sugar and cinnamon or with nutmeg, as desired. Raisins are good with thick cookies. Simply press onto tops as many as desired. Bake approximately 15 minutes. Watch both thick and thin cookies carefully near end of baking time as they burn easily. Both types of cookie are soft and fragile while warm. Let set momentarily, then remove from baking sheet carefully.

This makes a very sweet cookie. Some may prefer to reduce sugar slightly.

Yield: 4–5 dozen small cookies;
2 dozen large

Schnitz are dried apple quarters, which were a staple in early Pennsylvania Dutch homes. In Schnitz Brodt they were probably substituted for some other European fruit, possibly dried pears. Black walnuts are another Americanization. We prefer the substitution of dried peaches and prunes for dried apples. The result is an especially good bread, which will be slightly brown in color, from the prunes. Schnitz brodt is especially good warm or lightly toasted and spread with butter; ideal for sandwiches, especially those made with cream cheese. It keeps well and freezes satisfactorily.

Schnitz Brodt

(Dried Fruit Bread)

1 cup dried peaches, cut in quarters	*9–10 cups flour, preferably white hard-wheat flour*
1 cup dried prunes or 2 cups dried apples	*1½ tablespoons salt*
1 package yeast	*½ tablespoon allspice*
2½ cups lukewarm water	*½ tablespoon cinnamon*
½ cup granulated sugar	*1½ cups brown sugar*
½ cup butter, lard, or shortening	*1 cup seedless raisins*
	1 cup roughly broken nut meats, preferably black walnuts

⅓ cup melted shortening and/or butter

Cook peaches and prunes until tender. Reserve liquid, which should be about ½ cup. Dissolve yeast in ½ cup lukewarm water, let stand 10 to 15 minutes, then stir. Add remaining 2 cups lukewarm water and granulated sugar. Melt ½ cup butter or lard and let cool.

Into a large bowl sift flour, salt, allspice, cinnamon, and brown sugar. Add cut-up prunes and peaches, raisins, and nuts. Make a well in flour mixture and pour in yeast mixture, melted shortening, and liquid from fruit. Stir thoroughly until dough can be handled. Add more flour if necessary. (This will make a very soft dough with regular flour.) Knead dough by lifting and stretching apart with hands, about 15 minutes. When dough is smooth and elastic, cover bowl with clean white cloth and place in warm place to rise. (The cooked dried fruit will completely disintegrate in the process of mixing and kneading.)

When dough has doubled in bulk, punch down and knead well again. Divide dough and place in well-buttered pans. (Large circular tube pans work particularly well.) Brush top with melted fat, cover, and let rise again.

When dough has doubled once more, place in preheated 400° F. oven and let bake 10 minutes, then reduce heat to 350° F. Bake another 35 to 45 minutes (depending on size of

67

loaves). When done, the bread will have a firm crust and will shrink slightly from sides of pan.

Remove bread from pan while still hot, place on rack to cool, and brush tops generously with melted fat.

Yield: two large circular loaves

Leckerli are another spicy honey cookie that must age. This old recipe is very highly spiced, and some may prefer to reduce spices somewhat. (We prefer it this way.) To bake leckerli, observe lebkuchen rules: honey heated, but not boiled; silicone or beeswaxed pan.

Leckerli

(German-Swiss Cookies)

½ cup honey
½ cup sugar
Grated rind of one half lemon
¼ cup chopped candied lemon peel
¼ cup chopped candied orange peel
2 tablespoons orange juice

1 cup slivered blanched almonds
2¼ cups sifted flour
1 tablespoon cinnamon
1½ teaspoons ground cloves
1½ teaspoons nutmeg
⅛ teaspoon salt
1 teaspoon soda

Heat honey and sugar in saucepan until well melted, but not boiled. Remove from heat. Add grated lemon rind, candied lemon peel, and orange peel. Cool to lukewarm. Stir in orange juice, sliced almonds, flour, spices, salt, and soda sifted together. Cover and let mellow at room temperature at least 2 days.

To bake, preheat oven to 325° F. On a well-floured cloth, roll out dough ½" thick. Cut into bars approximately 1½" x 3". Place on prepared baking sheets. Bake 20 minutes, or until cookies are lightly browned.

Glaze

½ *cup granulated sugar*   ¼ *cup water*

Prepare glaze while cookies are baking by cooking ½ cup sugar with ¼ cup water until it spins a thread (230° F.). Brush each cookie with hot syrup. When completely cooled, store in airtight container three weeks or more before serving.

Yield: 55 to 60 cookies

In addition to the seven (or more) sweets and sours, the Pennsylvania Dutch always serve this pea salad with turkey on Thanksgiving and Christmas. It offers a delightful change from some of the more common Christmas dishes, especially since it is so very easy to prepare. It would be pleasant also for a summer lunch or picnic with cold ham or chicken.

Pennsylvania Dutch Pea Salad

1 *jar stuffed olives, sliced*   1½ *cups diced celery*
  (3 *oz.*)   1 *small onion, diced*
1 *hard-boiled egg, sliced*   2 *tablespoons or more*
2 *cans* (17 *oz.*) *green peas*   *mayonnaise*
5 *hard-boiled eggs, chopped*   *Salt and pepper to taste*

Slice olives vertically and set aside a portion for decorating top of salad. Likewise, slice hard-boiled egg for top. Mix remaining ingredients, adding mayonnaise and seasoning to taste.

Serves 8 to 10

CHAPTER IV

SECTION B

The Moravians

"When Christmas comes on Sunday—whew! Besides the regular morning service, there is the Children's Love Feast at 3; and then the two Christmas Eve vigils at 5:30 and 7:30. I never worry about the children upsetting a burning candle. It is the adults who jiggle them around."
—Moravian adult, Bethlehem, Pennsylvania

In the first years of Pennsylvania, no one made as much of Christmas as the Moravians who settled a 5000-acre tract in "The forks of the Delaware" in 1740. The people in this community—with an unusual concentration of the nobility—were distinctly different from the Pennsylvania Dutch refugees of the German Palatinate. Though they came here from Germany, most were born in Moravia or Bohemia (both now part of Czechoslovakia). Their traditions were both Bavarian and Bohemian.

The Moravians—so named in the eighteenth century by their patron-instructor, Count Zinzendorf—were followers of John of Husinec, later known as John Hus. Born in Bohemia, Hus defied the Catholic Church one hundred years before

Luther, and was burned at the stake in Switzerland in 1415. Repressive measures and war followed, but his teachings spread until there were some 200,000 members in 400 congregations in Bohemia, Moravia, and Poland.

In the first half of the seventeenth century many Moravians engaged in the Thirty Years' War. It decimated their members and forced the Moravian movement underground. It might have died completely had not Count Zinzendorf, a well-educated Lutheran, offered sanctuary on his estate in Saxony. In 1722, the Moravians established a village named Herrnhut there.

Although other refugee groups shared his lands, the Moravians captured Zinzendorf's imagination and attention. He became an active leader in the faith, and it was under his guidance that training for overseas missionary work began in 1731. The first settlement in America, in Georgia, had to be abandoned. But the Nazareth-Bethlehem venture of 1740 was so successful that in 1752 an expeditionary force set out for North Carolina. A year later, a temporary settlement, Bethabara, was begun with the official blessing of Great Britain and German-born George II. Never intended as an enduring settlement, it lost many inhabitants to the village of Salem, which the Count had envisioned. Today, Old Salem is a living restoration in the heart of thriving Winston-Salem. Happily, it has so far escaped the museum character that plagues many similar endeavors.

In 1741, soon after the Moravians settled in Pennsylvania, Count Zinzendorf joined them and took part in the official ceremony to name the village Bethlehem. Appropriately, it was planned as part of the Christmas Eve Vigil, one of the most important ceremonies of the Church year.

When the prayers had been concluded and the congregation began singing an old German hymn, the Count took up a lighted taper and led a procession to the other end of the room. As they paced the length of the rude log cabin they sang, "Not Jerusalem [but] lowly Bethlehem it was that gave Christ to save us." When the zealous band reached the other end, they probably found an indoor stable, a common arrangement, and sleeping animals.

In both Bethlehem and Old Salem, preparations for Christmas today begin in early October with candle-making. The process is essentially the same as in early times except that steel molds, yielding one dozen candles every seven to ten minutes, are employed. According to Moravian tradition, candles must be made of beeswax because it most properly represents the sinless purity of Christ. Until the fifteenth century, beeswax candles were used almost exclusively in churches because of an ancient belief that bees originated in Paradise.

When the candles harden, volunteers trim the base with red and green paper frills that serve as decoration and protection against the drip of hot wax. It is considered a distinct honor to be asked to help with this chore. A great number of candles are needed. Over 3,000 were used in Bethlehem alone for the 1965 Christmas Eve Vigils.

On the first Sunday of Advent, a carefully preserved Herrnhut star is hung in many homes, in the hall, on the porch, or as part of an Advent wreath, and is not taken down until all Christmas greenery is removed. In Bethlehem, a Herrnhut star is hung directly over the pulpit. It is moved on Christmas and a painting of the Nativity hung on the wall instead.

The Herrnhut star originated in Germany around 1850, and was shipped abroad from the Herrnhut Star Factory with instructions in four languages. When production was halted during World War II, Moravians in Winston-Salem began making them, but now German stars are once more being imported.

The star is made of parchment-like translucent paper, cut in such a way that, when it is put together, it has 26 points. It comes unassembled, but once the points are all fastened together, it cannot easily be taken apart. A light bulb is placed inside the star.

The Herrnhut star has threefold significance for Moravians: It testifies to the Creator who made the "numberless" stars on the fourth day of Creation, "each differing in glory"; it represents the star that guided the Wise Men; and it symbolizes the promise given in the Old Testament of the star to come out of Jacob and David, and the words in the New Testament that Christ is "the bright and morning star."

In autumn, some Moravians begin preparations for the Nativity scene. The German word for it is *Krippe* or crib, but the Moravians chose *putz* because of more profound implications. Putz comes from the verb *putzen* meaning to decorate, and especially to adorn a church. The putz, they believe, should provoke thoughtful meditation and be a religious experience.

St. Francis of Assisi is often cited as having originated the Nativity scene. In 1223, he arranged a grotto setting with live animals, but it is still debated whether or not any human figures were included.

A tradition dating from the second century is that Christ was born in a grotto or cave on the outskirts of Bethlehem. There is no Biblical foundation for the notion of a stable. Luke mentions a manger, but does not say it was in a stable. In fact, mangers were often placed outside the house, by the front door. Matthew uses the word "house" to describe where the Holy Family stayed.

As far back as the fourth century, St. John Chrysostom urged the congregation on Christmas Day to try "to see the Lord lying in the manger." The impulse to fulfill his instruction literally must have soon followed with the emotional people. In the Middle Ages there were numerous attempts to recreate the atmosphere and setting of Christ's birth. Holy grottos and settings with or without figures were reconstructed everywhere in Europe, and monumental groupings were permanently installed in chapels dedicated to the Nativity. In smaller form, placed in little boxes for easy transportation, they were known as "Bethlehems."

The Jesuits were quick to recognize the possibilities of propagating the faith by a cult of the Infancy of Christ, and spread the custom around the world. They made drama of it by arranging still-life figures in sequence. Entire chapels, or the center of the church were transformed into a stage for the Nativity. In a sumptuous, realistic setting, characters associated with the Christmas story were placed so as to present views with brilliantly effective perspective. Scenes were changed in consecutive order according to the Church calendar —Advent, the Nativity, the Slaughter of the Innocents (December 28), and Epiphany. Franciscans and other orders enthusiastically followed the Jesuit lead, as did laymen and Protestants. The first mention of elaborate reconstructions of the Nativity in a church are in Bavaria and Bohemia, and Portugual.

The personality and nationality of each group that adopted it modified the original concept. In Italy and France the town of Bethlehem was depicted as a contemporary city bustling with the daily life of trade and commerce. Countless extraneous figures were added, dressed in elaborate costumes of the period, thus preserving an accurate record of the style and taste of the times.

With the Moravians, the Nativity was pastoral rather than baroque. Greenery was and is profusely used, greatly enhancing the basically barren setting of Jerusalem, and creating an air of festivity around the manger.

In the autumn Moravians gather moss from the woods and water it occasionally to keep it green for Christmas. When the putz is built—on a low platform that allows it to be easily seen and protects it against crawling youngsters—the moss is laid over a landscape of hills and valleys constructed from wadded wet newspaper and other materials. The paper fills in gaps between stumps, logs, rocks, et cetera. It adds reinforcement and helps keep the moss green. Along the sides and back of the stage, fir, spruce, or cedar boughs and trees are set upright in cans of wet sand and rocks hidden underneath the stage. Sometimes there is a running stream, a much-admired *tour de force.* Overhead there may be a painted canvas with stars, moon, and clouds, and frequently a host of angels is suspended from the ceiling.

Scenes are chosen both for their relation to the Biblical story and the family's sentiment. In addition to the manger, all scenes connected with Advent may be portrayed: the journey

74

of Mary and Joseph, shepherds watching over sheep grazing on a hillside, the Magi, and somewhere in the distance Herod's castle. The community putz in Bethlehem has seven scenes, beginning with the prophecy of Isaiah.

Carved wooden figures of characters and animals are then placed in the putz setting. Some Moravians say there must be rabbits for simplicity, and white flowers for tenderness. Above all, there must be at least one thing that is "hidden," not easily noticed. Usually there are several hidden objects such as mountain lions and wolves. These secret parts play an important role: They force the viewer to stand and study the putz carefully. In so doing he experiences more keenly the impact of the miracle of Christ's birth and its meaning to mankind.

On rare occasion, a putz is set up underneath a decorated Christmas tree, but this goes against tradition. Sometimes, too, the trees in the background are lightly decorated, but traditionalists frown on it. The host of angels may be hung from the tree branches, and often are, but nothing more. The Moravian Christmas tree is usually in a different room and considered far less important than the putz.

Families who have preserved the custom of the putz usually add something new each year, and nostalgically point out each figure to friends, recalling when it was added and why. In fact, they think of the putz the year round. "You never pass up a piece of driftwood," observes the owner of a particularly lovely putz. "And you would not dare throw away a stump, no matter how big and heavy it might be!" One huge, petrified stump in her crib scene is older than Lehigh University, which was founded in 1895.

A putz is exhibited to visitors by darkening the area where it is, then lighting up the scenes one by one as appropriate Biblical texts are read aloud. Originally, children learned the verses by heart and recited them as the scenes unfolded by candlelight. In this way they were both educated and entertained. At the end of the narration, the entire putz is lit, so that one can examine carefully its myriad detail and see the scenes not mentioned in the Scriptures.

An old pun says that the term "putz" comes not from German, but from the English verb "to put," because so much work is required. Many Moravian families have given up constructing their own, and partly because of this both Old Salem and Bethlehem erect a community putz. It is open to the public at certain times and on certain days during the Christmas season. Elsewhere, Moravian churches install a putz.

Christmas Eve in Bethlehem is a busy time. There is an afternoon children's love feast and Christmas Eve Vigils after dark. The Bethlehem Vigil, a music and candlelight service, is so popular that for some years two services have been held to accommodate everyone who wishes to attend.

Moravian love feasts began in 1727, under the inspiration of Count Zinzendorf, who introduced light food in an effort to promote and prolong the fellowship of worshiping members. He took as model the act of the Apostles after Pentecost, when they broke bread together to signify their unity and equality. In the early days of the Church, this act was considered a concrete example of the highest form of love between individuals, and was given the Greek word for love, *Agape*. Love feasts were abandoned when they began to lose their devotional character.

In the eighteenth century, the Methodists had love feasts, and more recently some churches have instituted the custom during the Christmas season. The agape of the "free churches" of the Catholic Church is related to the Moravian ceremony only by the common name derived from the Greek term.

Moravian love feasts can be held at various times, but are customary at Christmas and Easter. They are musical services during which the congregation partakes of simple food and drink while the choir sings appropriate anthems and hymns.

The food can be anything, but for practical purposes it must be easy to distribute in the church pews. Usually it is baskets of slightly sweet buns and mugs of coffee brought in on trays. The entire congregation must be served in the time space of three hymns, no easy task. For the children's love feast in Bethlehem, chocolate milk and cookies are substituted. This presents something of a contradiction, as children regularly take part in other church love feasts at which coffee is served.

A trombone choir begins the Christmas Eve Vigil by playing Christmas chorales. Anthems and hymns and an eagerly awaited solo, "Morning Star," comprise the remainder of the service. The identity of the boy who has the honor to sing the solo is a well-guarded secret.

During the next anthem, sacristans enter with trays of lighted candles and begin passing them out. By the time the songs end, everyone holds one. At the final words, "Praise to our Heavenly King," all lift their flaming tapers high above their heads in an inspired gesture of beauty, reverence, and awe.

Each member of the congregation takes his candle home, for more than anything else it is the essence of Moravian Christmas. During World War II, two candles were mailed to each Moravian boy in the armed services for Christmas, one for the receiver and one for a friend.

The custom of distributing candles on Christmas Eve began with a 1747 service held for children in Saxony. The burning candle, wrapped with a red band, symbolizes the birth, passion, and wounds of Jesus Christ, the Light of the World. First mention of the custom in Bethlehem records was in 1756.

The trombone choir, so important to the Vigil service, was first formed in 1754. The Moravian religion has always stressed music, both as a means of enrichment in worship and as recreation. Today, over twenty musicians form the choir, which is unique in being divided into soprano, alto, tenor, bass, and double bass parts.

On important church-festival days the trombone choir mounts the church belfry at dawn to greet the day with "merry music," and announce it to the town population. An often-repeated story, said to have been revealed by a converted Indian, says that the music saved the lives of the first settlers in 1755. According to the legend, hostile Indians hid in the woods bordering Bethlehem and gathered to attack at dawn on

Christmas Day. As they were getting ready, the blare of the trombone choir sounded through the trees. The Indians fled in terror, believing the noise to be a warning from the Great Spirit.

The public is welcome to the Christmas Eve services in Bethlehem, and to view the putz earlier in the season, but it is not sought. The pastor and members of the Central Moravian Church hope to keep their church a vital, living organization and a non-commercial one. "If coming here makes it seem more like Christmas for you," one faithful member commented softly, after showing her putz to a stranger, "then it is worthwhile."

Love-feast buns, a feature of the Moravian celebrations, can substitute for any bread as they are only faintly sweet. The dough also makes an excellent bread that keeps very well. Half the amount given yields one small loaf.

Moravian Love-Feast Buns

1 cake yeast	1 teaspoon salt
¼ cup tepid water	¼ cup warm mashed potatoes
1 cup sugar	7–8 cups flour
1 egg, beaten	2 cups or more lukewarm water
¼ cup soft butter and lard or shortening, mixed	Melted butter or cream for glazing

Dissolve yeast in ¼ cup warm water. Add sugar to beaten egg, then softened butter and lard, salt, warm mashed potatoes, and yeast mixture.

Add alternately flour and warm water to make soft but firm dough. Knead until smooth on lightly floured board or in hands. Cover with clean, warm cloth and set in warm place to rise until double in bulk.

When dough has risen, punch down and make into buns 3″ to 4″ in diameter. (If preferred, any other type roll such as clover-leaf can be made with this dough.) Place so they do not touch on greased sheets. Cover with warm cloth and let rise again. Place in 400° F. oven and bake until golden brown, about 20 minutes. Brush with cream or melted butter just before removing from stove.

Makes 18 to 20 buns

Moravian sugar cake is served at Candle Teas held in early December in Old Salem, North Carolina. In a few years, this custom has become so popular that it is considered the opening of the Christmas season in Winston-Salem. The teas are given in the Brothers' House, where unmarried men lived in early days of the settlement. Hostesses wearing old Moravian costumes greet visitors and conduct them on a tour to watch beeswax candles being poured, and after having coffee and the sugar cake, they can study an enlarged putz.

This sugar cake is delectable, and could not be easier to make. It is best eaten warm or rewarmed.

Moravian Sugar or Coffee Cake

1 cup mashed potatoes, lukewarm	1 scant cup sugar
1 yeast cake	2 eggs
¼ cup lukewarm water	1 cup potato water, lukewarm
¾ cup butter and lard or shortening, mixed	1 teaspoon salt
	5 to 7 cups flour

Topping

2 teaspoons butter, in bits	½ teaspoon cinnamon
½ cup brown sugar, or more to taste	¼ cup table cream

Cook potatoes and mash, reserving one cup of the cooking water. Dissolve yeast in lukewarm water. Cream shortening and sugar, then beat in eggs one at a time. Add mashed potatoes and potato water, salt and yeast. Add flour gradually to make a soft, sticky dough. Cover bowl with clean, warm cloth and set in warm place to rise, 2 to 3 hours.

When double in bulk, punch down dough. Pat out in 2

well-greased pans 13″ x 9″ x 2″ and let rise again. When double, heat oven to 400° F.

With a sharp knife punch small holes over top of bread and insert bits of butter. Cover top with brown sugar and cinnamon and dribble cream all over. Bake 25 minutes, or until brown. Reheats very satisfactorily.

The crisp Moravian Spice cookies are especially popular for Christmas in Old Salem, but are sold there the year round. The dough is an exceedingly soft one, and best results in rolling out cookies are obtained by using a floured pastry cloth and a sleeved rolling pin.

Moravian Spice Cookies

2 tablespoons butter and lard or shortening, mixed	½ teaspoon ground cloves
	2 teaspoons ground cinnamon
2 tablespoons brown sugar	2 teaspoons ground ginger
⅓ cup black molasses	⅛ teaspoon salt
1¼ cups sifted flour	1 teaspoon soda (heaping)

2 teaspoons boiling water

Cream butter and lard with sugar. Add molasses. Sift flour with spices and salt. Add soda to boiling water. Add flour and spices and soda water to creamed mixture. Work with hands until well mixed. Cover and store in a cold place overnight, preferably longer.

To bake, turn oven to 375° F. Break off chunk of dough and roll to *paper thin* on floured cloth or board. Keep dough cold while cutting with fancy cutter. Put unused dough back in refrigerator. Place on greased cookie sheet and bake about 5 minutes, until cookies just begin to brown. Watch carefully and do not let burn or overbake. Cookies keep a very long time.

Dough keeps in refrigerator a very long time. Improves if ripened 1 to 2 weeks.

Yield: over 100

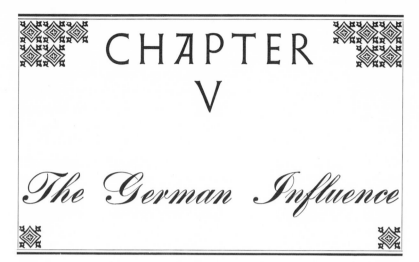

CHAPTER V

The German Influence

"We shall be told that the Quakers do not keep
Christmas. . . . But they keep it quite as much
as other Philadelphians. They do not rig out in
a spruce or hemlock; but they cram themselves
with stuffed turkeys, devour mincepies, and look
quite as full and as fat and as rosy and as happy,
and as satisfied with the inner man, as the dev-
otees of the green boughs. Therefore, we say
that, whatever the origin of Christmas elsewhere,
in Philadelphia it began in High Street market,
and as the Quakers founded the city and established that market, they must have had something to do with its contents. We believe, be-
yond all doubt, that in our city, Christmas is of
Quaker origin."
—*Public Ledger*, Dec. 25, 1847

The Germans went everywhere in America, and eventually
everyone capitulated to their sentimental Christmas traditions.
The way their secular holiday inevitably dominated wherever
they located is aptly illustrated by the history of the Quaker
City, Philadelphia.

From the beginning there was a mixture of customs there.
The English Quakers who founded the port were, like the New
York Dutch, a worldly people. Tolerance was a key tenet of the
Friends, and for that reason the New England Puritans loathed

81

Quakerism almost as much as they did the Church of England and the Pope.

The Quaker attitude toward life was positive. Whereas the Calvinists taught that the seed of sin is present in every new-born infant, the Quakers asserted that there is born in every man the seed of God. And since religion rested in man's inner being, there was no need for "hireling priests," nor for any of the outward sacraments to bring religion to man. The Quakers set aside "First day" as a day of necessary rest, but it was a civil institution, not a religious one.

They did not believe in keeping "vain holidays," but neither did they openly oppose them. Their silent disapproval, therefore, had little if any effect on those who kept Christmas enthusiastically—most notably, the German Pennsylvania Dutch, English Episcopalians, and a very small Catholic minority. The large Irish immigration in the 1840s greatly augmented the Catholic numbers, but by that time the year-end pattern was already well established.

If "the day called Christmas" happened to fall on a business day, Quaker shops and factories remained open. However, nothing in the religion specifically forbade feasting, and surviving accounts of holiday meals and parties indicate the Quakers never completely abandoned English appreciation of food and drink. A visitor in 1744 reported attending one party where the punch bowl was large enough to have "swimm'd half a dozen young geese." And John Adams, accustomed only to the "plain living and high thinking" of Boston, was astounded on one of his first trips to Philadelphia to see the "sinful feast" set before him by a typical Quaker.

Records indicate the tendency toward holiday indulgence increased while the seat of government was located in Philadelphia. One Christmas dinner given by President Washington for twenty guests included "an elegant variety of veal, turkey, ducks, fowls, hams, et cetera; puddings, jellies, fruits, and nuts, and a variety of wines and punch."

Toward the mid-nineteenth century, Quaker publications, which had formerly devoted their attention at Christmastime to

82

restating warnings against the celebration of "holy days and times," found a new cause for concern. Holiday "evening parties" were becoming exceedingly fashionable in Philadelphia. In 1854, one indignant Quaker editor suggested that, if evening parties could not be avoided, Friends depart for home no later than 10 P.M. He mentioned terrapins, oysters, calves-foot jelly, ice cream, champagne, brandy, punch, and hock as common fare.

A far more disturbing contemporary development, and one probably of German derivation, was the Christmas Eve Carnival of Horns. As the Carnival exploded, young and old from miles around gathered in the center of the city and created pandemonium until dawn. They banged tin pans, rattled metal kettles, rang sleigh bells, blew upon hundreds of penny horns, and played the horse fiddle, a well-rosined wooden drygoods case across which a wooden rail was drawn repeatedly. The Carnival was so popular and so raucous that it was outlawed in 1868.

The custom of holiday mumming also ran wild. The Swedes who settled along the Delaware River indulged in mumming at New Year's, calling it Fantasticals or Fantastics. It was customary with the German and English population during the pre-Christmas period, however, as it is today in Germany.

In England, mumming took the form of short drama that actors improvised extemporaneously on well-known themes. Plays centered around a savior figure, usually St. George, who overcame a fearful adversary. Additional characters ordinarily included the King of Egypt, Old Father Christmas, the Lord of Misrule, a fool, and a Turk.

Until the turn of the century, mumming was popular in other areas, most notably in Baltimore and parts of the South, and in Missouri. In Alabama there were Fantastic or Christmas Riders who donned masks and "Spanish" or clowns' costumes early Christmas morning and spent the day riding from one plantation to another. At each place they were greeted with cups of punch or liquor.

In early Philadelphia, Christmas mumming was more English than German. Bands of costumed men went from house to house and recited humorous verse or presented short folk dramas. In return they received some refreshment or a small coin.

The idea of costumes appealed to those producing the Carnival of Horns, and they adopted it. Conversely, mummers observing the liberties taken by the noisemakers began to act with greater license. Bitter complaints followed. The mummers "behaved with desperate freedom," newspapers reported, "wantonly" kissing women unable to resist and seriously smashing bonnets and crinolines in the process. A second statute was passed in 1881 against the "tin horn nuisance" and Christmas Eve masquerading.

But men grown accustomed to holiday make believe and its possibilities evaded the law by postponing fancy dress till New Year's Day, a traditional time for friendly calls. And since darkness was better suited to grotesquery, they changed the visiting time to New Year's Eve. The innovation spread like wild fire. Groups organized into marching clubs and paraded down to Independence Hall. Many carried pistols loaded with blank cartridges which they shot off when they reached the Hall around midnight.

Once again city authorities compelled unruly groups to exercise restraint. On New Year's Day, 1878, the first march to Independence Hall by individual groups was organized. By this time George Washington had long since replaced St. George as the "savior" in Philadelphia mummers' plays. In 1901, the City Council issued permits for a grand parade on Broad Street, the first New Year's Day Mummers' Parade. Today a crowd estimated at 1.5 million lines the three-mile parade route, and millions watch on television.

The old custom of wearing costumes on Christmas Eve was not limited to Philadelphia. There was a rural German equivalent called Belsnickle, Bells Nickel, Bels Niggel, et cetera.

As previously noted, Belsnickle or Pelznichol came into being when the Reformation fought against St. Nicholas and saint days. The fact that Pennsylvania Germans closely identi-

These are typical late-nineteenth-century Christmas tree ornaments made from brightly printed paper. The bird's nest (center) is made to be tied to the tree with velvet ribbons, while the others shown are string-tied and typical of sets sold at the time. (*From the Smithsonian Institution Collection*)

Tenderhearted sentiments such as these prevailed in the 1800s and 1890s. The Christmas card at upper right has not only a silk fringe but also a silk inner lining, which shows through cutouts. A different design was pasted to the back. The two lower cards were printed by Louis Prang. (*All are from the Collection of the Department of Cultural History of the Smithsonian Institution*)

A Merry Christmas

Though made to be worn by Indian bridegrooms, the tinsel headdress with the small sun-god face in the center is sold in New York City shops for use as a Christmas decoration

Cookie molds such as the one in the center, above, and the horse-man, opposite, are also used for wall decorations between cookie moldings at Christmas. These molds, carved in wood, are repro-ductions of antiques. (*Courtesy of the Smithsonian Institution Museum Shops*)

Dutch cookies are an ancient Christmas food, the dough shaped in wooden molds before being baked and often frosted in bright colors, as shown by the horsemen and the figures on the opposite page

A crèche, made recently in North Carolina from corn husks and cornsilk, used the old-time cornhusk dolls as inspiration. Husks are delicately tinted in pastel colors. (*Courtesy of the Smithsonian Institution Museum Shops*)

Japanese-American Christmas ornaments by Nancy Nishioka of Chicago, Ill., were made by interweaving gift-wrapping ribbons

Gingerbread crèche figures detailed above were designed and prepared by Mae Gerhard of Philadelphia, Pa., utilizing very dark dough, decorated in bright Byzantine shades of blue, red, green, gold, and white. She places the figures flat in her front window, just as Pennsylvania Dutch women did in olden days. (See following page also)

fied the two is clearly revealed in the title of an 1843 gift book, *Bellsnickle's Gift or A Visit from St. Nicholas*, printed in Lancaster. (The story was not related to Clement Moore's poem, but the coincidence of title seems hardly accidental.)

St. Nicholas brought presents and delegated punishment of the naughty to an assistant, but Belsnickle attended to both good and bad rewards. On Christmas Eve he frightened children out of their wits by peeping maliciously in at the window, then strode in carrying a pack of nuts and cookies and a switch or buggy whip. Upon entering a home, he cross-examined everyone present, including the parents. At times his performance was so effective—especially when he cracked his great whip in the air—that unwary children were startled into confessing previously undiscovered misdeeds. The impersonator obviously had to be someone well acquainted with the family.

This situation changed, however, as belsnickling grew more closely identified with mummery, and costumed individuals felt free to call on anyone they pleased. Even when it was known from past experience that a belsnickle's actions bordered on cruelty toward children, the door was never barred to him.

Belsnickles began coming in groups. Young and old men disguised themselves and went from house to house, begging and offering entertainment similar to mumming. If twenty-five to fifty belsnickles did not call, some prosperous farmers felt ill at ease with their neighbors. Some cookbooks contain recipes for belsnickles, cookies habitually given the holiday visitors.

Belsnickling continued as late as the 1930s in this country. It may be that the traditional plate of fruitcake left out for Santa Claus on Christmas Eve derived from the custom of rewarding Belsnickle. As Santa Claus became more popular, he assumed Belsnickle's habit of punishing unmindful children, but only with the threat of lack of gifts.

Sometime during the second half of the nineteenth century the holiday-hating Scotch-Irish, who poured into Pennsylvania in the eighteenth century, made accommodation with Christmas, perhaps because the possibility of extracting good behavior from rebellious youngsters outweighed other disadvantages of Christmas. Robert Blair Risk wrote in 1912 that, although his Presbyterian parents never allowed a Christmas tree because it was "too German," they did permit Santa Claus. Early in December his parents would promise a Christmas gift to children who kept out of mischief. "We felt we were paying pretty dear," he said, "for what might turn out to be inadequate reward."

When the Germans who landed in Pennsylvania in the early eighteenth century became economically free, they pushed on into what they called the hinterland. It was not long before they were spilling over the western borders into Ohio and Iowa and into the nearest southern province of Maryland.

The more cosmopolitan individuals moved into the city of Baltimore, and they must have made a considerable impact on English eating. Among the first arrivals there were a butcher and two men from York who established the first brewery in Maryland. Soon after that migrating Germans opened two inns (in the 1750s) and a tavern (1761).

The Pennsylvania Dutch brought all their old Christmas traditions to Maryland, as well as a recently adopted one called "Christmas Tree Yards," their version of the Moravian putz.

The Moravian communities of Lititz and Bethlehem were closed to outsiders when the first generation Pennsylvania Dutch were growing up, but at Christmastime the unschooled German children pushed on in regardless and demanded to see the putz in various homes. Later, they constructed the Christmas Tree Yards from their childhood memories.

Evidently, what had impressed the German children most in the crib scene were the water-power effects such as running streams and moving windmills. In the Pennsylvania Dutch Christmas Yards the Nativity was discarded and motion became paramount, with figures and carriages flying about, spouting fountains, water-powered mills and threshing machines, et cetera.

Christmas Tree Yards inevitably combined with the Christmas tree. In Pennsylvania today one often sees both a Nativity scene and a Christmas Yard, as they are now called, underneath the tree. Sometimes an elaborate electric train is set on a low table beneath the tree and the Nativity omitted. In Baltimore, the tradition of Christmas Yards is also preserved, in private homes and in certain firehouses.

In Philadelphia and many other cities, the Lutheran Church holds a Weihnacht service on Christmas Eve. At midnight four acolytes robed in red and white bear huge flaming candles down the aisle, as the congregation sings the famous Austrian carol "Silent Night," in German. Members who take part are careful to deposit their own lighted bayberry candles in a bathtub or sink before departing, for tradition says the Christmas Eve candle must burn down completely. Very bad luck will result if it is extinguished.

The first New Year's Watch Night Service in the United States is believed to have been in 1770 at St. George's Methodist Church. It seems likely that when John Wesley instituted the vigil to welcome the new year, he must have overlooked the original pagan connotations of the term.

The Germans in the second great immigration to the United States in the mid-nineteenth century settled throughout the land. Everywhere they took their irresistible Christmas customs. In 1844, a Protestant minister in Port Lavaca, Texas, decorated a large oak with lights and hung presents for the colony children upon the branches, while not far away Comanche Indians still gathered at night around campfires.

In 1851, Boston children of the parish of the German Catholic Church of the Holy Trinity gave what is believed to be the first American Nativity play. (The first known one in Germany was in the thirteenth century.) Dressed in Oriental costumes and singing Christmas carols, they marched solemnly down the aisle of the church to a Nativity set before the altar and handed the priests gifts for the poor.

The performance was so well received in the Puritan city that it was repeated twice for both Protestants and Catholics anxious to see the pageant widely acclaimed as "so charming" and "so edifying." The Christmas procession became a tradition in Holy Trinity Church, but costumes were abandoned in later years and the action simplified. Since 1851 Nativity plays and scenes have been staged all over the United States, in almost every form imaginable.

German Christmas foods have become almost as pervasive as German Christmas traditions in America. "Dutch" housewives introduced dozens of cookies and breads, as well as their favorite holiday fowl, goose.

Of all the German Christmas cookies, *pfeffernuesse* or peppernuts are probably the most popular and well known. There are many varieties, and all are not German. A Latvian version is given on page 213.

Peppernuts

¾ cup sugar	¼ teaspoon ground cloves
⅔ cup golden syrup	¼ teaspoon salt
¼ cup lard	½ teaspoon baking powder
¼ cup milk	1 teaspoon potash or
1 teaspoon anise extract	potassium carbonate
½ teaspoon vanilla	dissolved in
5 cups flour (or more)	1 tablespoon hot water
¼ teaspoon ground cardamom	Optional: confectioner's sugar

Heat together in a saucepan sugar, syrup, and lard. Add milk just as boiling point is reached. Cool. Add flavorings. Sift 2 cups of flour with spices, salt, and baking powder, and add to liquid. Add potash dissolved in hot water. Gradually add remaining 3 cups of flour, or more, if needed to make stiff dough. When mixture can no longer be mixed with spoon, knead in flour with hands. Knead until a very stiff dough is obtained, and for at least ½ hour. (The longer, the better. Old-time cooks used to knead it half a day, they say.)

This dough can be baked at once, or kept in refrigerator for a week or more. It is better if aged several days.

To make cookies, preheat oven to 350° F. Let dough warm at room temperature until soft enough to shape into rolls about

¼″ thick. With a sharp knife cut rolls into ½″ chunks. Bake on silicone-treated cookie sheet until golden brown, 8 to 10 minutes. Let cool momentarily to harden before removing from pan.

If desired, these cookies may be rolled on a board lightly dusted with powdered sugar.

Store these tasty nuts in a tightly closed container at least three weeks before dipping into them. They will keep forever, and are perfect with coffee.

Yield: 6 to 7 cups peppernuts

All Central Europeans make spätzle. It is said that Hungarians make the smallest, Germans the largest. They are delicious with any meat, especially with pork, and offer an interesting substitute for potatoes. One advantage is that they can be made in advance, then rewarmed in the oven in a covered casserole. An imported gadget slivers the dumplings into boiling water, but they can be broken with a spoon, or mashed through a large-holed collander.

Spätzle
Little Dumplings

2 cups flour, sifted with   *3 eggs, lightly beaten*
½ teaspoon salt   *½ cup to 1 cup milk*
3 tablespoons melted butter

Beat flour into lightly beaten eggs (using mixer), then gradually beat in enough milk to make soft dough with just enough consistency to be cut. Bring a large pan of salted water to a rolling boil. Break off dumplings into boiling water (using about ⅓ of dough at a time). Lower heat to gentle boil. Cook 2 to 3 minutes, until dumplings rise to top. Lift out with wire or slotted skimmer and put in serving bowl. Continue until all dough is cooked. Toss with melted butter.

Serves 12

Additional methods of serving spätzle: Toss with butter (2

tablespoons or more) and any of the following: ¾ cup warm sour cream, ½ cup grated cheese, or ½ cup crumbled bacon bits. Delicious added to any soup in which dumplings are suitable, and ideal with goulash or stews.

German-Americans often stuff goose or turkey with dumpling dough. Here is an especially good traditional recipe.

Fill-Up Dressing
German Dumpling Stuffing

4 tablespoons or more butter	¾ cup milk
½ cup finely chopped onion	1 egg, well beaten
½ stalk celery, chopped	1 teaspoon dried parsley
2 cups flour	Tops of one stalk celery, finely
½ teaspoon salt	chopped
2½ teaspoons baking powder	Optional: ¼ pound sausage,
⅛ teaspoon nutmeg	lightly fried out, or
	12 raw oysters

Lightly sauté onion and chopped celery in 2 tablespoons butter. Cool. Sift together dry ingredients. Add milk, 2 tablespoons melted butter, and egg. Stir in dried parsley and chopped celery tops. For turkey or capon, sausage or oysters may be added. If used, these should be stirred in at this point.

This stuffing will be stiff, but the fat from the fowl will make it quite juicy by the end of baking period. Fill neck cavity first, close, then fill bottom cavity.

To serve, dressing may be spooned out, or removed in a chunk from the fowl and sliced like bread or dumplings.

Sufficient for a 10-pound fowl

Of all the Christmas breads, this traditional German one is among the very best. It is very easy to make, and it keeps for weeks in an airtight tin.

Christmas Stollen

1½ packages yeast
½ cup lukewarm water
pinch salt plus ½ teaspoonful
½ cup sugar plus 1 tablespoonful
4½ cups sifted flour, approximately
½ cup milk
¾ cup sweet butter
1 whole egg, beaten with
2 egg yolks
Grated rind of 1 lemon

3 ounces chopped candied fruit (½ cup)
1 ounce slivered citron (¼ cup)
3 ounces raisins (½ cup)
1 ounce currants (2 tablespoons)
3 ounces slivered blanched almonds (½ cup, heaping)
1 tablespoon flour
1 egg, slightly beaten
¼ cup soft sweet butter

Granulated sugar, preferably vanilla sugar

(Note: This bread rises 3 times. Vanilla sugar may be obtained by storing granulated sugar in a closed container with a vanilla bean.)

In a large mixing bowl, dissolve yeast in lukewarm water, adding pinch of salt, tablespoon of sugar, and ½ cup sifted flour. Mix well, cover and let rise 10 minutes. Meanwhile, scald milk. Add butter and remaining sugar, stirring until dissolved. Set aside to cool to lukewarm. Add beaten egg and egg yolks and lemon rind.

Put yeast mixture in electric beater turned to speed for thin batters. Alternately add milk mixture with 2 cups of flour sifted with ½ teaspoon salt. As batter thickens, lower mixer speed. Beat well when 2 cups of flour have been added. Continue to add flour. When dough becomes too heavy to mix with beater, remove and stir in remaining flour with wooden spoon. When all flour has been added, stir vigorously until dough loosens from side of bowl. This should be almost immediately if dough was properly beaten when first 2 cups of flour were added. Cover with wet towel and place in warm spot to rise until doubled, about one hour.

Dredge chopped fruits in tablespoon of flour. When dough has risen, punch down and mix in fruit and nuts. Cover with

91

wet cloth and let rise once more until double, 40 minutes or more.

Turn dough out on floured board. Divide dough in two. Roll each chunk into an oblong about 12″ x 4″. Place each loaf on large baking sheet. Brush with slightly beaten egg. Cover with wet towel and let rise once more, about 30 to 40 minutes.

Bake in 350° F. oven until golden brown, 20 minutes or more. Remove from oven. Brush with softened butter and sprinkle with vanilla sugar.

Rewarm to serve.

The following recipe was so closely guarded by the woman who brought it to America that she would not give it even to her daughter. Shortly before her death she left it to her son, by giving it to his wife! The Loevinger children nicknamed the cookies moon cookies because of their shape.

Ruth Loevinger's German Filbert "Moon" Cookies

2 egg whites, beaten until stiff
½ pound superfine sugar
½ pound filberts, ground very fine, like flour

1 tablespoon citron, finely chopped

Powdered sugar and flour

Turn oven to 300° F. Grind filberts in blender or mouli-type grinder. Mix egg whites, sugar, ground filberts, and citron well. This will make a rather stiff dough. Sprinkle rolling board with powdered sugar and flour in equal amounts. Shape dough into a flat roll, as for icebox cookies. Slice off ½″ pieces and shape into crescents. Place on beeswaxed baking tin or on silicone-treated baking sheet. Bake about 12 to 20 minutes until just done. Do not brown. If using a silicone-treated baking sheet, watch carefully as it bakes faster. Store in a tightly covered container.

Cinnamon stars offer a perfect use for leftover egg whites. This recipe can be made two ways: Roll the dough very thin, and ice after baking. The result is a Swiss star, a crisp cookie that keeps indefinitely. Roll thick and ice before baking, and a macaroon-type cookie comes out, something very special, but a cookie that should be eaten right away.

German-Swiss Cinnamon Stars

Zimet Staerne or Zimsterne

4 egg whites, beaten stiff
4 cups confectioner's sugar

2½ cups ground unblanched almonds or filberts

2 teaspoons cinnamon, or more to taste

Add 2 cups confectioner's sugar gradually to well-beaten egg whites until meringue results. Remove one cup of mixture and reserve. To remainder add finely ground nuts and cinnamon.

Sprinkle board or pastry cloth (preferably) very liberally with about half of remaining 2 cups of sugar. Work with small portions of dough. Place on sugared board, then sprinkle liberally with more sugar. This will be a soft dough that must be handled carefully.

For crisp cookie: Roll as thin as possible. Cut into star shapes and place on silicone or beeswaxed pan. Bake in slow oven (250° F.) 20 to 30 minutes. When cookies are lightly browned, remove from oven and frost with egg-white mixture which has been set aside. Dry thoroughly before storing in a tight container with a slice of apple.

To make soft cookie: Turn oven to 325° F. Roll out dough on sugared board as directed above, to ¼" thickness. Cut out stars and place carefully on well-greased tin, leaving 2" between. Frost with icing which has been set aside. Bake 8 to 10 minutes, until icing just begins to turn brown.

Swiss Weihnachtkuchen

(*Adapted from* Swiss Cookery *by Marie Matzinger*)

½ cup butter
1 cup granulated sugar
½ cup milk
1½ cups sifted flour

½ teaspoon salt
2 teaspoons baking powder
4 egg yolks
1 teaspoon vanilla or
½ teaspoon orange extract

Meringue

⅛ teaspoon cream of tartar
Pinch salt
4 egg whites
2 cups superfine granulated
sugar

1 teaspoon vanilla
½ cup chopped nuts,
preferably pecans

For assembling: 1 cup or more heavy cream.

Bring all ingredients to room temperature before mixing. Preheat oven to moderate, 325 to 350° F. Grease and flour two 10-inch pans or three 9-inch pans. Cream butter, then cream in sugar. Cream in alternately milk and flour, salt, and baking powder sifted together. Beat well after each addition. Finally fold in well-beaten egg yolks and vanilla. Spread in pans. This will make a thin layer, but it will rise at least twice in bulk.

Add cream of tartar and salt to egg whites. Beat until stiff. Gradually add sugar and vanilla and beat 2 minutes more. Divide equally and spread lightly on unbaked layers of cake. Sprinkle with chopped nuts. Bake 30 minutes in lower half of oven. Meringue will be golden brown when cake is done and may pull slightly away from cake. Take out layers, place upside down on rack to cool. This will cause cake and meringue topping to settle together. Do not remove until completely cool. Be careful to have one layer without cracked meringue, for this will be the top of cake.

Place one layer, meringue side down, on cake plate. Cover with whipped cream. Place other layer on top, meringue side up. If there are three layers, in one instance meringue and whipped cream will come together.

To make a festive cake, decorate around top edge with glazed red and green cherries.

Swiss Hazelnut or Filbert Cookies

2 cups granulated sugar
4 eggs, beaten until very light
Additional granulated sugar

1 pound filberts, ground fine
¾ to 1 cup flour

Preheat oven to 300 to 325° F. Gradually beat sugar into beaten eggs, then add nuts and enough flour to make workable dough. Roll or shape into balls the size of marbles. Roll in granulated sugar. Place on well greased tin. Bake 20 minutes, or until delicately browned.

Yield: approximately 250

In some instances German dishes combined with American products and something new like turkey and sauerkraut resulted. In Baltimore, and other cities where there is a notable German influence, the combination is mandatory. In the Midwest, German descendants often cook turkey and sauerkraut together and lavishly dollop sour cream over it all.

Sauerkraut as prepared in the following recipe is an ideal foil for turkey as the sharpness of the kraut cuts the richness of the fowl. Sauerkraut is also delicious with capon, especially when it is stuffed with Fill-Up Dressing (p. 90).

Sauerkraut for Turkey

2 pounds sauerkraut
2 apples, peeled and sliced, or
¼ pound dried apples
1 onion cut in quarters
1 carrot, roughly chopped
½ bay leaf

10 peppercorns
Salt to taste
Water to cover
Optional: ham broth or turkey broth

Put sauerkraut in large saucepan, together with other ingredients, and cover with water, or half water and half ham or turkey broth. Cover pan and simmer 3 hours. This is best prepared in advance and reheated.

Serves 6 to 8

Just as German cooking affected other peoples, so did other national habits change the German. The following recipe for goose stuffed with fruit and served with rice is probably a result of German and Southern cookery meeting. The Germans frequently stuffed goose with apples and raisins, and sometimes they simmered or basted it with a mixture of water and wine or water and vinegar. (This makes sour goose.)

Germans ate potatoes with fowl, but Southerners prefer rice. More fruits were added to the apple rings so dear to Pennsylvania Dutch cooks, and apricot brandy was substituted for wine. The result is truly sublime.

In selecting goose, allow 1¼ pounds per person. One cup of stuffing is needed for each pound of meat. To increase amount of stuffing given, retain equal parts of fruit. Some persons like to save goose fat and eat it with pumpernickel bread.

Goose with Fruit Stuffing

1 12-pound goose

Stuffing

2 cups of pitted prunes, soaked overnight in sherry to cover

2 packages thawed frozen peaches

2 cups dried apple rings, cut in half

2 cups white raisins, rinsed in hot water

2 fresh pears, peeled and chunked

2 cups dried apricots

1 cup dry or toasted bread crumbs

½ teaspoon ground ginger

½ teaspoon cinnamon

8 cloves

¼ teaspoon nutmeg

Salt and pepper for goose

For basting: apricot brandy, about ¾ cup
For serving: green grapes if available, red otherwise

96

Preheat oven to 325° F. Salt and pepper goose inside and out. Toss together lightly fruit and juices (including sherry in which prunes were soaked), bread crumbs, and spices. Stuff goose and truss. If possible, bake in a pan from which the fat can be easily extracted, as it should be removed periodically. Place goose breast side up in pan. Baste initially with melted goose fat, and as often thereafter as seems needed. Goose is practically self-basting from the fat which oozes out; but it does require occasional attention. If legs and breast begin to brown too quickly, cover with foil paper until about 1 hour before removing from oven. For a 12-pound goose, allow 5 hours; for 8 pounds, 4 hours; for 10 pounds, 4½ hours; and for 14 pounds, 6 hours. Remove fat as it accumulates, and reserve if desired.

During the last hour, baste with apricot brandy. Fifteen minutes before serving, add grapes and baste them along with the goose. Serve with white rice cooked by favorite recipe.

Serves 8

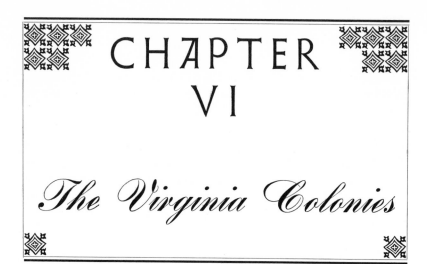

CHAPTER VI

The Virginia Colonies

"*Rode 7 miles to Mr. Stevenson's and preached. The hearers mostly Virginians . . . several present, appeared almost intoxicated. Christmas and New Year holly days, are seasons of wild mirth and disorder here.*"
—Presbyterian minister DAVID McCLURE in 1773

We know little about Christmas in the first century of the Virginia Colony, except that it was plain—not from choice, but necessity. The Virginians came to the new world not for spiritual-political reasons, but to better their fortune. They were remote enough from Cromwell and the Puritans to defy their anti-"Christ-tide" edicts, but they had not the means for an elaborate celebration.

There was little to celebrate on the first Christmas in Jamestown in 1607. Captain John Smith was away trading with the Indians, and in mortal peril. Those holding fort in his absence were at the point of admitting defeat and abandoning the settlement. Of the original party of one hundred, fewer than forty remained. All others had succumbed to famine and disease, or the massacres of the Indian Wars.

On Christmas Day they gathered forlornly for a sermon, and

offered up fervent prayers that reinforcements arrive before the end of the year. Their prayers were answered. The ships came and Jamestown was saved. Captain Smith returned, too, telling a hair-raising story of how his life had been saved by Pocahontas, the daughter of Indian Chief Powhatan.

The next Christmas day one of Powhatan's sons invited the Jamestowners to feast with him, and the brave band enjoyed the biggest meal they had eaten in a long, long time. They were "never more merrie," recorded one present, "nor fedde on more plentie of good oysters, fish, wild foule and good bread; nor never had better fire in England than in the warm smokie houses."

Little is recorded about the years following the feast of 1608, but it seems probable that celebrations were few as getting together at any time was difficult. The threat of Indian attacks made travel hazardous, and distances between the few scattered settlements were vast. A report to the Bishop of London in the early eighteenth century by the Virginia clergy is candidly revealing.

Owing to "the circumstances of this colony," they wrote, "no Holydays except those of Christmas Day and Good Friday," were observed because the Virginians were "unwilling to lose their dayly labour."

When Christmas celebrations finally began in Virginia, they did so with a bang. Every musket in town was exploded on Christmas Day. According to old records, faculty members of William and Mary often paid for the ammunition used to shoot off "Christmas guns." Farther south in Carolina, at least one family kept a small fieldpiece solely for Christmas morning, when it was placed on the piazza at early dawn and all members roused by its reverberations.

The holiday season in Virginia began about a week before Christmas, with a round of church-going, feasting, drinking, gaming, hunting, and balls. "All over the Colony, an universal hospitality reigns," the *London Magazine* reported in 1746, with "full tables and open doors." Settlers who had lived so long in isolation made so much of entertaining that they virtu-

99

ally waylaid strangers in order to have a great number share their pleasure.

From Christmas Eve through New Year's Day, Negro slaves were generally given a holiday from all tasks. In Missouri and Louisiana they selected the largest and greenest Yule log they could find because any work done while it was still burning had to be paid for. The final remnant was given to an elderly Negro woman to preserve for lighting the next year's log.

On Christmas day slaves were given an abundant supply of metheglin—a concoction of fermented honey, spices, and water —as well as an extra ration of food. In Virginia many used the backbones (spareribs, then generally scorned) to make a favorite pork pie. "Possum sizzlin" and "taters roasting" (yams) are also mentioned in Christmas songs and oral tradition, as well as "stuffed coon in a bath of 'lasses sauce."

Ordinarily, the area of the plantation house was the exclusive and privileged domain of the house servants; but at Christmas, and at this time only, field hands seem to have been both welcome and encouraged to come near and celebrate the entire day with singing and dancing. An English visitor to Austin, Texas, in 1846 noted in his diary that the Negroes in that vicinity gave a Christmas Ball in an unfinished store, "through the kindness" of the owner.

The Africans brought here as slaves had a highly developed animistic religion of their own, and in their suffering were easily persuaded to add Christianity to it. Naturally, they added also the white man's Christmas superstitions, such as the belief that those born on Christmas can "see sperrits." Some of our most beautiful American Christmas carols came from the Negro slaves, and one of the most famous of Negro spirituals is intimately connected with Christmas. "Go tell it on the mountains," its refrain runs, "Our Jesus Christ is born."

Christmas apparently was more a time for adults than for children in Colonial Virginia. For young women approaching a marriageable age, there was the excitement of young men visiting (and encouraged by a variety of kissing games, as in

New York City Christmas Week parties). But there was no gift exchange until New Year's Day, and no Christmas tree. The first was introduced in 1842 by a German professor at William and Mary.

Since the Christmas period was one when Virginia planters had free time between harvesting and planting, it became a favorite time for weddings. These, also, were great entertainment, and the holiday season so convenient that the custom of Christmas weddings spread throughout the South to New Orleans.

A long-remembered wedding took place at White House, the home of Martha Dandridge Custis, on "Old Christmas," January 6, 1759. Almost a month had been given to preparations for the wedding, and during the week before, the bride herself superintended the selection of spirits for punches and toddies and the preparation of sweets. There were quavery molded jellies, so dear to Colonial hearts; rich, creamy cakes packed with fruit; and thick pies, without which no Christmas wedding would have been complete.

There are no early records of Christmastime decorations in early Virginia, but there was a plenitude of native greenery— holly loaded with red berries, ivy, laurel, running cedar, pine, et cetera—and it seems likely hardpressed housewives used them to brighten dreary Colonial life and remember old England.

Possibly Christmas greens are not mentioned in the meager records of early Virginia because they were taken for granted. One of the first references, in fact, criticizes the amount of decoration. In 1712, *The Spectator* observed that the middle aisle of one church resembled "a very pretty shady walk, and the pews look like so many arbours on each side of it. The pulpit itself has such clusters of ivy, holly, and rosemary about it that a light fellow in our pew took occasion to say that the congregation heard the 'Word out of the bush, like Moses.' "

That would not have amused the people over on the frontier of Virginia, where the Scotch-Irish had settled, and brought their Christmas antagonism. In The Great Valley there were no decorations, no explosion of guns, no feasting, and certainly no parties. Christmas was a day like every other day, according to a note in 1773 by Philip Fithian, a Princeton divinity student in charge of a small school on the Carter Plantation. When offered the position, he was initially alarmed at the thought of moving to Virginia, because he understood the people were "wicked" and careless in all things. But he soon adjusted to colonial ways, and so did the Scotch-Irish. A year later, it is said, they comprised a majority of those attending a Twelfth Night Ball that ended the Christmas season in Alexandria.

Turkey and venison, augmented by a bountiful supply of oysters, replaced English boar's head and peacock in Christmas feasts in Virginia and Maryland. William Byrd II of Westover, Virginia, wrote that on Christmas Day, 1709, he had broiled turkey for breakfast, and that during the holidays he and his party feasted upon turkey and chine (pork), roast apples and wine, tongue and udder. From the outset, pork fed on native corn was a great favorite. *The Williamsburg Art of Cookery* gives the following colonial recipe for ham, which Byrd recorded in 1674 on the flyleaf of his Bible, one book not likely to be lost.

> *"To eat ye Ham in perfection, keep it in half Milk and half Water for thirty-six Hours, and then having brought the Water to boil, put ye Ham therein and let it simmer, not boil, for 4 or 5 Hours, according to Size of ye Ham—for simmering brings ye Salt out and boiling drives it in."*

The plenitude of oysters and the observance of Christmas Eve as a fast day combined in this country to make oysters perhaps the most universal American Christmas food. At Christmastime, a great store were gathered by the colonists. One early host noted contentedly in his diary that the supply of oysters lasted for three days of the lengthy feasting period.

This oyster and ham "pie" is just as good today as it was in early colonial times. If desired, a rich pie crust may be added.

Oyster and Ham "Pie"

1 pint fresh oysters
   with liquid
1 onion chopped
½ cup butter
½ cup flour
½ cup milk

½ cup white wine
¼ cup chopped cooked ham,
   preferably cured ham
2 cups green peas or
   1 package frozen

Turn oven to 400° F.

Separate oysters from liquid, and reserve both. Sauté chopped onion in 2 tablespoons butter until golden. Remove onion and reserve. Add remaining butter, melt; then add flour gradually, blending well. Let cool. Stir milk gradually into butter-flour mixture, then simmer, stirring constantly. Add wine and oyster liquid. This will make a very thick white sauce. Do not thin. Dish can be prepared to this point, then refrigerated until time of final cooking. Add oysters, cooked onion, ham, and peas to wine-oyster liquid mixture and turn into ovenware pot or dish. Put in preheated 400° F. oven and cook 15 minutes, or until peas are just done. Serve with tiny biscuits. If pie crust is added, bake until crust is golden.

Serves 4 to 6

One of the greatest contributors to Southern cuisine as it developed was a crop that flourished as it had nowhere else: rice. This 1801 recipe, using already cooked rice, is a find for busy women today. It is perfect with fowl, or in any way rice is served.

Pilau of Eastern Rice

¼ pound butter
¼ cup pine nuts (unsalted)

¼ cup pistachio nuts
1 teaspoon mace

2 cups cold, cooked rice

Melt butter in skillet, then add nuts and sauté. Add mace and rice. "Lift" rice with large spoon until it is thoroughly warm and butter has been absorbed.

Serves 4 to 6

Thrifty colonial housewives knew that yeast would make butter and cream, always scarce, stretch much further in a cake. Sometimes they even prepared plum pudding with yeast, by boiling the risen dough.

An eighteenth-century *Manuscript Household Receipt Book* displayed in the housekeeper's room at Tryon Palace, New Bern, North Carolina, contains the following recipe for a typical huge yeast cake. Until 1775 the English ruled New Bern, which had been settled by a Swiss nobleman and some 700 Swiss, German, and English followers. Tryon Palace is a beautiful restoration well worth a special visit.

"To Make a Great Cake"
From *A Tryon Palace Trifle* published by Tryon Palace

Take half a peck of fine flower, and Nine pound of Currans well picked and dried and warmed by the fire; take 3 pound of butter and a pinte & a half of Cream; Set the cream over the fire, & the Butter, till it be hott and the butter Melted but not to boyle; take 20 Eggs, but 10 whites; beat them well; take a quart of Ale Eaſt half a pinte of Roſe water; ſtrain the Eaſt into the Eggs and put the roſe water to it; then Mingle amongſt your flower 3 quarters of a pound of Shuger, & one ounce of Mace, and a little Salt; ſo mingle all together as you do a Pudding; then ſet it by the fire to riſe half a Quarter of an Hour, when you ſee it riſe work in your Currans; work it in a Bowle, not on a Table; So make what haſt you can to get it into the Hoope then ſet it in a prity quick oven, let it ſtand an hour and a half. To Ice it, take 3 whites of Eggs, beat them to a froath, then take a pound of double refinde Shuger, beat it, ſmall Searce it throug a hair Sive, then put it to the white of Eggs, and beat it till it be as white as Snow, then put a little Muſk and Ambergreece to it. And when the Cake is ſomething Coole Ice it over. Butter the Hoope well, and the paper you ſet it on muſt be three Sheets.

N.B.   Ale Eaſt, yeaſt left after Ale is brewed
        Hoope, a ſhort metal cylinder uſed as a ſhape for cake
        Searce, ſift finely
        Ambergreece, Ambergris

American fruitcakes are uniquely our own, a combination of several types of national cakes.

As black cakes became popular in the South, so did their

degree of blackness. Cooks vied with each other to produce the blackest cake, and often browned flour before mixing, to make it darker.

The following Maryland black cake is far easier to make than most Christmas cakes, and far superior. It has a chewy consistency, something like candy, and the temptation to keep having one more bite is irresistible. Since this cake is so moist, it keeps a long time. The cake is perfect without any addition of liquor.

The original recipe called for more fruit, which may be added by those preferring a very fruity cake.

Maryland Black Cake

½ cup butter	½ teaspoon cloves
1⅓ cups dark brown sugar	1½ teaspoons ginger
3 eggs, separated	1 teaspoon nutmeg
1¼ cups sifted flour	2 cups currants
1 teaspoon baking powder	2 cups seeded raisins
¼ teaspoon salt	¼ cup black molasses
1 teaspoon cinnamon	¼ cup sherry or fruit juice

2 cups shredded candied citron

Grease pan (loaf pans or tube), then line with greased paper. Turn oven to 275° F.

Cream butter, then cream in sugar thoroughly. Beat egg yolks until foamy and cream with butter and sugar. Add baking powder, salt and spices to sifted flour. Sift over currants and raisins. Gradually add to egg mixture, alternating with molasses and sherry. Beat to mix well, then fold in stiffly beaten egg whites.

Pour ¼ batter into lined baking pan. Sprinkle ⅓ chopped citron on top of batter. Pour in another ¼ batter, then layer with citron, and continue alternating layers until both citron and batter are used (3 layers citron, 4 layers batter).

Place large pan of hot water in oven, then put cake pan in hot water. Cover rim of cake pan with heavy greased paper.

Bake cake 3 to 4 hours, testing with straw for doneness. If batter is divided into smaller cakes, baking time will be cut.

This recipe makes about 4¼ pounds cake. Keeps indefinitely, but can be eaten immediately.

Making fruit cakes with layers of fruit is a trick we should relearn from the colonials. This white fruit cake, adapted from *The Williamsburg Art of Cookery*, is one of the best ever tasted, according to all who have tried it.

Williamsburg White Fruit Cake

1 stick butter (½ cup)	*1 pound citron, shredded*
1 cup sugar	*or cut in slivers*
2 cups flour, sifted	*¾ pound almonds, blanched*
½ teaspoon soda	*and sliced as for almadine*
1 teaspoon cream of tartar	*½ coconut, shredded*
¼ teaspoon salt	*(2 packages frozen may be*
6 egg whites, beaten until stiff	*substituted)*

Preheat oven to 325° F.

Cream together butter and sugar, then cream in flour sifted with soda, cream of tartar, and salt. If necessary in order to work in entire amount of flour, add a little of the beaten egg whites. Finally fold in beaten egg whites. Add about ⅓ of the citron to batter.

Pour thin layer of batter in prepared and lined loaf or tube pan or pans. Sprinkle with layer of citron, nuts, and coconut. Pour in second thin layer of batter; then cover with citron, nuts, and coconut. Repeat layers of batter, then fruit and nuts, ending with layer of batter. For two cakes, there will be three layers of batter. As the cake bakes, some of the batter will seep into the fruit, binding it all together. Bake until done, about one hour. This cake keeps well as the coconut makes it moist.

Yield: 2 large round cakes

Colonial cooks undoubtedly made English jumballs or jumbles for Christmas. With a blender, they are much easier to make these days.

Jumballs

Almond Cookies

(Adapted from The Art of Cookery,
Made Plain and Easy *by Hannah Glasse, 1747)*

1 cup sifted flour	*½ teaspoon rosewater,*
¾ cup powdered sugar	*or almond or vanilla extract*
¼ pound blanched, ground	*1 egg white*
almonds	*2 to 4 teaspoons cream*
	Powdered sugar

Turn oven to 450° F.

Sift together flour and sugar, then add almonds. (The almonds can easily be ground in the blender.) Mix as for pie crust, adding rose water or other flavoring and unbeaten egg white. Add cream—just enough to make a stiff paste.

Roll dough thin on floured board. Cut in fancy shapes and bake for 10 minutes, or until lightly browned. Watch carefully, as cookies will brown quickly, once they are done. Dust with powdered sugar. These cookies keep very well in an airtight tin.

As soon as the colonials learned how to make bourbon, they began to substitute it for brandy in cooking. Whiskey snaps probably resulted from one such happy exchange.

Whiskey Snaps

1 cup soft butter	*Confectioner's sugar*
¾ cup sugar	*plus 1 teaspoon cinnamon or*
2 egg yolks (or 2 small eggs)	*optional spices*
½ pound pecans, ground	*1 teaspoon ginger (optional—*
2 cups flour, approximately	*see directions)*
⅛ teaspoon salt	*1 tablespoon cinnamon*
½ cup bourbon	*(optional—see directions)*
Granulated sugar (optional—see directions)	

Turn oven to 400° F.

Cream butter and sugar until smooth. Stir in egg yolks,

mixing well. Dredge ground pecans in 1 cup flour, then add to sugar mixture, alternating with part whiskey if necessary for use in mixing. Alternately add remaining flour and bourbon until dough is stiff enough to roll out, but still quite soft. Roll out thin, about ⅛″, and cut in diamonds. Place on greased baking sheet and bake 5 to 8 minutes. Watch carefully; cookies should not brown.

Let cookies cool momentarily, then sprinkle lightly with confectioner's sugar and cinnamon mixed.

For a spicier cookie, add ginger and cinnamon to flour in which nuts are dredged. Sprinkle these cookies lightly with granulated sugar before baking.

Both versions will keep indefinitely. Both are so delicious, it would be hard to make a choice between them.

Yield: 100 to 120 cookies

CHAPTER VII

The South

"When I was young, Christmas was the only holiday we had. It was Fourth of July, Thanksgiving, and shivaree all rolled up in one."
—Former resident of East Texas

"Selling fireworks is supposed to be illegal, but someone must have them. A few nights before Christmas the firecrackers begin popping so much they keep me awake all night."
—Resident of Birmingham, Alabama

Remnants of many kinds of Christmas can be found today in the Southern states—French, Spanish, English, Greek, German, Moravian, Italian, especially—and on New Year's Day a tradition that the slaves must have brought is universal. From the District of Columbia to Texas, black-eyed peas are cooked with hog jowl or ham and served in Southern homes for "money in the pot" or good luck. Restaurants that happen to be open often place a sign in the window to reassure patrons that the precious dish is available.

In some areas, especially in Charleston, South Carolina, peas are combined with rice to make Hopping John, a dish quite similar to Jamaican and Puerto Rican staples. Hot pepper sauce is served with it, and often boiled okra and baked yams. It seems probable that the tradition of peas for New Year's Day

109

originated centuries ago as a year-end fertility ritual, in the same way that mandatory bean and pea dishes for Christmas Eve and New Year's began in Europe. The planting and harvesting of yams is still an important fertility ritual in Africa today.

In Williamsburg, Virginia, an old English Christmas is annually re-created. Festivities begin about a week before Christmas with a torchlight parade headed by costumed militia and fifes and drums. On that night, and for every succeeding one of the holidays, lighted candles are placed in every window. A Yule-Log ceremony, candlelight concerts and recitals, firing of Christmas guns, and authentic firework displays of "Illuminations" follow in a daily progression.

It is particularly appropriate that special Christmas carol services are held annually in Williamsburg, and in such historic spots as Gunston Hall in Alexandria. Undoubtedly some of the oldest and most beautiful Christmas carols would have died out completely had they not survived in this country, for in Europe they were opposed by both the Reformationists and the Puritans.

According to ancient tradition, the first carol was sung by the angels, the "heavenly hosts" who announced the birth of Christ the Saviour to the shepherds. The majority of early carols concerned the good news the angels brought, a fact which supports the theory that the French Christmas term "Noel" comes from "nowells" or "novelles," old French for "news."

The first known use of the phrase "Christmas Carol" was in the sixteenth century. Carols in England started as part of ring dances, then later became detached as songs alone. Initially, they were sung in connection with performances of mystery plays and not limited to Christmas because the plays were more often given in summer than winter.

Luther discouraged the singing of Christmas carols, especially those referring to the Virgin; and the Puritans abolished them altogether in 1652 by the edict forbidding any Christmas celebration. When the bans were lifted, the lords and ladies of the Restoration did not resume the practice of carol-singing. Perhaps they felt too sophisticated to indulge in songs of such idyllic innocence.

In Virginia and Kentucky, however, neither the Reformation nor the Restoration were effective. Old, old carols have been found there in many variations, and distinctly American carols that grew out of the older forms. "The Cherry Tree Carol," for instance, goes back to performance of mystery plays in Coventry, England.

Researchers found that each area developed its own favorite mode for singing, and that the scales vary from five to seven notes each, often with gaps between successive degrees. Furthermore, colonists adapted the old English carols as they saw fit, sometimes replacing the old tune with a different melody. In other instances, they altered the melody to fit contemporary major scales, and in still others, they gave completely new words to old carols.

In the Appalachian Mountains one ancient Christmas song was found and so successfully revived that today it rivals religious subjects as a theme for Christmas cards. This was the ancient counting song, "The Twelve Days of Christmas." Counting songs were magical or pagan in origin, and no one knows what this one originally meant (See Chapter I). In England it became a forfeit game, played by adults and children alike. Typically American modifications were made in "The Twelve Days of Christmas," such as the substitution of "part of a juniper tree" or "part of a june-apple tree" for "a partridge in a pear tree." The long list of gifts ends with a true Americanism, "Twelve fiddlers fiddling."

In Albemarle County, Virginia, Christmas carols have revived the custom of wassailing. In England on the Eve of Epiphany or Twelfth Night, farm people would go to the apple orchard at sunset or after dark to toast the most promising tree with a cider drink. Often they poured some of the wassail on the trunk or branches and on the roots to promote fertility. Some of the Christmas carols we sing today began as wassail songs, and are just as heathen as the partridge in the pear tree.

In several Southern cities Christmas carols have inspired a development that could come about only in the United States. Choir members are grouped on a giant triangular platform in such a way that they give the appearance of a huge decorated Christmas tree, and hence become "Singing Christmas Trees." Best known are those in Charlotte, North Carolina, and at Belhaven College, Belhaven, Mississippi.

In some places in Kentucky and farther south, in North Carolina, "old Christmas" is celebrated, also. For many years after the change of calendars in 1752 the isolated inhabitants of Rodanthe, Hatfield Island, North Carolina, stubbornly refused to accept December 25 or "New Style" Christmas. The old calendar was right, they declared, and they independently kept the holiday as they always had.

In the argument about the right day to celebrate Christmas, it seems never to have occurred to anyone that the way they celebrated was more pagan than Christian. The day began with a parade of fife and drums inherited from forebears. The march took hours, with a pause at noon for an oyster roast.

Shortly before dark, the remaining townspeople, dressed appropriately for an evening of mumming, in colorful or grotesque costume, wandered about aimlessly, playing tricks until "Old Buck" came out of hiding. Old Buck, the villagers said, represented an animal that had once been a scourge, the terror of Hatteras Woods. Where he stayed all year was a dark secret (and still is today), but once a year he wandered out of the woods to cavort in town. Old Buck had a magnificent steer's head with a fine pair of horns, on a pole body covered with quilts and hung with a bell. His rushes and passes at the crowd were guided by a rider who called out directions.

By the time Rodanthians became reconciled to Christmas in December, Old Buck had become a firmly established tradition that no one wanted to give up. So today, Old Christmas in Rodanthe is something of a combination of medieval mumming, Santa Claus (who inevitably got into the act in modern times), and an old-fashioned church supper. However, the exact date of January 7 has given way to the Saturday nearest to it. A huge oyster roast is held on the front lawn of the Rodanthe Community Center before dark; then, when all have feasted sufficiently on oysters and hot dogs, they file into the building for a program of Christmas carols, Santa, and Old Buck's capers.

Texas and Oklahoma are not part of what was once known as the Deep South, being more western than southern, but their Christmas customs illustrate a corresponding variance. In Southwest Texas a strong Spanish-Indian influence is evident. (See Chapter IX.)

In West Texas, Christmas comes ranch-style. Records of an 1872 surveying party record fourteen varieties of "local" meat for Christmas—buffalo, antelope, deer, bear, rabbit, prairie-dog, possum, turkey, goose, ducks, prairie chicken, brant (a type of small goose), curlew, quail, and "other birds." The most expensive meat the men had was bacon, which was hauled 500 miles. There was also honey, which the group had discovered as a result of killing a bear trying to rob a hive. One of the hunters offered "a mess of rattlesnakes and polecats," but was refused. Two excellent cooks, a Negro and a Mexican, vied with each other in preparing the feast.

In 1885, M. G. Rhoads, operator of the Morning Star Hotel at Anson, decided to give a grand ball for the cowboys the Saturday night before Christmas, in honor of the recent marriage of a popular local cowboy. At the end of the hard working season it was the practice of the hotel proprietor to entertain the cowboys who patronized his hotel. An invitation to Rhoads' Ball was considered a great honor, and "the finest people in the community" attended. Thus began an annual social occasion similar to the Twelfth Night parties of Colonial Virginia.

Because of the centennial celebration in 1922 of the coming of Stephen F. Austin to Texas, there was a revival of public interest in the Christmas Ball, which was restaged for the Centennial, as part of the pageant "Texas Under Six Flags."

Today, the Cowboys' Christmas Ball has become a folk festival, so popular that it is given on four successive nights with over a thousand people attending.

"Approved costumes for the dancers," the official notices read, "are those of the 80's and 90's," but are not absolutely required. However, women in modern "western" clothes or pants are not allowed on the dance floor. "Masculine make-up" is that of an "Old-time Texas Cowboy . . . colorful with red bandana, plaid shirt, etc." The Ball begins with a Grand March, usually led by a bridal couple, representing the pair honored at the first Cowboys' Christmas Ball.

In Oklahoma City, the townspeople have found a practical way of celebrating the close of the Christmas season. On Twelfth Night, everyone takes his Christmas tree and Christmas greenery to be burned in a grand bonfire in Wiley Post Park. Other American cities also follow this custom, in keeping with ancient superstition that Christmas greenery should be burned and that bad luck follows if it is left up after Twelfth Night.

Christmas is a time when Southern cookery comes into its own. Misunderstood and abused by those who have sampled it only in second-rate restaurants, it is a unique cuisine that would honor any nation. In the Virginia Colony, it began as English cooking. When Thomas Jefferson returned from Paris with a cache of French recipes and enthusiasm for French food, there were those who criticized him for abandoning the good American ways.

Elsewhere in the South there was always a mixture of influences. French refugees from Huguenot persecutions established a foothold in South Carolina and Florida in 1680, and after 1730, German refugees from the Rhineland settled throughout the Southern states.

Most important of all, perhaps, were the Negro slaves, the first real "Southern" cooks. By taking basic recipes taught by their mistresses and making changes by instinct, often substituting natural products at hand for foreign ingredients, they evolved a kind of cookery neither they nor their masters had known before.

Nature provided a bounty for their use and experimentation. There was a variety of incomparable native nuts—pecans, hickory, and black walnuts—wild berries and fruits, and that versatile vegetable, corn. It was good to eat, made the pigs grow fat and tasty, and provided flour or meal for bread and puddings. In addition to what nature already provided, vegetables and grains introduced to the new land thrived so well that they were to all intents and purposes native.

In 1789, someone in Bourbon County, Kentucky, realized the potential of the native corn and produced a native liquor. On May 4, 1964, the United States Congress passed a resolution declaring bourbon to be a "distinctive product of the United States," the only American liquor to be so designated. Southern cooks were quick to substitute it for much more expensive brandy in their recipes.

Eggnog is a particularly Southern holiday specialty. It is usually traced back to syllabub, but the English drink contained no eggs and eggnog never became popular in New York, where syllabub was a favorite New Year's Day drink. It seems more likely that eggnog is related to German egg punch made with milk and wine and still popular in Germany today.

Until around World War II, eggnog parties were exceedingly popular in the nation's capital. Typically Southern specialties such as biscuits filled with chicken salad or ham and plates of fruitcake and sweet cookies were served with it.

In many Southern homes today a jar of eggnog is kept in the refrigerator during the holiday season, and refilled when emptied. According to contemporary taste, it is perhaps more often served as a dessert than as a cocktail. It also seems an ideal pick-me-up to strengthen the cook for the labors of the big Christmas feast, and sometimes serves as a substitute for the midday meal on Christmas Day.

Recipes for eggnog are many and varied, from the very rich Kentucky bourbon version to those requiring a variety of liquors. When making a quantity of eggnog to serve over a period of time, it is more satisfactory to divide the egg whites and use only as needed, beating them up at the time of serving.

Holiday Eggnog

6 eggs, separated	2 teaspoons vanilla
½ cup sugar, or to taste	3 cups heavy cream
1½ cups bourbon	1 pint milk
½ cup rum	3 tablespoons sugar
½ cup brandy or Cointreau	Nutmeg

Beat egg yolks well, adding sugar gradually. While still beating, add liquor gradually. Add vanilla, and put mixture into refrigerator to chill at least one hour. Then add cream and milk from time to time, preferably over a period of 24 hours. Stir well with each addition.

When ready to serve, beat egg whites (or as many as needed for first serving) until stiff. Fold half into mixture. Add 3 tablespoons sugar to remaining portion and swirl on top of eggnog if served in a bowl or drop by spoonfuls on top of individual cups. Sprinkle with nutmeg.

Eggnog can be frozen satisfactorily, but will not freeze hard because of the large quantity of alcohol.

Serves approximately 25

In 1845, a German visitor to Galveston, Texas, noted that whiskey punch "is the national drink here with which Christmas is celebrated." Below is one version of a whiskey punch which is known in our family as Texas punch. It is good any time of year.

"Texas" or Bourbon Punch

1 dozen medium-sized lemons	1 quart water
1 cup sugar	1 fifth bourbon

Cut lemons in half and squeeze juice into saucepan. Add sugar, water, and rinds to juice, and bring to a boil. Remove from heat and cool slightly. Add bourbon and let steep several hours or overnight. Remove lemon rinds, squeezing out any liquid. Strain and refrigerate. Will keep in a covered container in the refrigerator for a month. Serve over ice.

One of the most Southern of Christmas specialties is cornbread stuffing or dressing. My mother worked out the following recipe after a conversation with a locally famous Negro cook who was not eager to share the secret of her unusually light filling.

"How many eggs do you put in that stuffing?" mother asked.

"Oh, quite a few," was the reply.

"Three?"

"Oh, more than that!"

"Five?"

"More than that!" And so it went. . . .

The dressing should be quite thin—"soupy"—when it is put in the fowl. It will thicken and expand in cooking.

Cornbread Stuffing or Dressing

1 pan cornbread (recipe follows)	1 tablespoon sage
	1 teaspoon poultry seasoning
2 cans chicken with rice soup	1 teaspoon pepper, or more to taste
1 small loaf bread, preferably French bread, toasted very dry	1 tablespoon chopped parsley
	⅓ cup celery leaves, chopped fine
2 large onions, chopped fine and sautéed in butter	1 cup (or more) turkey broth made with wing tips, giblets, et cetera
7 eggs, beaten	
3 tablespoons butter, melted	

Salt to taste

Crumble cornbread into a large mixing bowl. Heat the soup. Pour half of it over toasted bread and soak until bread is soft.

117

Reserve remainder of soup. Add bread to cornbread, together with onions, eggs, butter, spices, and celery leaves. Mix well. Add remaining warm soup and sufficient turkey broth to make dressing almost thin enough to run from a spoon. Adjust salt to taste. Warm water may be added instead of turkey broth, but there is some loss in flavor.

This stuffing is best if made a day in advance and allowed to mellow. In stuffing turkey, be sure to stuff neck first, as this thin dressing will run right through cavity otherwise.

Sufficient for 14 to 16 pound turkey

Cornbread for Stuffing

1 cup cornmeal
1/4 cup flour
1 teaspoon baking powder
1/2 teaspoon salt

1/8 teaspoon soda
1 cup buttermilk, or more
1/4 cup shortening
1 egg

Turn oven to 400° F.

Mix together cornmeal, flour, baking powder, and salt. Stir soda into buttermilk. Heat heavy skillet and melt shortening in it. (In the South, bacon fat would be used.) Gradually add buttermilk to cornmeal mixture, mixing well. Stir in egg. If necessary, add more buttermilk in order to make thinnish batter with the consistency of cake batter. Pour melted shortening into batter. (This will thicken it.) Pour all into heated skillet and bake 20 to 25 minutes, or until done.

We use an 8-inch enameled iron skillet to make cornbread, but any baking dish of approximately the same size may be substituted.

Packaged cornbread mixes are too sweet to use for dressing without some adjustment. (No true Southern cook puts sugar in cornbread.) One package of mix may be used if 1/2 cup cornmeal and 2 eggs are added. 1 egg can then be omitted from the stuffing recipe.

Some Southerners say that the best part of Christmas is having hominy grits with leftover turkey gravy for breakfast.

The word "hominy" came from an Indian term, but grits were probably first created by Negro slaves. A similar dish prepared from ground cassava root is a staple of contemporary African diet, and is known as *foo foo*. Some visitors who have eaten foo foo at African embassies say they can taste little difference between it and steamed hominy grits.

In old cookbooks the terms "hominy" and "grits" are often used interchangeably. Grits are ideal for making another well-known Southern specialty, spoonbread, which is really a soufflé. The version given below goes well with any meal, beginning with breakfast or brunch. We prefer to make it with unsifted stone-ground grits, which give a certain texture, but regular grits are more commonly used.

Hominy Grits Soufflé

1 cup hominy grits	*4 cups milk*
2 tablespoons butter	*Salt*
1 to 2 tablespoons sugar	*2 eggs, separated*
	Additional butter

Cook grits, 2 tablespoons butter, sugar, milk, and salt to taste together in double boiler until thick and tender. The time for this will vary. Stone-ground grits may take as long as one hour, while quick-cooking grits will be done in 15 minutes. If necessary, add water for additional liquid while cooking. Let grits cool.

Turn oven to 350° F. Whip egg yolks into cooled grits. Pour into buttered baking dish and gently fold in egg whites beaten stiff with a pinch of salt. Dot with butter. Bake 30 to 45 minutes, until brown.

Serves 8 to 9

Southerners have always specialized more in making cakes than in baking cookies for Christmas. A man who grew up in Charleston, South Carolina, recalls that friends and neighbors used to exchange plates of cake during the Christmas holidays.

"There would be half a dozen kinds, or more," he said. Pound cake was a favorite throughout the South. It was served at both Mount Vernon and Williamsburg. Our light fruitcake is actually a glorified pound cake, but there were dozens more. In Kentucky and Tennessee, a specialty was jam cake, made with the fruit of wild blackberry. In Charleston, South Carolina, the elegant Lady Baltimore cake, said to have originated there, was favored as well as a "white" fruitcake, actually a black cake covered with almond paste, then iced. It is a sort of cross between black cake and the English almond-iced simnel cake which is traditional at Christmas and Easter.

In Virginia, in addition to pound cakes there were banana, pineapple, caramel, gold and White Mountain cakes. White Mountain was similar to the snowball cake for which recipe is given in this chapter. And in Texas a luscious pecan cake came into being, probably through the substitution of pecans in a recipe for English walnut cake.

Not surprisingly, someone in Kentucky decided to try putting bourbon in cake, and created a new one, Whiskey Cake. Light and delicate, it is as good in summer as in winter.

Whiskey Cake

½ pound candied cherries	3 eggs, separated
⅓ cup white raisins	1 teaspoon baking powder
1 cup 100-proof whiskey	¼ teaspoon salt (optional)
½ pound butter	1 teaspoon nutmeg
1 cup white sugar	2½ cups sifted flour
½ cup brown sugar	½ pound pecans, lightly floured

Soak cherries and raisins in whiskey overnight.

When ready to make cake, turn oven to slow, 250° to 275° F. Cream butter well, then add sugar gradually and cream until fluffy. Add egg yolks and beat well. Add baking powder, salt, and nutmeg to flour. Add liquid from fruit to egg mixture gradually, alternating with flour mixture. Add soaked fruit.

Beat egg whites until stiff, then fold into cake. Finally add floured pecans. Pour into a greased tube pan and bake 3 to 4 hours, until cake tests done. Cool thoroughly, then remove from pan and stuff center hole with cheesecloth soaked in whiskey. Store in tightly covered container. This cake does not need time to ripen, but will keep indefinitely if stored in a cool place.

Coconuts are not native to the South, but they have always been plentiful and inexpensive. And, as they began to appear for sale in December, they became synonymous with Christmas holidays. The great Coconut Snowball Cake which is traditional in many Southern homes is one of the most impressive of creations.

Coconut Snowball Cake

⅔ cup butter, softened	*3 teaspoons baking powder*
2 cups sugar	*½ teaspoon salt*
1 cup warm water	*8 egg whites, room temperature*
3 cups sifted flour	*and beaten stiff*

1 teaspoon orange extract

Grease two 9″ or 10″ round cake pans and line with paper on the bottom. Then grease again and dust with flour.

If using electric oven, turn to 350° F.; if using gas, turn to lowest heat.

Cream butter and sugar well together, about 10 minutes. Begin to add warm water, ¼ cup at a time, alternating with flour to which baking powder and salt have been added. When all water has been added, alternate remaining flour with stiffly beaten egg whites. Add flavoring last.

Divide batter equally between two prepared pans, and put in oven to bake. If baking in a gas range, increase heat 25° after 15 minutes, then increase 25° every 10 minutes. Remove cakes from oven when they are just well done, not brown or crusted. Turn out on rack.

When cake layers are cool, place one upside down on a large flat platter to be iced.

Icing and Filling

4 cups sugar

2 cups hot water or juice of coconut

4 egg whites, beaten stiff

2 large or 3 small coconuts, grated

1 teaspoon orange extract

Place sugar in a saucepan and pour hot water over it. Boil together very rapidly until it forms a soft ball in cold water. Pour ½ cup of hot syrup over stiffly beaten egg whites. Let remaining syrup cook until it spins a long thread or reaches the hard-crack stage when dropped into water. Pour slowly over egg whites, beating constantly. Add flavoring and beat until icing begins to be thick and smooth.

Spread layer of icing 1" thick on cake. Then spread 1" layer of grated coconut on top of icing. (Do NOT mix coconut with icing; it would completely change the character of the cake.) Top coconut with a second 1" layer of icing. Place second layer on top and cover with a layer of icing 1" thick. Spread icing down sides until cake is white and icing thick. Sprinkle grated coconut very generously on top, at least one inch thick. Dab coconut down the sides also, as thickly as it will stick.

If icing will not stand up one inch thick, it is too soft and needs more cooking. In that case, steam in double boiler until icing will hold its shape when dropped from a spoon.

Coconut balls can be made from this recipe by baking the cake in a loaf pan. Then cut cake in to 1" squares. Dip squares into icing, then spread with grated coconut and press into round ball. The soft icing will shape easily.

Store cake in refrigerator.

The following is a luscious traditional holiday cake from Carter County in Eastern Kentucky. Hickory nuts make a more authentic cake, but pecans or toasted almonds may be substituted.

Kentucky Hickory-nut Cake

1 cup butter	3 cups sifted flour
2 cups sugar	8 egg whites (unbeaten)
½ cup milk	1 cup hickory nuts
¼ teaspoon salt	1 tablespoon flour
2 teaspoons baking powder	1 teaspoon vanilla
Confectioner's sugar (optional)	

Turn oven to 350° F.

Cream butter well. Add sugar gradually, beating after each addition. Add milk. Sift salt and baking powder with flour. Add small amount to butter mixture, then beat in two egg whites. Alternate remaining flour with egg whites, adding one at a time and beating well after each addition. Dust nutmeats with tablespoon flour and mix well into batter with the vanilla.

Pour batter into a greased and floured tube pan. Bake 50 minutes or until the top browns. Cool in pan and turn out on a clean cloth or rack.

This cake is moist enough without any frosting, but if desired it can be dusted lightly with confectioner's sugar or iced with white frosting given for coconut ball cake, omitting the coconut.

Garnish with holly sprigs.

Arguments abound as to when and where the Lady Baltimore Cake originated, and whether it is a white or a yellow cake according to strict tradition. One version has the Lady Baltimore Cake as a white cake, with a companion cake, called *Lord* Baltimore, created from the leftover yolks.

Lady Baltimore Cake

¾ cup butter or shortening	1 cup milk
2 cups sugar	7 egg whites, room temperature
3 teaspoons baking powder	¼ teaspoon cream of tartar
¼ teaspoon salt	1 teaspoon vanilla extract
3 cups sifted flour	½ teaspoon almond extract

123

Turn oven to 350° F.

Cream butter well, then add sugar, and cream until fluffy. Add baking powder and salt to sifted flour and add to creamed butter mixture, alternating with milk. Beat thoroughly after each addition. The final addition should be flour.

Beat egg whites with cream of tartar until stiff, but not dry. Fold into cake batter. Flavor with vanilla and almond extract.

Pour into three 9″ greased round layer-cake pans and bake 20 to 25 minutes, until well done but not brown. Cool in pans 10 minutes, then turn onto cake racks for further cooling.

(Note: For a firmer, closer, slightly more tender texture, cake flour and superfine sugar may be used. Instructions remain the same.)

Frosting

3 cups granulated sugar
1 cup water
3 egg whites, stiffly beaten
1 cup pecans, chopped

½ cup glacé cherries, cut in quarters
½ cup additional candied fruit or chopped raisins (optional)

To make frosting, boil sugar with water until it spins a long thread when dropped from a spoon. Add gradually to the stiffly beaten whites of 3 eggs. Beat until almost ready to spread, then add pecans and fruit. Spread between layers and on top and side of cake.

Pecan Loaf Cake

1 cup butter
2 cups sugar
6 eggs
½ teaspoon salt
2 teaspoons baking powder
3 cups sifted flour

½ cup orange juice
1 teaspoon vanilla
1 pound pecans, broken in large pieces
1 cup flour
½ cup rum

½ teaspoon rum flavoring

Turn oven to 275° F.

Cream butter, then add sugar gradually, and cream thoroughly. Add eggs one at a time, beating thoroughly after each addition. Add salt and baking powder to flour and sift together three times, then add gradually to egg mixture, alternating with orange juice. Add vanilla.

Set aside ½ cup pecans, then sift 1 cup flour over those remaining. Fold into cake.

Pour into well-greased tube or loaf pan and bake about three hours, until done. Mix ½ cup rum and teaspoon rum flavoring and pour over cake. Let cool in pan.

Ice with favorite white frosting, adding remaining pecans to frosting.

This old-time favorite is worth reviving. It makes a very moist cake which will keep (or freeze) for a long time.

Dried Apple Fruit Cake

2 cups dried apples	1 teaspoon cinnamon
1 cup molasses	¾ teaspoon cloves
1 cup butter	½ teaspoon nutmeg
1 cup sugar	4 cups sifted flour
2 eggs	1 cup buttermilk
2 teaspoons soda	1 cup raisins (or more)
¾ teaspoon allspice	½ cup citron, chopped
	1 teaspoon vanilla

Soak apples overnight in water, then cut in quarters and cook with molasses until thick. This will take about an hour. Let cool while preparing cake batter.

Turn oven to 250° F.

Cream butter until fluffy, then add sugar, and cream again. Add eggs one at a time, beating well after each addition. Mix soda and spices with sifted flour, then fold into egg-sugar mixture alternately with buttermilk. Mix raisins and citron with apples and fold into batter. Add vanilla.

Pour into a well-buttered and floured tube pan or two loaf pans and bake about 2 hours, until cake tests done. Remove from oven and let cool. Be careful in removing from pan, as this is a very tender and moist cake. It will keep well in a cool place in a tight container.

Sometimes an "Oriental" fruitcake was made for Christmas by putting a fruit filling between layers of a common yellow cake, most often the cake known as 1–2–3–4 cake because of the proportion of its ingredients.

This cake has an "old-fashioned" taste, something like that of jam or jelly-filled cakes. Much lighter than true fruitcakes, it is one men will love.

Oriental Fruit Cake

1 yellow-cake recipe making three layers

Icing

1 cup water
2 cups sugar
1 cup shredded coconut
(fresh or frozen)

Juice of 2 oranges
2 cups seeded raisins
1 teaspoon cinnamon
1 teaspoon allspice
Large pinch of salt

Combine all ingredients thoroughly. Cook over low heat about 45 minutes, stirring occasionally. When thick, spread between layers and over top and side of cake.

In the South, the preparation of homemade candies was second only to cake-baking in the pre-holiday period. Butter-creams, stuffed dates, white fudge and black fudge, divinity, pralines, caramels, panocha—there were dozens of kinds filling several big tins. Recipes for a few of the best follow. The caramels originally called for hazelnuts or filberts, but of course in the South pecans were substituted. It is interesting to note in this connection that pecans were never considered special in the old days because they were so plentiful or common. "What I really looked forward to," an old-timer recalled, "was the handful of Brazil nuts that were always in my Christmas stocking."

Pecan Caramels

1½ cups sugar
¾ cup light corn syrup
½ teaspoon salt

3 cups light cream
1 teaspoon vanilla
1 cup pecans, roughly broken

Combine sugar, corn syrup, salt, and 1 cup of cream. Cook over moderate heat, stirring constantly, until sugar is dissolved. Reduce heat and continue to cook, stirring occasionally, until 236° F. is reached, on a candy thermometer. Meanwhile, heat remaining 2 cups of cream, covered, in a double boiler. When syrup reaches 236° F., slowly add 1 cup of warm cream and heat again to 236° F. point. Slowly add remaining 1 cup of warm cream and continue cooking, stirring occasionally, until 244° F. is reached. Add vanilla and pecans.

Pour into buttered 8″ square pan. When cold, cut into 1″ squares or 1″ x 2″ pieces, and wrap in waxed paper.

These caramels may be flavored with bourbon or rum if desired.

Chocolate Apricot Fudge

2 cups sugar
2 tablespoons corn syrup
6 tablespoons or more cocoa
¼ teaspoon salt
¾ cup milk

2 tablespoons butter
1 teaspoon vanilla
1 cup dried apricots, ground fine

Combine sugar, corn syrup, cocoa, salt, and milk in a large saucepan. Heat until melted, stirring often. Bring to a boil and boil without stirring until mixture makes a soft ball (236° F.). Remove from heat. Add butter. Cool. (This can be hastened by placing pan in another pan of cold water.) When nearly cold, add vanilla and beat for about two minutes. Add apricots. (If candy begins to harden earlier, stop beating at once and add fruit.)

Pour into an oiled container, in a layer ½″ to ¾″ thick. Mark in squares, then leave to set. Cut when cold. Store in tight container.

Yield: About 60 one-inch squares

In olden days, taffy pulls were common Christmas holiday entertainment. In 1843, William Bollaert, an English visitor to Texas, described such a party in which "some 50 lads and lassies congregated to assist. The great fun and sport," he reported, "is to approach slyly the person whose candy appears to be well pulled and snatch it from them. This produces great hilarity." Black walnut taffy is a refinement of more common varieties.

Black Walnut Taffy

1 cup light Karo syrup	2 tablespoons butter
1 cup sugar	1 teaspoon soda
1 cup thin cream	1 cup black walnuts, chopped
1 tablespoon vinegar (or more to taste)	

Boil first three ingredients to syrup stage. Add vinegar and continue boiling to firm-ball stage (254° F.). Add butter, soda, and walnuts and pour into a well-buttered platter. Let cool to handling stage, then with buttered fingers begin pulling edges to center. When candy has cooled sufficiently to pull, pull apart until firm and glossy, ending with a small rope. Cut into 2" bars and wrap in waxed paper.

We discovered recently that the following cookie bar, a childhood favorite, is just as inviting as we remembered it to be.

Gumdrop Cookies

2 eggs	¼ teaspoon baking powder
1 cup brown sugar, firmly packed	1 cup flour
1 tablespoon corn syrup	¾ cup chopped nuts, or more to taste
1 tablespoon orange juice	1 cup small gumdrops, or large gumdrops cut up
1 teaspoon cinnamon	
¼ teaspoon salt	

Turn oven to 325° or 350° F.

Cream one egg with brown sugar and beat well. Add second egg and beat well. Stir in corn syrup and orange juice, and mix well. Mix cinnamon, salt and baking powder with flour and add gradually to egg mixture. Add nuts and gumdrops.

Spread about ¼″ thick in buttered 8″ x 12″ pan. (Mixture will triple in bulk.) Bake 15 to 20 minutes, until an inserted toothpick comes out clean. (Do not brown.) Let cool slightly, then cut in squares.

Store and let ripen at least three days.

Sweet potatoes in some form were always served with holiday meals. Most often, they were candied in a buttery sugar syrup (after boiling). But they were also used in puddings and soufflés, and plain baked sweet potatoes were served with great globs of country butter. Sweet potato pie might also be a part of Christmas entertaining.

Southern Sweet Potato Pie

1½ cups cooked, mashed
sweet potatoes (yams)
¾ cup sugar, half brown,
half white
1 cup evaporated milk
3 medium-sized eggs,
well beaten

¼ cup soft butter
½ teaspoon salt
¼ teaspoon cinnamon
¼ teaspoon ginger
½ teaspoon nutmeg
1 unbaked pie crust

Preheat oven to 450° F.

Mix ingredients thoroughly. Pour into unbaked pie shell. Bake ten minutes, then reduce heat to 325° F. Bake 30 minutes or longer. Serve cold.

CHAPTER VIII

The French Louisiana Territory

"*What I remember most about Christmas in New Orleans was the réveillon, and what I remember most about the réveillon was the gumbo. There was always a huge pot of it.*"
—Former resident of New Orleans

For over two centuries Spain and France fought for control of Louisiana and the area along the Mississippi River; but at Noel or Christmastime and *Le Jour de l'An* ("New Year's Day") the French always won. Today in the French Quarter in New Orleans, in Acadian Louisiana, and in isolated spots like Ste. Genevieve, Missouri, French customs are still predominant during the Christmas-New Year period.

In conquering the New World, the French set up routes of commerce and trading posts, but as a rule did not establish large settlements or intermarry with the Indians. In 1698, the French established a port near the mouth of the Mississippi, the great route to Canada, and in 1722 New Orleans became the capital of French Louisiana. In 1764, French colonists pushed up to Kansas and Missouri and founded St. Louis.

In the same year the first Acadians began to arrive in Louisiana, nine years after being expelled from Nova Scotia because they refused to swear loyalty to the British Crown and to forsake Catholicism. Within a period of twenty-five years, over 5,000 French refugees from Canada settled in the area west of New Orleans. During the same period, refugees from the French Revolution appeared. These were members of the aristocracy, who brought to the frontier an appreciation of *la bonne vie*, the good life of costume balls, silks and satins and jewels, opera and ballet.

During the administration of Thomas Jefferson, the United States purchased Louisiana for $15 million. As had happened with every port city in America, a mixture of peoples flocked to New Orleans when it opened up, especially English, Spanish, and Germans. The prestige of the French, however, was so effectively established that many families of other nationalities changed their names into literal French equivalents in meaning.

The exact meaning of the term "Creole" is still disputed. It first came into use while New Orleans was under Spanish rule in the eighteenth century. According to the final authority—namely, the Public Relations Office of the City of New Orleans—it was applied originally only to French settlers and their descendants, connoting from the beginning a "certain excellence of origin." Because of this implication, Spanish offspring whose pure blood entitled them to top social rank also adopted the designation. Technically, only the pure in blood were ever entitled to call themselves Creole. "Much later, the term was adopted by, but not conceded to, the natives of European-African or Creole-African blood, and is still so used amongst themselves," the authority continues.

The clearest of blood lines did not necessarily entitle a French descendant to the privilege of calling himself Creole, however. To this day New Orleans Creoles stubbornly refuse to acknowledge the Acadian French as being anything except "cajuns." Any other strangers who happened to make their home in Louisiana—English, Scotch, Irish, and Creoles from any other area of the United States—are lumped together "under the distinctive terms, Americans or 'Snow Diggers.'"

Both the French and Spanish settlers brought to America a tradition of Christmas Eve midnight mass followed by a huge feast. How a mass at midnight became customary on Christmas Eve is not known. The reason often cited is that midnight is thought to be the hour of Christ's birth, a belief without Biblical foundation. The time prescribed for the first Christmas Day mass is in nocte ("while it is still night"). During the early years of Christianity, Romans set the time as that of the first cockcrow, ad galli cantum, reckoned to be around 3 A.M. Spanish-speaking people still call the mass Misa del gallo or mass of the rooster. They have no name for the meal that follows.

Réveillon, the French name for the early morning feast, was a time when Creole cooks shone. A simple réveillon for an affluent nineteenth-century Creole family re-created for a 1959 national Home Demonstration Agents Convention in New Orleans consisted of the following: deviled eggs with mushrooms and baked eggs with shrimps; a French laced loaf of sweet bread with dates, apples, almonds, wine, and spices in the filling; orange praline rolls; a glacé coffee loaf; daube glacé (recipe on page 138); spiced peaches, dates in port, and réveillon wine cake; white, red, and dessert wine. Daube glacé is a jellied meat dish which a New Iberia Creole once described as fit to "take on a trip to Heaven."

The Acadian country cousins of the New Orleans French gave less attention to Christmas Day. "The dinner was about like the usual Sunday meal," a correspondent writes of the 1910–1925 period, and the day itself like a special Sunday. Children were generally given fruit as a present from L'Enfant Jesus ("the Baby Jesus").

In Acadia, New Year's Day was the important holiday. It was the day for family reunions, and the time when Le Bon St. Nicolas brought good children Les étrennes, gifts of dolls, wagons, store-bought candies, et cetera.

Older Negro members of the community were also given

étrennes. They wished the givers good health and prosperity in exchange, ending always with the litany, "Paradise to the end of your days." This was a literal translation of the customary French New Year's salutation between family members for *Bonne année, bonne santé, et paradis a la fin de vos jours*. The Negroes, too, had become "Acadian," having taken up the religion of their masters (Catholicism), and their French language with its particular expressions. In some areas of Acadia today, one occasionally hears the French term *étrenne* used in referring to Christmas gifts.

Celebration of *Le Jour de l'An*, which translates literally as "the day of the year," started the night before with an explosion of firecrackers and Roman candles. The day itself began with early morning mass, followed by a country breakfast, eagerly anticipated by all: baking powder biscuits and country butter, *boudin* or blood sausage, hog head cheese, and café au lait.

But the New Year dinner, "That was the feast to be remembered." The table was loaded with roast suckling pig, *chaudin* (stuffed stomach of a young hog), baked chickens and ducks, ham, rice dressing, "store-bought" bread, country butter, winter vegetables (no frozen foods in those days), and baked sweet potatoes. Wine was served, of course, and at the end a demi-tasse of pure black coffee made from home-roasted beans. For dessert there was ambrosia and an assortment of cakes, as well as pecan and benne-seed pralines for visitors who stopped by during the day-long celebration. For children there was an ample supply of popcorn balls.

Today, of course, Santa Claus has replaced St. Nicholas as bringer of gifts in Louisiana, and he comes on Christmas rather than on New Year's Day. But the French crèche is still a revered part of Christmas in French families, and New Year's Day a day when members of the family come into New Orleans from outlying areas to pay respects to older relatives.

For a few young women in New Orleans, the most important thing about Christmas is that it signals the approach of Mardi Gras. On Christmas Day they receive invitations to be Maids at the Carnival Ball of the Duke's Krewe, in the form of notes tucked into bouquets of long-stemmed red roses.

On Twelfth Night, the beginning of Mardi Gras, the Twelfth Night Revelers choose their Queen by cutting a special cake containing a golden bean. In many countries the practice of selecting a King and Queen of the Bean on Epiphany still exists—in France, Spain, and most Spanish-speaking countries—and the custom is maintained in some French-American families. "In many homes," a correspondent writes from New Orleans, "the *gâteau des rois* (king's cake) is still a must for the celebration of Epiphany, and the drawer of the bean must give the party the following year." Holding open house on Christmas and New Year's Day has replaced réveillon to a great extent, he adds.

So long as the French influence was predominant in St. Louis, *La Guignolée*, an old French New Year's masquerade, was a part of the New Year revelry, and a brightly burning candle was placed in each home to signal that visitors would be welcome. Suddenly, on New Year's Eve there would be a burst of song and the sound of a fiddle, as a group of masked men appeared out of nowhere. Upon being welcomed by the master of the house, they entered, singing a song of many verses, some sense and some nonsense. After singing and dancing, eating and drinking, they departed, taking with them contributions of food for the Twelfth Night Ball.

In St. Louis today, residents place a lighted candle in the window during the Christmas season as a signal to carolers that they are welcome and will receive a contribution. The St. Louis Christmas Carols Association accidentally came into being in 1911 when nine persons organized a caroling expedition that eventually became an annual event. Others asked to join, and the idea spread until now thousands take part each year. They perform where requested, in hospitals and other public places, and raise thousands of dollars to help others.

Since the word "Creole" meant something superior, it was naturally applied to the style of cookery developing in the New Orleans area. In time, "Creole" became synonymous with any indigenous product—local tomatoes, for instance, were labeled "Creole tomatoes." Similarly, other foodstuffs claimed such distinction, as well as any other item that might be promoted.

Creole cuisine, quite unlike the European settlers who proudly called themselves Creole, was anything but pure-blooded. Its distinctive characteristics derived from the very fact that so many contributed to its lineage. Most notably they were Negroes, French, Spanish, Indians, and perhaps Italians.

Negro slaves brought from Africa a taste for foods highly spiced with red pepper, which grew so well in the Louisiana area; more important still, they planted okra seeds brought from their homeland, thus introducing an ingredient essential to many Creole dishes. When okra could not be obtained for making gumbo, in the winter, Negro cooks used the ground sassafras leaves that the Indians had been using for centuries as medicine. They added a little thyme to it, and the result became known as filé. For benne or sesame seed, brought from the West Coast of Africa in the earliest days of slave trading, they found new uses and employed it lavishly.

Creole cookery was not the sole creation of Negro cooks, of course. French and Spanish recipes which they learned from their mistresses were its basis. But without their ingenuity and imaginative way of using the natural gifts of the sea and land, Creole cuisine would have developed into something quite different.

"Gumbo" is an Americanization of the African name for okra. Yankee cookbooks and ignorance have led to some confusion and misconception regarding this Creole masterpiece. An explanation which could stand for all time was given some years ago by a famous Natchez cook to a visitor who did not understand about it. The non-Creole complained that "Some recipes for gumbo are quite thin," and asked if they were correct. The imperious cook drew herself up to her full height.

"There's gumbo," she explained disdainfully, "and there's gumbo soup. Gumbo means to be *thick*."

The following recipe is for gumbo, and it means to be very thick, indeed. It will make a very hearty meal, noon or night, and one which may be prepared well in advance. If okra is fried out first, as it should be for any proper gumbo, it will not be stringy or slippery. Frozen okra can be thawed, then fried satisfactorily. Filé powder may be substituted if okra is not available. Filé should not be added until just before serving, and should never be boiled, as that makes it bitter.

Crab, shrimp or oysters may be omitted. Every gumbo is different, but this one will not be quite the same without them.

Creole Gumbo

2 teaspoons lard, or shortening
  (more if needed)
1 small ham bone or
  1 pound raw ham
½ pound veal
¼ pound chicken, raw or
  leftover cooked
1 pound fresh shrimp,
  preferably medium size
2 slices bacon
2 large onions, minced fine
1 tablespoon green pepper,
  finely chopped
1 pound okra, fresh or frozen
2 cloves garlic, through the
  press

1 bay leaf
Pinch thyme
2 teaspoons sugar
2 large fresh tomatoes, skinned
  and chopped, or 1 medium
  can
3 tablespoons chopped parsley
Tabasco to taste (several
  dashes)
2 tablespoons Worcestershire
  sauce
2 tablespoons lemon juice
1 pound fresh crab meat
½ pint oysters
Salt and pepper to taste

Put lard in heavy skillet and heat. Brown ham bone or ham, veal, and chicken, adding more lard if necessary. Set aside.

Remove shrimp from shells and put shells in water to boil about 10 minutes. Strain out shells. Save cooking water. Clean shrimp and set aside.

In another heavy pan (the deep one in which gumbo is to be cooked may be used), fry out bacon. Remove bacon and set aside. Using half of the bacon fat, sauté onion and green pepper until onion is golden and pepper wilted. Remove and set aside.

Add remaining bacon fat and fry okra until it is browned and has lost its gummy consistency. Add garlic, bay leaf, thyme, and sugar and cook one minute. Add chopped tomatoes and parsley and ingredients which have been set aside: ham, veal, and chicken; shrimp, shrimp water, crumbled bacon, and onion-green-pepper mixture. Add remaining ingredients except salt. Cover with water. Cook one hour and taste for salt. Add more if needed. (Ham will give some salt and more may not be needed.) Simmer one hour more or longer. Cool and chill.

Gumbo is better if made at least one day in advance and rewarmed. When ready to use, skim off fat, and reheat.

Serve with fluffy white rice and crusty French bread.

Yield: 4 quarts or more

Rice is a favorite dish in all the South, but never more so than in Louisiana. Baking is an easy way to prepare it when entertaining.

Baked Rice

4 tablespoons butter   *4 cups boiling water*
2 cups rice   *1 teaspoon salt*

Preheat oven to 350° F. Melt butter in one-quart ovenproof casserole. Stir in rice, boiling water, and salt. Cover and bake for 30 minutes in oven. Check at this time and stir gently. For some tastes, it may be sufficiently cooked. Otherwise, re-cover and cook a little longer, but not more than 15 minutes.

Yield: 6 cups

In Louisiana, Creoles and Acadians discovered how to make stuffing for fowl with rice and oysters, a delectable combination.

Oyster and Rice Dressing

¾ cup rice
1 can chicken stock
¼ cup minced onion
¼ cup minced celery
(stalk and tops)
1½ tablespoons minced parsley

¼ cup butter
1 pint oysters, well drained
1½ cups toasted bread crumbs
1½ teaspoons poultry seasoning
Salt and pepper
1 egg, well beaten

Cook rice in broth, adding water if necessary. Sauté onions, celery, and parsley in butter until tender. Add oysters and cook until edges begin to curl. Remove from heat. Add to other ingredients. Toss lightly with fork until well mixed.

Yield: enough for 6-pound fowl

Years ago, the Christmas season was ushered in at Vicksburg, Mississippi, when *le grand boeuf*, the big Christmas beef, arrived. Shortly before the holidays, a fine animal wearing ribbons and colored garlands or a piece of holly on his head was led through the streets by a proud young boy.

One of the dishes prepared from the Christmas beef was *daube glacé*, still a classic Christmas dish in New Orleans. It is also delightful in the summer, when jellied meats are so inviting.

Daube Glacé

¼ pound salt fat pork, cut in
larding strips
1 sprig thyme
2 bay leaves, crushed
2 sprigs parsley, chopped
Salt, pepper, cayenne
1 onion, chopped fine
2 cloves garlic, minced
4 pounds beef round or
lean beef
1 tablespoon or more lard or
shortening

2 onions, cut in quarters
5 carrots, cut in thick slices
1 onion, finely chopped
¼ cup sherry
Stock for boiling
3 pounds veal
2 pig's feet
1 crumbled bay leaf
1 sprig thyme
2 sprigs parsley
½ clove garlic
½ cup sherry

Season larding strips with chopped sprig of thyme, bay leaves, parsley, salt, pepper, and cayenne. Mix well with 1 chopped onion and 2 minced cloves garlic. Cut incisions in beef and fill with larding strips and herb mixture. Make insertions across the width of the meat, so that when it is sliced the strips will show in an attractive pattern.

Brown meat well in lard or shortening in a heavy pan or Dutch oven. Add quartered onions and brown lightly. Add sliced carrots and 1 chopped onion. Cover and cook gently 10 minutes. At end of time, turn meat. Simmer gently 10 minutes more. Add sherry and enough boiling stock (made with bouillon cubes) or water to cover meat. Cover pot tightly. Simmer 3 hours, or until meat is very tender.

Meanwhile, season veal and pig's feet with salt, pepper, and cayenne. Simmer in 4 quarts of water until very tender. Remove veal and pig's feet. Mince meat and discard bones. Put bay leaf, thyme, parsley, garlic, and sherry in pot. Simmer a few minutes, enough for flavors to combine. Adjust seasoning. Add minced veal and pork.

Transfer the cooked beef to a casserole or serving dish slightly larger and deeper than the chunk of meat. Pour the prepared minced-meat and stock over beef. Set casserole in refrigerator overnight. The stock will form a firm but tender jelly.

Slice to serve, jelly and all.

Serves 20

Anyone who has wandered through the French Quarter of New Orleans has discovered another Creole pride—pralines.

There are dozens of recipes for making them, but the greatest secret about their perfection is that pralines must be eaten very fresh. Each day a praline is stored, it deteriorates.

In olden days, Acadian and Creole cooks often used benne or sesame seeds instead of the native pecans. They were toasted or "parched" before using. Here is one very good praline recipe, a favorite from my childhood:

Pralines

1½ cups light brown sugar	⅓ cup butter
½ cup white sugar	1 tablespoon corn syrup
½ cup water	2 cups pecan halves

Mix sugar, water, butter, and corn syrup. Place over heat and cook until sugar is dissolved. Cook about 10 minutes. Add pecans and cook to soft-ball stage, stirring occasionally. Beat, but watch carefully. Overbeating will cause pralines to be too sugary. Drop by spoonfuls on buttered plate or tray. Work very fast when spooning out pralines, as candy hardens rapidly.

Many Southern cooks prefer to substitute milk for water in making pralines.

In Acadia, that German Christmas specialty, lebkuchen, finally met its nemesis. The French Cajuns took the basic idea, added a little of this—mostly eggs—and took away a little of that—honey—and out came a new cookie. Even the name changed in the process. The result adapted from *First—You Make a Roux*, a cookbook compiled by the Lafayette Museum in Lafayette, Louisiana, does not age as well as the German original. But no one would want to keep it that long, anyway.

Acadian "Lep Kuchen"

7 egg yolks	2 teaspoons baking powder
5 egg whites	1 teaspoon allspice
1 cup granulated sugar	1 teaspoon nutmeg
1 cup syrup	2 teaspoons cinnamon
1 cake sweet chocolate, melted	2½ cups sifted flour
½ teaspoon salt	¾ cup chopped citron
1 teaspoon vanilla	1¼ cups chopped nuts
1 cup raisins (optional)	

Preheat oven to 325° F.

Beat egg yolks and whites together until very light. Add sugar gradually, then syrup, melted chocolate, salt, and vanilla. Sift baking powder and spices with flour. Remove 2 tablespoons for dredging citron, nuts, and raisins (if used). Gradually stir remaining flour into egg mixture. Stir in dredged fruit and nuts.

Pour into two large greased tins 15″ x 14½″ with raised edges. Bake 8 to 10 minutes, or until just done. Remove from oven. Ice while still warm. Cool, then cut into bars.

Icing

2 egg whites   1 cup confectioner's sugar
                    1 teaspoon vanilla extract

To make icing: Blend egg whites and confectioner's sugar and flavoring. Beat for five minutes.

Ambrosia was an integral part of Christmas everywhere in the South, Creole or otherwise. Ordinarily, it was served as a dessert after the heavy Christmas meals, but in our family it has been the chief component of Christmas breakfast as long as anyone can remember.

An Ambrosia Cake has been evolved from the original light dessert. It is made by combining ¾ cup cream whipped stiff, 2 cups powdered sugar, and the juice and grated rind of one orange, plus the chopped orange segments and grated coconut. Half the grated meat of one coconut is added to the cream mixture, which is then spread between layers of yellow cake. The remaining coconut is sprinkled lavishly on the outer cream topping.

Ambrosia

1 fresh coconut, grated
4 oranges, peeled, sectioned,
    and seeded

½ fresh pineapple, cut in
    bite-size chunks
Milk from the coconut
½ cup orange juice, or more
Sugar to taste

In a large glass bowl, or in individual glass sherbet dishes, place layer of coconut, layer of oranges and pineapple, and top with layer of coconut. Pour coconut milk and orange juice over all. Lightly sprinkle with sugar, and pass sugar for individuals to add more if desired.

Some Southerners add sherry to ambrosia when serving it as a dessert.

Serves 8 to 10

CHAPTER IX

Spanish, Mexican, and Indian Influences

"*A New Mexico Christmas is* luminarias, farolitas, achones, Las Posadas, Los Pastores, Naci-
mientos, Los Matachines, *Indian dances. . . .*"
—"Anglo" resident of Santa Fe,
New Mexico

The Spanish celebrated Christmas in New Mexico long before
the Puritans landed at Plymouth. In 1540, Coronado and his
men spent Christmas at a winter camp near Albuquerque, and
may very well have feasted on the native "cocks with hanging
beards," or turkeys. Probably the first happy celebration was in
1600 in San Gabriel. Twelve *luminarias* or tall stacked pine-
bough fires were built in the plaza, one for each of the Apostles, and there was a performance of the miracle play, *Los
Pastores*, the shepherds. At midnight, the music and singing
ceased, as the new colonists, conquistadors, and Indians filed
into a little adobe church for *la Misa del Gallo*, the midnight
mass of the rooster.

By the time the Spanish influence reached the Southwest, it
had been altered by a sojourn in the South. "The Twelve
Apostles of Mexico," the first brown-robed Franciscans, had

143

come to the New World in 1524. In Mexico, they discovered two important December celebrations: one in honor of the war god Huitzilopochtli, at the time of the solstice, and one celebrating the birth of the Earth Mother, Tonantzín, who was represented as a "child coming down from heaven."

In Arizona and New Mexico they found that the Pueblo Indians also had strong religious beliefs, based on natural phenomena and fetishes, and elaborate religious rituals governed by a calendar calculated according to the sun. In each pueblo there was at least one kiva, the center of religious experience and a symbolic connection with the underworld.

The Franciscans introduced the birthday of Christ to the Indians, and the Spanish traditions attached to it. Soon the warriors were coming from far and near on December 25 to celebrate the birth of the strange God-Child. They shot arrows in the air, sang, and danced, and, at midnight gathered for mass in the chapel, where a lifelike *nacimiento* cradling the Holy Infant was prominently displayed. "They celebrate also with great festivity the Kings' Day, *el Dio de los Reyes Magos*, and represent the drama of gift offerings of the Three Kings to the Christ Child," Padre Toribio de Motolinía noted in his *History of the Indians in New Spain*, written sometime before 1568. The subterranean kivas remained untouched.

Today, Indians in New Mexico, numbering around 60,000, participate fully in all aspects of the old cultural triad. There are over 25,000 Pueblo Indians among nineteen pueblos or villages. These people were citizens of Mexico after the Republic won its freedom from Spain, and only recently have adopted constitutions and by-laws patterned after those of the United States. Until 1930 the state legislature of New Mexico was officially bilingual; and today, a number of inhabitants still prefer to speak in Spanish.

SHÁLACO CEREMONIES

In the far western part of New Mexico, the Christmas season is said to begin with the last day of Shálaco in the Zuñi

Pueblo, the date varying from late November to mid-December. The ceremonies have hardly changed since the village was discovered by the Spaniards in 1539.

Shálaco is a forty-nine day re-enactment of Zuñi legend which shows that the Indians began life in a subterranean home, which they gave up for one on earth. The dead are believed to enter the village with the Shálaco, but are invisible. There are many secret ceremonies that outsiders may not witness until the last night, when new homes built during the year are blessed and dedicated. The rites go on all night and owners of the houses must traditionally feed all who attend, a very expensive obligation, indeed. At dawn, the dancers return to the underworld, but dances continue for four days, culminating with a final prayer for rain to fructify the earth and fill all watercourses, wells and springs.

THE FEAST OF OUR LADY OF GUADALUPE

Many in the Southwest consider that the Christmas season begins with the feast honoring Our Lady of Guadalupe, Patroness of the Americas. The Virgin first appeared to an Indian convert in 1531, at the very spot where the shrine of Tonantzén had stood, near Mexico City. Now she is worshiped in many spots in the Southwest. In Albuquerque there is a street procession with Indian Matachine dancers, and a mass with music furnished by mariachis, a Mexican brass band. At the Mission of San Luis Rey in California, another procession is an annual event.

Perhaps the most elaborate celebration is that at Tortugas, New Mexico, three miles south of Las Cruces. The three-day ceremonies begin on December 10 at nightfall with the image of the Virgin transported from Her private chapel to the pueblo's Ceremonial House. Shotguns are fired and all night long there is Matachine dancing to the music of wailing violins, booming tom-toms, clattering maracas, and Indian chanting.

At dawn, in a candlelit procession, the Virgin's image is returned to the church. The Tortugeños then begin a fourteen-mile climb to a shrine atop Tortugas Mountain. They spend the day in prayer, meditation, and making elaborate walking sticks called *quiotes*, which represent the staffs carried by the shepherds journeying to Bethlehem. At nightfall they return. Enroute, they set afire piles of firewood gathered on the way up, and a crucifix set halfway between heaven and earth.

Before making a triumphal re-entry into the village, men and women in separate columns surge toward a huge bonfire. On December 12, the Virgin's own day, the men don high-feathered headdresses and lead a great primitive dance at one o'clock in the morning.

THE MATACHÍN DANCES

A remarkable dance that reveals the elements and background that shaped the culture of the Southwest, the Matachines, is given in the Jémez Pueblo on December 12. The dances took their name from the Spanish Dancers who performed in a sixteenth-century Spanish morality play about the triumph of Christian Spain over invading Moors. In Mexico the Spaniards gave the play for the Aztecs, hoping to convert them as the Moors in the play had been converted. The Aztecs could not understand Spanish, however, though they loved the silk costumes of the Moorish characters with their high-crowned turbans. The Mexican Indians, themselves superb dramatists, reworked the drama, converting the Moors into Apostles in brilliant satin capes and gaily ribboned mitres.

Each tribe reinterpreted and rearranged the play as it spread throughout the Southwest, and in New Mexico local Indian music and serpentine dance steps were added that converted the pageant into a prayer for rain and fertility. At the Jémez Pueblo, both versions, Mexican and Indian, are given; and at various times during the holidays variations are presented in other pueblos, the most notable being at Taos on Christmas Day and at Nambe on Three Kings' Day or Epiphany.

LAS POSADAS (THE INNS)

On the sixteenth of December, the ancient Mexican-Spanish tradition of *Las Posadas* begins. For nine nights, Nativity figures of Mary and Joseph are carried through the streets in search of lodging, to the accompaniment of songs of praise. Each night, they are finally admitted at some home, and a party ensues. On the last night, the figure of the Holy Infant is added.

The custom derives from an idea of St. Ignatius Loyola, who suggested a novena (prayers on nine successive days) that would be reminiscent of Mary's and Joseph's journey to Bethlehem. St. John of the Cross put it into practice in 1580 as a pageant, recalling perhaps how the figure of the Holy Infant was carried in procession at the end of Nativity mystery plays.

Seven years later, Friar Diego de Soria obtained permission to celebrate special Christmas masses with a similar re-enactment in Mexico, hoping to replace pagan Indian celebrations held at the time of the winter solstice. Thus began *Las Posadas*.

Initially, it took place inside the church, and was a very serious celebration. Not surprisingly, the irrepressible Mexicans transferred it to the outside, where it became one of the gayest fiestas of the year.

Las Posadas continues in several ways. In California there are traditional observances in the Old Town of San Diego and at the Mission of San Luis Rey, and staged performances in the Padua Hills, where Mexican Players have been re-enacting *Las Posadas* for over thirty years with performances beginning about the middle of November and continuing until the first week of January.

In Santa Fe, *La Sociedad Folklorica* preserves the tradition with enactments in private homes or at churches; in San Antonio, Texas, and in other cities where Mexicans have taken root, including Chicago, they themselves hold the nightly processions and parties.

In the Newman Center of New Mexico State University, at Las Cruces, *Las Posadas* is conducted by students. Many come from areas where they have had no previous encounter with Spanish and Mexican customs. By taking part in the Center's extensive Advent program, they become aware of the rich Spanish heritage.

LOS PASTORES AND OTHER MYSTERY PLAYS

When the Franciscan fathers introduced the mystery plays in Mexico, they became so popular and successful that the complete Christmas cycle of plays became traditional. Eventually, as in Europe, the Mexicans added so many of their own ideas and so much ribaldry that their greatest favorite, *Los Pastores*, was banned from the church. But the play continued in private indoor and backyard performances given by small troupes of Mexican players who became known as *pastoreles*. Words and action were passed on from one actor to another by word of mouth, since most could neither read nor write, and they presented the drama as an *Auto Sacramental*, an obligatory act of devotion. In their hands, the play became a mixture of sacred teachings, Indian imagery, and Mexican folklore. Basically, the theme is the eternal conflict between good and evil as shown in the tribulations and temptations of the shepherds making their way to Bethlehem.

Costuming is unique and traditional, with continued innovations by the actors. The homemade creations for Lucifer and his imps are wild and bizarre, with distorted masks of vermilion-painted tin and real hogs' tusks and deers' antlers; those for the shepherds, bright and gay with tinsel, artificial flowers, ribbons, and a multitude of tiny bells that jingle with every movement; and the Holy Family traditional.

The most colorful and complete performances are probably

those given in San Antonio; but the tradition survives also in New Mexico in small towns where Spanish continues to be the mother tongue. In Mesilla a number of performances are given, not only in Catholic churches, but also in the Methodist Church.

CHRISTMAS EVE AND CHRISTMAS WEEK IN THE PUEBLOS

Many Indians no longer live in the pueblos, but all try to return at Christmas for a family reunion, and for the great Indian pageants and accompanying feasts.

From ancient times the Indians held religious dances to coincide with the natural phenomena of summer and winter solstices and vernal and autumnal equinoxes. The Franciscans succeeded in bringing the Indian celebrations and Christian holy feast days together. As consequence, on one night of the year, Christmas Eve, Indian fertility dances are given in the church. Some take place before the midnight mass, others afterward, when the Host has been removed from the building. At Acoma, Indians bring small clay figures of horses, cattle, and sheep in baskets or bowls and a cross in a bowl for God, and leave them in the church for four days, then bury them in the fields beneath cedar bushes, in hope of multiplication of their animals and crops.

The most unique Christmas Eve dances are held in San Felipe Pueblo, thirty-five miles south of Santa Fe. Shortly after the priest departs, there is a burst of birdcalls from the loft, sounds produced by blowing into a shallow bowl of water with a split perforated hollow reed. The warbling dies down as an insistent drum throb reaches the doorway and dancers move into the blazing candlelight of the altar. Dressed in masks, animal skins, shells, coral, turquoise, downy feathers and headpieces with real antlers, they perform deer, buffalo, turtle, and eagle dances. Women who take part carry a sprig of *hakak*, the sacred spruce tree which they believe helped create mankind and that represents eternal life.

149

In Taos a statue of the Holy Mother is carried in a procession lit by *achones*, great pitch-pine torches fastened to the ends of long poles that make the fires appear magically suspended in midair. From time to time, rifles are fired to frighten away evil spirits.

During Christmas week and until Epiphany or Three Kings' Day on January 6 game dances are given repeatedly in the pueblos, as well as on February 2, Candlemas.

Children in the San Juan Pueblo are on their best behavior before Christmas, in fear of *Tash-ve-yohs*, a mythological boogeyman who devours naughty children. Children who have reason to expect punishment beg their mothers to bake many loaves of Indian bread to assuage him. In San Idlefonso Pueblo, *Tsaviyo*, another form of the same spirit, has become recognized as a sort of Santa Claus because he distributes gifts.

LUMINARIAS AND PIÑATAS

Padre Motolinía noted in the sixteenth century that on Christmas Eve the Indians set "many luminarias [bonfires] on the patios of the churches, and even on some of the flat roofs of the houses, so . . . since their houses join one to the other, the bonfires light . . . as much as a league. The whole impression is that of a brightly lit sky." Thus had the European custom of placing a candle or lantern to light the way for the Holy Couple been dramatized in the Southwest.

The Indians built luminarias by stacking piñon boughs in a three-foot high circle, and in small Spanish-Indian villages in the mountains they still follow this procedure. In the cities, however, bonfires were replaced by an ingenious arrangement in which a brown paper bag is weighted down with sand and a small candle placed inside. Some say this type of luminaria began when the first overland wagon trains arrived from St. Louis early in the 1820s. Some purists, on the other hand, maintain that only the bonfires are luminarias, that the paper lights should be called *farolitas*, and that they are an American version of Mexican festival lights.

On Christmas Eve some homeowners put hundreds of paper-bag lights along paths and fill their lawns with them. They place luminarias anywhere colored lights might be used, as along roof-tops. For the annual Nativity pageant in Cavecreek, Arizona, five thousand are set in the rugged granite boulders of the desert, and along highways entering the village.

Visitors to the Southwest have been so entranced with the luminaria displays, especially in the "luminaria city" of Albuquerque, that the custom has spread north, south, and east to Schenectady, New York; the Coastal Islands of Georgia; and Fairbanks, Alaska.

The piñata, a colorful and whimsical creation of tissue, crepe paper, tinsel, and sequins in almost any shape and form, has also spread everywhere. A sunburst type with flowing streamers was the only decoration in the White House when the Johnsons began their stay.

Piñatas are a unique blend of European and Indian influences. They began in Italy during the Renaissance, as *pignattas*, sweet-filled clay pots that were hung from the ceiling and broken with a stick as part of the entertainment at masquerade balls.

In Spain, the game was adopted for Lent, and the first Sunday called Piñata Sunday. Often there were Lenten masquerade balls or a Dance of the Piñata. During this period, the name piñata referred only to the game of pot-breaking, not the container.

Simultaneously, in Mexico there was a parallel which existed from Aztec times. Sometime near the end of the year priests prepared an offering for the god of war, *Huizilopochtli*. They filled a clay pot with treasures and delicacies, covered it with fine woven feathers and brilliant plumes, and stood it on a pole in the temple. When Aztec New Year came, they broke the pot with a club, and the gifts spilled at the feet of the idol as a sacrifice.

The Franciscan padres converted the Indians to secular use of the piñata, and today it is part of a game at the party following *Las Posadas*. Children are blindfolded one at a time, then spun round and given a stick to hit the pot, which is manipulated by a rope and playfully pulled out of reach until someone is allowed to smash it. Then candies and gifts spill out and there is a mad scramble for them. Theoretically, this game teaches a religious lesson that all things come through faith, the act of faith being to put on a blindfold.

"Anglos," persons who are neither Indian nor Spanish, have taken up *Las Posadas* and the piñata, and often hold piñata parties alone, without the *Posadas*. Piñatas meanwhile, have developed into such fascinating creations that often they are never broken.

As the holidays approach, tantalizing aromas of *biscochitos* (rich cookies), and empanaditas fill the air in southwestern homes. Empanaditas are Spanish fried pies that have adopted American mincemeat for filling. Traditionally, they are served between meals with wine. One friend recalls that when he was a boy, fellow schoolmates used to make exchanges with him because his mother's empanaditas were known to be the best made.

The original recipe for empanaditas uses leftover roast or boiled beef, but ground fresh meat can be substituted and is perhaps preferable. If meat is uncooked, simmer with spices in a small amount of water until meat is well done, then add remaining ingredients and cool. If meat is cooked, put through a meat grinder, then mix with other ingredients, adding a little broth if mixture seems too dry. Both fillings may be prepared several days in advance and refrigerated until needed. Often prepared mincemeat is substituted for the homemade filling, and sometimes sweetened fruit or jam is used.

A contemporary practical adaptation of empanaditas is one in which some sugar is omitted, and the pie converted into an intriguing hors d'oeuvre. Empanaditas are really best when fried in deep fat, but baking is permissible and much less caloric. In New Mexico they are usually eaten cold, but they are much, much better when reheated.

Empanaditas
(*Little Spanish Mincemeat Pies*)

Dough

1 package yeast	3 tablespoons melted lard
2 tablespoons sugar	3 cups flour (approximately)
1½ teaspoons salt	Deep fat for frying or
1½ cups warm water	melted butter to brush before
1 egg, beaten	baking

Dissolve yeast, sugar and salt in warm water. Then add beaten egg, melted lard, and flour. Roll out dough about ⅛" thick and cut with a biscuit cutter. Place a heaping teaspoon of filling in center of dough round, fold over and seal edges. If empanaditas are to be fried, heat fat to 375° F., then drop in empanaditas and fry until golden brown. If baking is preferred, brush empanaditas with melted butter and bake in hot oven (400° F.) until golden, about 15 minutes.

Empanaditas can be rolled out and filled, then refrigerated for half a day before cooking. The dough will keep satisfactorily in the refrigerator for several days, as will the filling. Empanaditas freeze very satisfactorily. Reheat to serve. This recipe yields a great many, the number depending upon size.

Fillings

For dessert or sweet:

1 pound beef, ground
    (fresh or cooked)
¼ teaspoon allspice
½ teaspoon nutmeg
¾ teaspoon cinnamon
¼ teaspoon salt, or to taste
1 can applesauce (16 ounces or
    1¾ cups)
1 cup sugar
¼ cup pine nuts
1 cup raisins

For hors d'oeuvre:

1 pound ground beef
⅛ teaspoon allspice
¼ teaspoon nutmeg
½ teaspoon cinnamon, scant
¼ teaspoon salt, or to taste
1 can applesauce (16 ounces or
    1¾ cups)
¼ cup sugar
¼ cup pine nuts
1 cup raisins

No performance of *Los Pastores* in San Antonio would be complete without Mexican food—cinnamon chocolate, tamales

153

kept hot over a charcoal brazier, and *buñuelos*, a festive Christmas specialty from Spain.

Almost every country has a tradition of some sort of rich cruller or doughnut for the holidays. Ask a Scandinavian about Christmas and his eyes light up. *"Fattigmand!"* he exclaims. (*Fattigmand*, or "poor man's cake," was named in irony, for the ingredients are many and very expensive.) For Poles it is *chrusti;* Ukrainians, *pampushky;* Lebanese, *zalabee;* and so on. For Spanish-speaking people all over the world, it is *buñuelos*.

Buñuelos

1½ cups flour, sifted
½ tablespoon sugar
½ teaspoon baking powder
¼ teaspoon salt
1 egg, well beaten
¼ cup milk or water, approximately

2 tablespoons butter, melted
Deep fat for frying
Sugar and cinnamon, or thin syrup of honey, or brown sugar and water

Sift dry ingredients together into a bowl. Add the beaten egg and melted butter, and enough liquid to make a soft but not sticky dough. Place on floured board and knead very well, until dough is smooth and glossy. Brush with a little shortening, cover and let stand an hour or longer. At time of cooking, pinch off pieces of dough the size of a small walnut and roll on a well-floured board to paper thinness. Extra thinness may be achieved by taking up the round and stretching it by hand, especially on the edges. Let rolled-out buñuelos stand 5 minutes while fat is heating. Before frying, try out a small sample. If deep fat is right temperature, dough will not sink, but will float, and air bubbles will form all over top surface. Cook momentarily, just to a golden brown, then turn. Watch carefully, as buñuelos overcook very easily. When golden brown on bottom side, remove to absorbent paper and drain. Sprinkle with sugar and cinnamon, or place in shallow plate or bowl and pour thin syrup over. Syrup may be flavored with cinnamon stick if desired.

Yield: About 2 dozen buñuelos, 6 to 8″ in diameter

In New Mexico cooks often cheat in making buñuelos. Instead of whipping up a new mixture, they pinch off bits of bread dough and fry them. Empanadita dough is excellent for this purpose. Occasionally a fancier sauce is made for buñuelos by boiling till thick 6 tablespoons brown sugar, ½ cup each water and wine, ½ cup seeded raisins, and ½ teaspoon cinnamon.

In Mexico and in San Antonio, Texas, *capirotada* is a favorite dessert for Easter, and absolutely traditional at that time. The New Mexicans, however, adopted it for Christmas. It sounds like a strange combination—cheese and caramelized sugar—but it is a delicious one. This dessert can be assembled in advance, then cooked at the last minute. It does not rewarm very satisfactorily.

Capirotada
(*Mexican Bread Pudding*)

1 cup sugar	6 slices toasted bread,
2 cups water	crusts removed
1 teaspoon cinnamon	1 cup grated cheese, Jack or
2 teaspoons butter	munster type
1 cup raisins	

Turn oven to 350° F.

Pour sugar into saucepan and let cook over medium heat until golden brown. Add water and cinnamon and boil until sugar dissolves. (Sugar mass will at first harden, but will dissolve with cooking.) Add butter and let melt, then set aside.

In a 6-cup casserole place a layer of bread. The container should have extra depth, as the dessert is likely to boil up in cooking. Sprinkle on cheese and raisins. Repeat to make at least three layers, until all ingredients are used. Pour syrup over mixture.

Place in oven and bake until syrup is absorbed by bread, about 30 minutes. Serve warm.

Serves 6

Miss Frances Apodaca has contributed much toward preservation of Spanish folk arts, particularly in the realm of decorative cookies and breads. For the celebrations of Our Lady of Guadalupe in Mesilla, N.M., she makes cookies shaped by specially designed cutters executed by a local blacksmith. They are figures of the Virgin, iced in the traditional blue and red which the Virgin wears. The dough she uses is excellent for making any fancy cutout cookies, especially those to be hung on the tree, for they are firm and not easily broken.

Cookies de Guadalupe

¾ cup shortening or butter
¾ cup granulated sugar
1 egg, lightly beaten
1 teaspoon anise seed
1 teaspoon vanilla

2½ cups sifted flour
¼ teaspoon baking powder
⅛ teaspoon salt
Cold water
Decorator icing

Turn oven to 375° F. Cream shortening and sugar. Add egg, anise seed, vanilla. Sift flour with baking powder and salt, then blend into egg mixture. Add enough cold water, one teaspoon at a time, to make firm dough. Roll to ¼-inch thickness on well floured board. Cut with fancy cookie cutters. Place on greased cookie sheet and bake for 10–12 minutes. Cool and ice with decorator icing. If cookies are to be hung, pierce with darning needle while still warm.

Decorator Icing

1 egg white
⅛ teaspoon cream of tartar

1⅔ cups sifted confectioner's
sugar
Food coloring (optional)

Beat egg white with cream of tartar until stiff, then gradually beat in sifted confectioners' sugar. Since egg whites vary in size, amount of sugar may be varied according to consistency desired. To add food coloring, divide and remove amount to be used to another bowl and add coloring until correct shade is obtained. Spread with a knife, or use decorator tubes or wax paper cornucopia. (Directions for cornucopia, page 245.)

CHAPTER
X

Other Latin Influences:
Puerto Rican, Filipino,
French, and Italian

"*My husband asked me the other day, 'When are you going to take down that Christmas star?' I told him, 'It's so big, I'm afraid it might get crushed. I think I'll leave it up all year!' So it's still hanging from the living room ceiling near the door.*"
—March conversation with a Philippine-American

"*Between my sister and brothers and their children and grandchildren, there are thirty-two now in our family. I'm the oldest, so I try to keep up the tradition of a big dinner together on Christmas Eve, even though it is a lot of work. If you skip it just one year, the family begins to break apart.*"
—Italian-American

In America, descendants of persons from two widely separated areas of the world—Puerto Rico and the Philippines—retain Christmas customs directly related to those Spanish customs so noteworthy in the American Southwest.

In Puerto Rican communities, the most important holiday is Epiphany, January 6. In New York City, there is such gaiety among the Puerto Rican population that many of their non-Spanish-speaking neighbors have begun to adopt their Christmas habit of honoring the day of the Three Kings.

Much of the general merriment is furnished by gay street parades in the manner of contemporary Spain, but the idea non-Puerto Ricans in Harlem appreciate most is gift exchange. In Puerto Rico, as in Spain, Epiphany was the time children received presents, supposedly left by the Three Magi or Los Tres Reyes Magos.

Some schools in New York City, as well as the Puerto Rican Community Development Project, have encouraged the preservation of Puerto Rican Christmas songs called *aguinaldos*, a Central American term. Aguinaldos are gifts or special treats, and the use of the word for Christmas carols may be due to the custom of rewarding aguinaldo singers with gifts of food. The more usual Spanish name is *villancicos*.

There are a few aguinaldos about the three wise kings, but the majority center around Christmas foods. "Have you some *pasteles?*" one asks. In Puerto Rican families pasteles are always a part of the Christmas season, especially for the Christmas Eve feast. They are something like a very complicated tamale, with ground pork and cubed ham tucked in lye-soaked corn meal. The filling also includes olives, raisins, capers, chick peas, green pepper, onion, and seasonings. The recipe is not given here because it is so complicated.

"Let us eat some pudding that the cook is making," the same song suggests. The pudding might well be this superlative sweet-potato pudding made with coconut milk. It looks spectacular—a golden orange round topped with melted caramel—and tastes so unusual few will be able to guess its chief ingredient.

Budín de Batata

(Puerto Rican Sweet Potato Pudding)

1 large ripe coconut, cubed, or
about 1¼ cups packaged
flaked coconut
1¼ cups hot water
¾ pound sweet potatoes
(about 2 large)

1½ cups sugar
4 eggs, lightly beaten
¼ teaspoon salt
¾ cup butter
½ cup sifted flour

Make a hole in the coconut and let liquid drain out. Crack coconut, extract meat and peel. Cube meat. Pour ¾ cup hot water into an electric blender. Add coconut meat. Blend at high speed until coconut is finely grated. Pour blended mixture into a piece of cheesecloth over a bowl. Squeeze and twist cloth to extract liquid. Set liquid aside. Return coconut to the blender and add remaining ½ cup hot water. Repeat procedure. Discard grated coconut. If using packaged coconut, soak in hot water several hours, then squeeze out.

Peel and slice potatoes. Cut in pieces and cook in salted water to cover until tender.

Meanwhile, place ½ cup of the sugar in a 2-inch-deep, 8-inch round metal pan. Caramelize by placing pan over low heat and cooking until sugar is melted and golden brown, stirring constantly. Remove from heat and swirl pan to coat sides also.

Preheat oven to 400° F.

Drain potatoes, & mash well. Add coconut milk, beaten eggs, remaining sugar, and salt. In a separate container, melt butter. Cool and cream in flour. Reheat until flour and butter melt together, stirring constantly. Mix carefully but thoroughly into sweet-potato mixture.

Place pan containing pudding in a larger pan of hot water. Bake 40 minutes, then lower heat to 350° F. Bake until just done, about 1¼ hours. Cool completely before turning onto a deep serving platter. Carefully cut around edge of pan with a thin spatula and turn pudding out onto a deep serving dish, letting the caramel syrup run down over the pudding. Chill several hours or overnight in refrigerator.

Serves 6 generously

In Philippine-American homes the Christmas season begins on December 16, the traditional day for hanging up an elaborate paper Christmas star, and for setting up the *Belen* (Bethlehem) or Nativity Scene.

The Filipino Christmas Star lanterns are a distinct contribution to Christmas culture, for nothing remotely like them exists anywhere else in the world. They are put together with three ingredients readily available in the Philippine Islands—bamboo, paper, and imagination. The lanterns are constructed somewhat in the same manner as kites, by covering a star-shaped bamboo frame with thin paper, and illuminated by inserting some kind of light. Lanterns take many forms: Some are almost abstract, like delicate white snowflakes; others are simple five-pointed stars, glorified by the addition of long fantastic tails. In the United States, members of the Philippine-American Women's organization find the lanterns a highly desired item for Christmas bazaars.

The date of December 16 was established as the beginning of Christmas in the early 1900s by a canny priest to win his people away from their older pagan ways. Following an extraordinarily rich harvest, he called the farmers together and suggested that they conduct a novena, prayers of thanksgiving on nine consecutive days, to assure repeated grace from God and good fortune the following year. He selected December 16 as the beginning date so the end would coincide naturally with the festivities of Christmas and supplant a pagan feast held to promote fertility. His scheme worked perfectly.

"In the Philippines we would have a great many things for the Christmas feast," a friend says, "but here it is most often a boned stuffed chicken served only with fruit salad."

Filipinos usually serve the stuffed chicken lukewarm, but many will prefer it cold like a paté.

Filipino Gallina Rellenada
(*Boned Stuffed Chicken*)

1 large chicken for roasting
2 tablespoons lemon juice
1 tablespoon soy sauce
1¼ pounds veal, ground fine
1 pound pork sausage
3 unbeaten eggs
¼ cup grated Parmesan or
cheddar cheese (optional)
2 tablespoons raisins, black or
white

½ pound cooked ham,
sliced in strips
2 sweet gherkins,
sliced lengthwise
2 chorizo Bilbao, "Spanish
sausage," skinned
2 hard-boiled eggs,
quartered lengthwise
1 small jar pimento strips
Butter for basting if baked

Have butcher bone chicken, taking care to make no breaks in skin. (If there are any tears, sew them up with white thread.) Remove meat from skin, and put skin to soak in lemon juice and soy sauce while preparing stuffing. Grind chicken meat and combine with ground veal, sausage, eggs, cheese, and raisins. Mix thoroughly. Remove skin from marinade. Arrange stuffing, ham strips, pickle slices, *chorizo*, egg slices, and pimento in layers in an attractive pattern so that they will show prettily when the chicken is sliced. Bring skin together and sew up. Refrigerate until ready to cook.

This stuffed chicken can be baked, or it can be steamed. The latter method is recommended, as little of the flavor cooks out. To bake, preheat oven to 350° F. Place chicken in pan and cover with tin foil. After 30 minutes, remove foil and baste well with melted butter. Re-cover. At end of another 30 minutes, uncover, baste, and leave uncovered. Cook 1 hour longer, basting from time to time.

Gravy can be made by adding a little flour and water to the juices in the pan.

To simmer, wrap chicken in towel or cheesecloth and tie ends tightly to keep firmly packed. Bring to a boil three quarts chicken broth made with bouillon cubes, drop in chicken and simmer slowly 1 hour and 45 minutes, or 25 minutes per pound. Remove from broth and let stand until cool enough to handle. Take off towel. Wrap in clean towel and lay on platter with enought weight on top to press chicken slightly together, but not to squeeze out juice. Cool and refrigerate until time to serve. Chicken will keep in refrigerator a week or more. The stock in which it was cooked may be strained and jellied to serve as a garnish, or used for soup.

The donor of this recipe says she has seen chicken wings boned and stuffed in the same manner. The wing swells up so with stuffing that one will serve one person.

Yield: approximately 40 slices

French-American homes feature the Provençal version of the Nativity, known as *santons*. In recent years, these figures— like the Philippine star lanterns—have become increasingly popular with Americans through discovery at pre-Christmas bazaars.

The French say that the family of St. Francis of Assisi introduced the crèche in France sometime between 1316 and 1334; but it was not until the sixteenth century that the tradition became widespread. In southern France it is believed that itinerant peddlars, perhaps gypsies, brought the custom of the theatrical figures from Naples and popularized them. The peddlars called the pieces "*Santi Belli*," or beautiful saints, and the French shortened the term to santons. The figures, based on everyday Provençal life, include gypsy caravans and the three saints Mary that the gypsies worship at St. Marie-de-Mer. According to tradition, Mary, the wife of Cleophas; Mary, mother of James and John; and Mary Magdalene were cast up there after fleeing persecution in Judea. Their swarthy servant Sara, also cast up with them, became patron saint of the gypsies.

In New York City, a gift to the Metropolitan Museum of Art of an extensive collection of *Italian* crèche figures has created a new tradition, that of decorating a Christmas tree with them. Under the supervision of the donor, Mrs. Howell H. Howard, a Nativity scene is placed underneath the 14½-foot blue spruce tree and angels and cherubs placed about on it so that the tree seems to be filled. Tiny stars and electric candles complete the heavenly combination.

The figures were executed by some of the most famous Neapolitan crib artists. Flesh-colored heads and shoulders modeled from terra cotta or wood are fastened on wire bodies clothed in eighteenth-century costumes of lovely pastel shades, enriched with jewels, embroideries, and other accessories.

Mrs. Howard alone is responsible for creating the tree, and she believes she is the only person to trim one in such a fashion. (Few such collections are available.) One observer several years ago commented that the tree has universal appeal because, as in all fine popular art, the simple figures offer both poignant and comic relief.

An Americanization of Italian Christmas tradition is the fashioning of a Christmas tree from panettone dough. The bread, ordinarily round and flattish, is the most typical of Italian Christmas breads, but Christmas trees are still hardly known in Italy. A panettone Christmas tree would make a lovely centerpiece for a holiday coffee or brunch, though it is almost too pretty to cut. Any similar stiffish dough could be substituted.

Panettone

1¾ cups milk	*5 cups sifted flour*
5 tablespoons shortening	*1 teaspoon salt*
1 cup sugar	*½ teaspoon anise extract*
1 package yeast	*½ cup raisins*
¼ cup lukewarm water	*½ cup thinly sliced citron*
2 eggs, well beaten	*1 cup shelled pine nuts*

Additional flour, about 2 cups

Scald milk. Add shortening and sugar. Stir until melted. Cool to lukewarm. Dissolve yeast in water. Add to lukewarm milk together with beaten eggs. Sift flour with salt and add gradually to milk-yeast mixture, stirring thoroughly. Cover with wet cloth and let rise in a warm place until almost double in bulk, about 1½ hours. Punch down dough and add flavoring, fruit, and nuts. Knead in as much additional flour as needed to make a dough easily handled. Knead until fruit and nuts are well distributed. This dough will make three traditionally shaped round loaves.

(Panettone Christmas Tree–I)

*1 egg white, lightly beaten
with spoonful of water*

*Red and green candied cherries
Silver dragées*

Grease a large cookie sheet well. Take a chunk of dough and form a trunk, about 1 inch thick and 10 inches long. Taper it at the top, and pull it out into a broad base at the bottom. Make a series of 1-inch diameter rolls. Make somewhat smaller rolls for the top "branches." Twist rolls into figure eights lengthwise down one side of the trunk, stretching loops out wider at the bottom to make a triangularly shaped tree. Follow same procedure for other side. If desired, cut a star for the top of the tree. Brush with egg white.

Fill holes in the figure eights with red and green candied cherries. Sprinkle tree liberally with silver dragées. Cover with damp cloth and let rise until almost double. Bake in 350° F. oven until golden brown, almost 40 minutes. There will probably be excess dough to make a small loaf, too.

(Panettone Christmas Tree–II)

*Melted butter
Tiny colored gum drops*

*Silver dragées
Candied fruit, optional*

White confectioner's-sugar icing

Roll dough into seventeen 1½" balls. Arrange on a well-greased baking sheet in form of Christmas tree: 2 balls for the stem, then remainder in rows of 5, 4, 3, 2, and 1. Cover with damp cloth and let rise until double. Brush with melted butter.

Bake in 350° F. oven until golden brown. Let cool, then decorate with icing, (see p. 156) gum drops, silver dragées, and candied fruits.

For Christmas day Italians prefer capon. This mushroom stuffing is typical, says an Italian-American, and "as festive as they come."

Italian Mushroom Stuffing for Capon

Stale bread—about 25 thin   ¼ *cup butter (or more)*
  slices   ¼ *cup dry Marsala wine*
1 cup milk   *1–2 eggs, well beaten*
2 cups mushrooms, finely   *2 heaping tablespoons ground*
  chopped   *Parmesan cheese*
            Salt and pepper to taste

Soak enough bread in milk to yield 4 cups when squeezed out. Sauté finely chopped mushrooms in butter, adding it a little at a time as needed. Additional butter may be necessary. Mix bread and mushrooms well with remaining ingredients.

This amount will stuff a 6 to 8 pound capon. To increase amount of stuffing, preserve ratio of half as much mushrooms as bread.

Capon stuffed in this manner would most likely be served with pan-fried potatoes, broccoli, or cauliflower browned in oil ("Never any garlic!" cautions the woman who donated the recipe).

"You know," said the Italian-American who contributed the mushroom-stuffing recipe, "the Yule Log (Bûche de Noel) is really Italian even though the French claim it! Anything made with *marrons* (chestnuts) is very Italian. The French did not know anything about cuisine," she continued, warming to the subject, "until Caterina de Medici married the French King and carried the art of Italian cooking to France!"

"In France there is no tradition regarding the dishes for the Christmas meal," a French-American explained recently. "It all depends on where one lives. In my family we most commonly ate goose, but it is difficult to find here. This year, I think I will make a good *boeuf braisé*, beef marinated and cooked with wine. It should be especially good for Christmas, when there is so much rich food everywhere." She added that the controversial Bûche de Noel is seldom served for réveillon. It is usually reserved for Christmas Day luncheon when the meal is a light one and a rich dessert can be fully appreciated.

Here is an easy braised beef which is delicious.

Beef Braised in Madeira

2 tablespoons bacon fat
⅓ cup each, finely chopped
   carrot, celery, onion
2 pounds lean beef
⅓ cup chopped tomato
1 tablespoon finely chopped
   parsley
1 small bay leaf

½ cup dry madeira
¼ cup cognac
⅛ teaspoon thyme
¼ teaspoon ground allspice
¼ teaspoon caraway seeds
Freshly ground pepper
Salt
Beef broth, canned or made
   with bouillon cubes

Turn oven to 325° F.

Heat ½ bacon fat in heavy, ovenproof casserole. When warm, add chopped carrot, celery and onion, and brown lightly, then remove vegetables, and fat, and any juices, and reserve. Add remaining bacon fat (More if needed), turn up heat and brown beef well on all sides on high heat. When brown, remove from heat and drain off any excess fat.

Put vegetables and any juices back in pan, then add remaining ingredients, with enough beef broth to cover. Cover casserole securely, put in oven, and cook 3 hours, or until meat is very tender.

Be sure to turn every 45 minutes.

When done, lift meat from casserole and remove any excess fat and bay leaf. Juice may be thickened if desired with a little flour mixed with water.

Serves 6

CHAPTER
XI

Swedes and Scandinavians

"*On Christmas morning everyone joins hands
and sings and dances in a circle around the
Christmas tree in the living room. Then, we
dance up the stairs to a bedroom where there is
another tree, and we dance and sing around it.
There is always a large straw goat under the
tree.*"

—Swedish-American teen-ager

Scandinavian-Americans who still hold a family *ringdans*
around their Christmas tree seldom realize that in ancient
times their tradition was part not only of the festivities of
Yuletide, but also of June 23 or Midsummer. At one time the
rituals of both periods were virtually interchangeable throughout the Germanically influenced area of Europe.

The relationship of summer solstice rites to those of Christmas are demonstrated in customs and superstitions involving
fire and light, greenery and decorated trees, and fear of pervasive evil. In primitive times, all the symbolic fires and fears of
the winter solstice described in Chapter I were repeated at the
time of the summer solstice, when solar decline commenced
once again.

167

In addition, certain Druidic May Day ceremonies became an accepted part of Midsummer. The Celts reckoned their year so that the second half began on May Day, and therefore they kept it in a way similar to Norse Midsummer. In an inevitable mingling, two important aspects of Celtic May Day, the Maypole and the May Queen or Bride, were permanently detached from the earlier time and adopted in Sweden for Midsummer.

Today in Sweden and in Swedish-American homes, the subtle links between May Day-Midsummer and Christmas are vividly exhibited in enthusiastic portrayals of St. Lucia or St. Lucy on December 13, her name day, when the Christmas season officially begins.

In her Swedish role, St. Lucy is portrayed as robed in white and wearing a traditional Swedish bridal crown of greenery or gold with seven lighted candles. For centuries, such candlelit bridal crowns were a symbol of purity and virginity and the sole property of the Church. They may still be seen today in churches in Sweden. In America, similar bridal crowns are available for rent in some Swedish communities. In recent years they have reappeared in photographs of girls impersonating St. Lucy.

Lucy means light, and is undoubtedly the reason lighted candles and lanterns have always been associated with the saint, who was condemned to death at the stake as a Christian in fourth-century pagan Sicily. Later a number of legends evolved round her bright image.

According to one, the flames would not go near Lucy's body when the faggots were lighted, and she was killed by the thrust of a sword. Contrarily, another says that she did die from the flames, and that simultaneously a blinding flash illuminated the entire village. According to still another story, St. Agatha, an earlier Sicilian martyr, comforted Lucy in a vision with the words, "Lucy, thou art indeed a light."

Yet another version says that Lucy and her noble mother, inspired by their conversion to Christianity, began to minister to the poor. Because of fear of discovery, they used to go about at night; but in order to see the way and to leave their arms free for gifts, Lucy placed a burning candle on her head.

The disclosure that Lucy was a Christian is attributed to her generosity. Just before she was to marry, it is said, she gave her entire dowry to a poverty-stricken village. This action aroused the suspicion of her fiance and he reported to the Roman Prefect that Lucy was probably a Christian.

In the years following her death, Lucy became renowned for her generous deeds, and many claimed to have seen her miraculously administering to the poor and starving. Sometime during the Middle Ages she first appeared in a vision to Swedish peasants in Värmland, on Lake Vänern. Early one morning, during a terrible famine, she emerged out of the mists, on a huge ship laden with fine food. She was robed in white, they said, and around her head there shone a circle of fire or light. So it had once happened with their former Nordic goddess Freya, who once visited on the longest night of the year and served the Swedes mead from a golden horn, in promise of a bountiful harvest.

Until relatively recent times, *Luciadagen* was kept only sporadically in Sweden, and then in the western provinces. Where it was observed, the Swedish firmly believed December 12, the eve of St. Lucy's Day, to be a witching night with evil forces threatening on all sides. On the day itself no one was allowed to work, for anything accomplished would only be undone or turned to dreadful purposes. There was, however, general feasting. Until the nineteenth century, many considered rich meals on Lucy's Day a good omen for the harvest in the following year.

In the 1920s, the celebration as it is observed today caught on, primarily because it was commercially introduced in the cities of Sweden. Shopping centers in Stockholm held outdoor Christmas processions headed by a white-clad Lucia. Since that time, St. Lucy has become so popular in Sweden that she is commemorated on December 13 in every family and by practically every organization of every community.

At the time of the mass Swedish immigration to the United States in the 1850s, not every family that came here brought the custom of St. Lucy's Day because the observance was not universal. As in Sweden, the day has become increasingly popular in America. It has been fostered by organizations such as the Scandinavian Foundation, the Swedish Historical Society, and Swedish churches. "The young people love it," a Swedish-American writes, perhaps revealing the greatest reason for Lucy's growing popularity.

In recent years the Swedish government has joined in promoting St. Lucy's Day, to renew the bonds between that country and ours. Contests held throughout the United States have inaugurated new light festivals in this country, such as a "Light of Christmas" ceremony in Portland, Oregon, where the Lucia Queen sets ablaze 70,000 lights with a light wave of her wand.

According to tradition, Lucy is represented by the oldest daughter of the family. Before dawn, the time household chores began in olden days, she dons a white robe and cautiously places on her head a crown of flaming candles. She arranges mugs of steaming coffee on a tray and special saffron buns called *Lussekatter* or Lucy "Cats" and goes to the bedside of each member of the household to offer them coffee and buns.

In some American areas the old custom of "star boys" has also been revived. Star boys are common in Central and Northern Europe at Christmastime, and in Sweden they ordinarily accompany the Lucia Bride. Carrying wands tipped with a lighted star, the boys are dressed somewhat like Lucy, but on their heads they wear pointed dunce caps. In America, a frankly contemporary modification has crept into their wands and Lucy's crown—for safety's sake, candles are often replaced by battery-powered lights.

From St. Lucia's Day on there is great excitement and activity in Scandinavian-American homes. The Christmas tree is decorated, often with straw figures including a straw goat in varying sizes. The goat provides one more link between Norse mythology and St. Nicholas. Long ago, Scandinavian parents told their children that Christmas gifts were brought by a *Julbuck*, one of the goats that pulled Thor's chariot through the sky.

In some Scandinavian homes a straw *Julnisse* is also prominently displayed. The nisser are dancing dwarfs that live under barns and farm buildings. They protect the animals and household from evil, and bring Christmas presents to good children. On Christmas Eve, a bowl of *Julgröt*, or cooked cereal, is left out for the Julnisse, a custom which may well be connected with the American tradition of leaving out a piece of fruitcake for Santa Claus.

The fact that the Julbuck, Julnisse, and other Christmas ornaments are fashioned from straw is evidence of the importance of grain as the staff of life. Its necessity to primitive man is demonstrated even more concretely in two important Christmas Eve ceremonies, that of beginning or ending the meal with a ceremonial bowl of porridge, and, in Swedish-American homes, that of *doppa y grytan*, or dipping in the pot.

Doppa y grytan is a peculiarly intimate tradition that takes place in the kitchen. Each member of the family and any close friend invited for the occasion spears a piece of heavy rye bread with a fork, then dips it deep into a big pot of broth in which the Christmas ham or *Jul skinka*, the Christmas sausage, and other porky meats have simmered many hours. Usually, several cups of hot *Julglögg*, a spicy alcoholic drink, are taken with the fat morsel. Consequently, according to one young Swedish-American devoted to the custom, the rich bite does not dim the appetite. Rather, he says, "By the time you eat, you have a good appetite."

How dipping in the pot developed has long since been forgotten, but one American who has enthusiastically taken up the custom of her Swedish husband has a logical explanation for it. Mrs. Sten Johanson of Minneapolis, Minnesota, believes it came about this way.

"During the time of famine in the days of the old manor houses, the owners spent days working with their servants preparing the food for the household Christmas," she writes. "Since boiling was the only method of preparing meats, there was broth left and it could not be wasted. At noon on Christmas Eve Day the manor folk and the servants assembled in the kitchen to taste the foods prepared and to dip the rye bread in the warm broth."

Some persons believe the custom goes back to the Vikings. They sacrificed to the sun at the end of the year by fasting and refraining from meat. In the time of dreary darkness and cold, they made their meals from broth and bread.

As Mrs. Johanson pointed out, the ceremony of dipping in the pot took place in the middle of the day in former times, and was followed by a light meal. The heavier evening meal came later, after dark. Today, the time of the traditional ceremony varies. Ordinarily, it takes place sometime during Christmas Eve. A practical solution is to hold it at cocktail time, and delay the big feast until several hours later. But in many families a big meal follows immediately afterward. In still others, friends are invited, and the dunking ceremony is held on the Saturday nearest Lucy's day.

The Christmas Eve feast in nearly all Scandinavian-American homes features *lutfisk*, a dish Scandinavians adore and that most other Americans abhor. *Lutfisk* is white fish that has been soaked in lye several weeks, then boiled. It is served with melted butter or white sauce. "I think you almost have to grow up with the tradition," a Swedish-American recently commented, "for the truth is, even though people who are not Scandinavian complain about its taste, *lutfisk* really has very little taste if it is properly prepared!"

The curing of *lutfisk* is such a time-consuming process (and such an odoriferous one) that few Americans today try to cure it at home. A packer in Chicago now ships frozen *lutfisk* all over the United States, wherever there are sentimental Scandinavian customers. In Junction City, Oregon, a *lutfisk* festival has been held annually for many years.

Scandinavian homes invariably feature some kind of pork for Christmas, as pig has been traditional in the Norselands since the time of Freya, when the ritual slaughter took place before dawn. There were solemnly sworn oaths; a heady liquor was poured over the sacrificial animal; and each man present dipped his finger into the blood and made a mark on his forehead to bring good luck in the following months. The vitality of the animal was believed to enter the bodies of all who ate it, endowing them with enormous strength and good health.

So, today. Blood sausage is a Christmas favorite, and "No Swedish home would feel like Christmas without the *Jul Skinka*," according to one enthusiast. Jul skinka is a ham soaked in salt brine, not smoked. In Scandinavian areas, jul skinkas are available in meat markets throughout the Christmas season. After the ham is baked, the words *God Jul* are often written across it with white frosting.

The Lutheran Church shunned midnight services in older times because of the Catholic connotations. In early days, a very early service, the *Julotta*, was held at 5 A.M. on Christmas morning. In America, a midnight service gradually replaced the *Julotta*, "Probably," one member suspects, "because the minister wanted to sleep!" In recent years, the traditional early Christmas morning service has been revived in New Jersey, Minneapolis, and elsewhere, and the churches are always filled to capacity, despite inclement weather.

Lucy's "Cats," the nickname for Lucia Buns, known also as *dovelskatter* or "devil's" cats, serves as a reminder that evil spirits were generally believed to be abroad at the time of the winter solstice, when St. Lucy's Day was originally celebrated. It was said that the devil frequently took the form of a cat, but that his evil powers could be dispelled by an open display of the same figure, an X with curled tails. This shape supposedly represents a cat's outline.

In more recent times, Lucia buns have developed a number of new forms, one of the most common being "priest's locks," made by placing three strands of dough together and curling the ends.

Lucia Buns

(Swedish Saffron Buns and Bread)

2 packages dry yeast	1 egg, beaten
½ cup lukewarm water	15 almonds, ground or finely
½ cup sugar	chopped (not blanched)
½ teaspoon salt	2 bitter almonds, ground or
1 teaspoon ground saffron or	finely chopped (optional)
cardamom	⅓ cup raisins (optional)
4½ cups sifted flour	1 egg white, lightly beaten
½ cup (1 stick) butter	Raisins
¾ cup scalded milk	Sugar

Additional chopped almonds

Soften yeast in warm water and set aside to dissolve. Into a large bowl sift together sugar, salt, saffron, 2 cups sifted flour. Set aside.

Melt butter in scalded milk. Cool to lukewarm, then make a well in flour mixture and add milk, yeast, and beaten egg. Cream in electric mixer (Speed 5) or beat by hand about five minutes, until batter is very smooth or falls from spoon in sheets. Remove dough from mixer. Gradually add remaining flour to make a medium dough.

Knead on lightly floured board until creamy and satiny, about five minutes. Place in greased bowl, turning dough to bring greased surface to top. Cover and let rise in warm place (80° to 85° F.) until dough is doubled in size, about 40 minutes to 1 hour.

Punch down dough and work in ground almonds and bitter almonds, and ⅓ cup raisins if desired. (Raisins should be added if bread is to be made instead of buns.) Cover and let rest 10 minutes.

Pinch off pieces of dough and roll into 12″ rounds ½″ thick. Curl each end and put two pieces together back to back, or cross on greased baking sheet. Put raisin in center of each curl. Or form dough in S shape, curling the ends and placing raisins in curls. Or make simple circular bun.

Let rise until double in bulk, brush with beaten egg white, then bake in 400° F. oven 10 to 12 minutes.

To make bread: Roll out dough and cut into four strips. Place on greased baking sheet and braid together. Cover and let rise until double in bulk. Brush with egg white and sprinkle with chopped almonds and sugar. Bake in moderate oven (350° F.) 15 to 20 minutes.

These saffron buns are not sweet. If sweet bun is desired, add more sugar to dough initially. Both bread and buns would be delicious for luncheon, with curry or fruit salad.

Yield: 18 buns

Julbröd

(Swedish Christmas Bread)

¾ cup milk
½ teaspoon salt
⅓ cup sugar
½ cup butter
2 packages yeast
¼ cup lukewarm water
2 eggs, well beaten with
1 egg yolk
4 cups sifted flour

1½ to 3 teaspoons powdered
  cardamom
½ to 1 cup raisins (to taste)
1 cup slivered citron
1 cup slivered blanched
  almonds
¼ cup sifted flour
1 egg white
¼ cup powdered sugar

Scald milk, then add salt, sugar, and butter, stirring until butter is melted and sugar dissolved. Pour into large mixing bowl. Cool to lukewarm. Meanwhile, dissolve yeast in water. Add to milk mixture, together with beaten eggs and egg yolk. Gradually add 2 cups of flour, sifted with cardamom (to taste; 2 teaspoons produces a delicately flavored bread, only hinting of the spice), beating by electric mixer or by hand. Beat well after mixing in first two cups of flour. Gradually add in remaining 2 cups flour, mixing on slow speed until dough crawls up beaters. Then remove from mixer and add any remaining flour, beating with wooden spoon. Turn dough out on board and knead until smooth. (This will take only a few minutes.)

Dredge fruit and nuts in ¼ cup flour. Add to dough. Put in well-greased bowl. Turn over (to oil). Cover with wet towel. Place in warm spot to rise until double, about one hour.

Punch down dough. Divide into two pieces. Roll out into loaf or into round mound. Place on well-greased baking tins. Brush with lightly beaten egg white.

Cover with wet towel and let rise once more, approximately 1 hour. Bake at 350° F. until golden brown, approximately 40 to 60 minutes. Dust with confectioner's sugar and place on rack to cool. This bread keeps very well. If preferred, it may be baked in well-greased loaf pans.

Limpa is everyday bread for Swedish people. "It's comparable to Jewish rye bread you get at the delicatessens," explains one young man who keeps it on hand all the time. To make the bread special for Christmas, grated orange peel was often added, especially in earlier days in this country. The recipe below dates back to 1850. It comes from *Mormor's Gamla Hemmet's Swedish Recipes*, or *Grandmother's Old Home Swedish Recipes*. It could not be an easier yeast bread to make.

Swedish Orange Limpa
(Rye Bread)

1½ cups lukewarm water	1 tablespoon salt
2 packages yeast	Finely grated rind of
2 tablespoons melted	2 small oranges
shortening	2½ cups rye flour
½ cup molasses	2½ to 3 cups sifted white flour
⅓ cup sugar	Cornmeal
Additional melted shortening	

Dissolve yeast in warm water. Melt shortening. Stir in molasses, sugar, salt, 2 tablespoons melted shortening, grated rind. Using electric mixer, gradually mix in rye flour, or mix in with spoon until smooth. Next add white flour (remove from mixer when dough becomes too stiff), working in enough to make dough easy to handle. The final portion may be kneaded in by hand. Knead well, then cover with warm wet cloth and set in warm place to rise until double. This should not take more than 1 hour.

Punch down, cover, and let rise 30 minutes, until almost double. Shape dough into two round, slightly flattened loaves. Grease baking sheet(s) well and sprinkle lightly with corn-meal. Place loaves on opposite ends, or in separate pans if oven is small. Brush lightly with melted shortening. Cover with damp cloth and let rise one hour. Bake at 350° F. 25 to 35 minutes. This bread keeps very well, and is delicious when warm, though ordinarily limpa is sliced very thin and served cold.

In Minnesota, where there is a large Scandinavian popula-tion, *lefse* begin appearing in the bakeries near the holidays. They are like a very thin, oversized pancake.

Ruth Loevinger's Lefse

(*Potato crêpes*)

3 cups mashed potatoes	*½ teaspoon salt*
1 tablespoon butter	*1¾ cups sifted flour*
½ teaspoon baking powder	*½ cup milk*

Mix warm mashed potatoes with butter, then set aside to cool. Sift baking powder, and salt with flour, then combine with potatoes and milk. If too sticky to roll out, add a little more flour.

On a floured board, roll out *lefse* very thin, about ⅛″. Cut into 6″ rounds.

Bake on ungreased *lefse* iron or griddle until speckled brown, about 2 to 3 minutes (they will rise a little), then turn. When speckled brown on other side, remove from pan. Fold into quarters to store.

Wrap in waxed paper and keep in refrigerator (they mold very easily otherwise), or freeze. Remove from cold and bring to room temperature before serving. Better still, warm in foil paper in the oven.

Mrs. Loevinger says *lefse* are easier to handle than the recipe sounds, but that it is really a job for two people—one to roll out the *lefse*, and one to flip them on the grill.

Yield: 15 pancakes

Danish *Festsuppe* is often served at special gatherings during the holidays. It is what its name implies—a special feast soup, not a family dish. As originally made, *festsuppe* was a great deal of work. However, with a little planning, all the ingredients can be prepared in advance, then quickly assembled at the time of serving. The original recipe called for six to twelve hours total cooking time, primarily to make a substantial broth. If desired, equal amounts of chicken and beef broth, about six cups each, can be substituted. *Festsuppe* is a very hearty dish, almost a stew in consistency. However, in an emergency, it can easily be made to serve more persons by the addition of broth, and the uninitiated will still find it delicious.

Danish Festsuppe

For Soup Broth:

1 four-pound chicken	2 ribs celery, chopped coarsely
1 pound lean stewing beef	1 large onion, quartered
1 cracked veal knuckle or large bone	6 sprigs parsley
	3 leeks, split, rinsed well
2 beef bones	15 peppercorns
4 carrots, chopped coarsely	Salt

For Soup:

Meatballs (See recipe)	4 carrots, chopped in small dice
Dumplings (See recipe)	4 cups cooked rice
Chopped parsley	

To prepare soup broth, place all the broth ingredients in a large kettle. Add water to cover (about 2 inches above meat).

Bring to boil and skim. Continue cooking, skimming surface occasionally, until meat is fork-tender. Remove meat and continue cooking broth until ready to serve.

Refrigerate beef for use some other time. The broth may be made several days in advance and refrigerated, as may the meatballs. (Broth should be strained before storing.)

Meatballs

1 pound round steak,   *3 tablespoons flour*
   finely ground   *1 egg*
       Salt and freshly ground pepper

To make meatballs, combine ground meat, flour, egg, salt, and pepper. Mix well and shape into small balls. Drop into boiling water and simmer 3 or 4 minutes, turning with slotted spoon. If meatballs are made in advance, refrigerate in broth in which they are made.

Dumplings

½ cup butter   *1 cup boiling water*
1 cup flour   *5 eggs*

To make dumplings (which can be prepared earlier in the day, or the day before, and stored in tightly covered container), melt butter in saucepan. Add flour and stir to blend. Gradually add the boiling water while stirring with a wooden spoon. Stir briskly until mixture leaves the side of the pan.

Remove from heat and add five eggs, one at a time, beating well after each addition. Bring a kettle of salted water to a boil. Use two teaspoons to break and shape dough into tiny dumplings about the size of an almond. Cook briefly on one side, a few at a time, then turn and simmer a minute or two longer. Remove dumplings, drain and set aside while cooking remainder of dough. Cover with waxed paper or cellophane wrap until ready to use.

Cook rice and keep covered until time of use.

To assemble soup: Strain broth. Roughly chop part or all of

179

chicken and return to pan. Put on heat and add freshly chopped carrots and cook until just done. Add rice and dumplings and heat only long enough to warm both sufficiently. To serve, sprinkle with parsley.

Serves 10 to 12 as main course

Cabbage is popular in all European holiday feasting. Prepared as in the recipe below, it makes a festive dish, indeed. One advantage is that the cabbage rolls can be stuffed in advance, then cooked just before serving.

Kal Dormor
(Swedish Cabbage Rolls)

1 head of cabbage	½ teaspoon allspice
1 cold potato, grated	½ teaspoon sugar
1 cup cooked rice	1 egg, lightly beaten
1 pound ground beef	3 tablespoons flour
1 pound ground pork	¼ teaspoon salt
1 medium onion, chopped	¼ cup butter, or more
1 teaspoon salt	1 tablespoon flour (additional)
½ teaspoon pepper	½ cup light cream

Wash cabbage and remove any damaged outer leaves and cut out core. Bring pot of water to boil and put in head of cabbage to wilt while preparing stuffing. (Turn off heat under water.) Mix together potato, rice, meat, onion, 1 teaspoon salt, ½ teaspoon pepper, allspice, sugar and beaten egg.

Separate cabbage leaves, and return any not sufficiently wilted to be manageable to hot water for additional wilting. Shape stuffing into oblong patties and place one in core end of each cabbage leaf. Fold over sides slightly and roll up, tucking in sides of leaf if possible. If necessary, toothpicks may be used to fasten rolls, but should be avoided on all except small leaves. When leaves are stuffed, roll lightly in mixture of 3 tablespoons flour and ¼ teaspoon salt. Melt part of the butter in a frying pan and sauté cabbage rolls until golden brown. Re-

Lithuanian mushroom cookies, frosted in a variety of ways, are set among greenery and look for all the world like real mushrooms

Swedish *papparkakor tree*, topped with the symbolic sheaf of wheat, has well-frosted cookie ornaments hung from the lady-apple-tipped wooden rods. Below are seen Mae Gerhard's Christmas stocking cookies and two Polish straw figures, imported by the Smithsonian Institution Museum Shops

A panettone Christmas tree, decorated with red and green candied cherries and embellished with silver dragees, was made by the author

Candied jels, cut in two and placed cut side up, when baked become transparent, glossy, and highly decorative on the browned panettone dough Christmas tree

White cake-decorator's icing with jewel-toned colored gumdrops adds a festive, gay note to traditional panettone Christmas trees

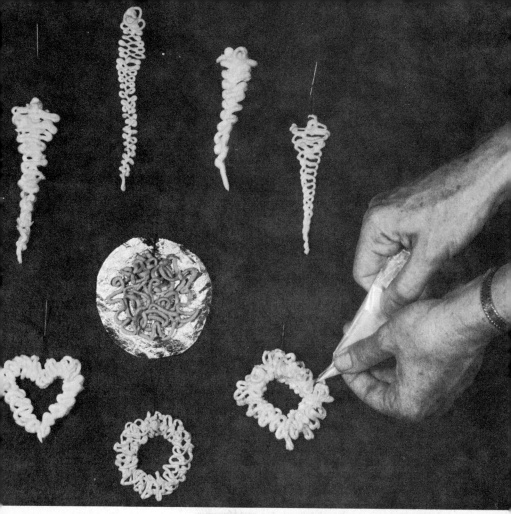

In a contemporary American version of Czechoslovakian baked meringue decorations, long spidery ornaments are backed by heavy string. The proper method of holding a wax paper cornucopia in the hands to squeeze out the meringue is demonstrated

Czechoslovakian traditional baked meringue decorations will last for years (if they are not eaten immediately). Except for the snowman (center), made by the author, all of these shown were designed and prepared by Mrs. Leopold Pospisil of Eugene, Ore.

Pirnik (gingerbread) Czechoslovakian Christmas decorations may be hung on the wall or tree. Two Madonnas and a round medallion of the Infant of Prague were made by Mrs. Leopold Pospisil of Eugene, Ore.

Christmas tree ornaments of today may be made of inedible bread dough, called baker's clay. The flying Santa Claus, painted with poster paints, is hung from yarn, while those on the right have their designs impressed in the dough with hanging hooks embedded in the back

Rhinoceros and sun face, designed by Edward Huber of the Hussian School of Art, were planned for hanging on the wall or framing. They and the sun face earrings are made of baker's clay

Colonial figure puppets with joints hinged with plastic cord are completely movable. William Crawford of the Hussian School of Art, Philadelphia, Pa., designed and made them, decorating them with pastel-toned paints

Gingerbread angels are decorated with bright pastel-colored icing, geometric patterns, and floral candies. Designed and decorated by Mae Gerhard. (*From the collection of the Hussian School of Art, Philadelphia, Pennsylvania*)

move and place in well-greased baking dish. Add more butter as needed for sautéing.

To cook cabbage rolls, heat oven to 300° F. Cover baking dish with cover or foil paper and bake 1 hour, basting from time to time with melted butter. Remove dish from oven. In a small pan mix 1 tablespoon flour and cream. Add liquid from cabbage rolls and simmer until thick like gravy. Pour over cabbage rolls and serve.

Serves 8 to 10

The Danes always serve "brown" potatoes for special occasions.

Danish Brown or Caramelized Potatoes

8 to 12 new potatoes or	*½ teaspoon salt for new*
old potatoes cut size of walnut	*potatoes*
	3 tablespoons granulated sugar
3 tablespoons butter	

If new potatoes are used, cook in jackets, then peel while warm. If old potatoes are used, boil in salty water until done, then drain and dry on paper towel. Put sugar in heavy saucepan or skillet and caramelize. When sugar is golden brown, add butter and cook one minute. Add salt if new potatoes are used. (Butter will separate from sugar momentarily, but blend when potatoes begin to coat.) Dump in potatoes. Cook quickly, turning potatoes constantly until sugar adheres. This will take approximately 5 minutes.

If potatoes are not served immediately, add ¼ cup of water, cover, and keep on warm burner. Evaporate water before serving.

Serves 8

Swedish Americans who are used to "dipping in the pot" are fond of *Potatis Korv*, potato sausage or, as it was called in early days, *Jul Korv*, or Christmas sausage. Mrs. Ragnor

Johnson in Seaside, Oregon, has made the sensational discovery that it is not really necessary to have a sausage casing and a cowhorn to funnel in the stuffing. Mrs. Johnson uses waxed paper instead. Cooking parchment is even better.

Potatis Korv

(*Swedish Christmas Sausage*)

2 pounds lean pork, ground
2 pounds lean beef, ground
6 medium potatoes, shredded
  (uncooked)
1 medium onion, chopped

3 teaspoons salt (4 if
  stuffing in parchment)
2 teaspoons ground allspice,
  or more to taste
½ teaspoon black pepper

Mix all ingredients well together. Form into rolls about 4 inches long, 2 inches in diameter. Cut waxed paper or parchment into 6-inch lengths and wrap sausage well, tying both ends tightly with string. Prick waxed paper with fork (do not prick parchment) and place in kettle of simmering salted water. Cook slowly about 45 minutes. This sausage is delicately flavored. Some Americans may prefer slightly more seasoning.

Makes 15 to 16 sausages

Swedish settlers used to take a bowl of *flyttgröt* made of rye or oatmeal, or a bowl of rice to welcome new neighbors. The porridge was supposed to insure that the new home would never be without the all-important, life-preserving grain. A similar tradition at Christmastime has lasted until this day, in the inclusion of rice porridge as a mandatory part of the Christmas meal.

In Sweden, rice porridge is very sensibly served at the end of the meal as dessert, but in other Scandinavian countries it precedes, indicating that its significance was once symbolic of the need for abundant harvest.

A single almond is placed in the pudding, and, according to tradition, whoever finds it will marry during the ensuing year.

In ancient times, it was believed that almonds offered protection against unseen evil forces, and it may well be that the first almond was put into the Christmas *gröt* for this reason.

The original pudding or porridge was a simple affair, served with cream or milk, sugar, and cinnamon. The Danes, however, have a knack for embellishing sweets and making something very special of them. They have turned the simple rice pudding into a dessert fit for a king.

Danish Rice Pudding

½ cup water	2 tablespoons rum or sherry
½ cup rice	½ teaspoon vanilla
2 tablespoons butter	2 tablespoons blanched
¼ teaspoon salt	almonds, chopped
3 cups milk	1 whole blanched almond
½ envelope gelatin	1 cup cream, whipped
2 tablespoons cold water	Strawberry or raspberry fruit
⅔ cup sugar	sauce

Red and green maraschino cherries (optional)

Bring ½ cup water to boil. Add rice and butter. Cook uncovered over medium heat until water disappears, stirring frequently. Add salt and milk. Cover and simmer over lowest heat or in top of double boiler until rice is tender and milk is absorbed.

Dissolve gelatin in 2 tablespoons cold water. Stir into hot rice. (The gelatin will give a thick consistency; not a jelled dessert.) Add sugar and cool. Add rum or sherry, vanilla, chopped almonds. Fold in ¾ cup whipped cream and hide single almond somewhere in mixture.

To serve, decorate with swirls of remaining whipped cream and red and green maraschino cherries if desired. Pass fruit sauce separately. Pudding is delicious even without sauce.

To MAKE FRUIT SAUCE: Heat raspberry or strawberry juice and thicken with 1 tablespoon cornstarch per cup juice. Chill before serving.

Serves 6

The Swedes often ate lingonberry sauce with their porridge, and in this country wistfully tried to duplicate the flavor with other berries. Their mock lingonberry sauce offers a new and effective way to prepare cranberries as a dessert sauce or to go with turkey.

Mock Lingonberry Sauce

1 can whole cranberry sauce   1 stick cinnamon
¼ cup port wine   ½ teaspoon allspice

Place all ingredients in saucepan and simmer 15 minutes. Remove cinnamon and serve hot or cold.

The addition of an unusual sauce sets Ost Kaga (Swedish Cheese Cake) apart from more well-known varieties. Sauce is best served warm with chilled cake, but may also be served cold.

In olden days, this cake was made by adding rennet to the milk to separate the cheese from the whey. By using creamed cottage cheese, it can be whipped up in just a few minutes.

Ost Kaga

(Swedish Cheese Cake with Almond Custard Sauce)

3 cups cream-style cottage   ¾ cup sugar
   cheese   ¾ cup sifted flour
4 eggs   1 teaspoon salt
        ½ teaspoon almond extract

Preheat oven to 350° F.

Put cottage cheese in blender and run until smooth, or sieve. Beat eggs with electric beater, gradually adding sugar, then sifted flour, salt, and almond extract. Pour into well-buttered 6-cup ring mold. Place in pan of hot water in oven and bake one hour. Turn off oven and open door. Let cake cool in oven one hour, then remove. In baking, the cake will rise up out of the pan, but in cooling it will settle back down. Chill to serve.

Almond Sauce

1 tablespoon butter
1 tablespoon flour
3 egg yolks, well beaten

2 tablespoons sugar
1 cup light cream
1 cup milk
½ teaspoon almond extract

Melt butter in small pan. Blend in flour and cook until smooth. Combine with it the beaten egg yolks and sugar in top part of double boiler. Gradually add milk and cream. Cook over lightly boiling water, stirring constantly. When done, remove from fire and add flavoring. This sauce can be made quickly just before serving cake; or, it can be made in advance, removed from water and covered, then very carefully reheated for serving.

Serves 8 or more

Ebbleskivers are a Danish invention requiring a special iron pan for proper preparation. The pan looks something like a popover pan, except that the holes are rounded. It is heated on a burner, and the butter dropped in. When one side browns, the *ebbleskivers* are turned and the other browned. The result is a rounded ball, a delicious morsel, indeed. They are especially good for morning coffee or brunch.

Danish Ebbleskivers

1 package yeast
1 cup lukewarm water
1 tablespoon sugar
2 eggs, separated

1 tablespoon melted butter
½ teaspoon salt
1 cup flour
Granulated or powdered sugar
Additional butter

Dissolve yeast in lukewarm water with tablespoon sugar. Beat egg yolks, then add melted butter and salt. Stir in flour and yeast mixture. Finally fold in well-beaten egg whites. Let stand 30 minutes, or until doubled in bulk.

To cook, heat *ebbleskiver* pan. Butter lightly. With spoon, half fill depression. When bottom has browned lightly, turn *ebbleskivers* with fork and brown other side. Dust with granulated or powdered sugar. If desired, small amount of applesauce or jam may be dropped into the batter when it is put in pan. When dough rises, jam will be in center of *ebbleskiver*.

Yield: About 56

Swedes say there should be seven kinds of cookies for Christmas, and among the seven, *Finnska Pinnar* or "Finnish Strips" would be one of the most delectable Swedish types. These unusual cookies are a favorite at the annual Christmas show sponsored by the Museum of Science and Technology in Chicago, Illinois.

Finnska Pinnar

(*Swedish "Finnish" Strips*)

½ pound butter
¾ cup sugar (approximately)
½ cup finely ground blanched almonds (If using commer-
cially packaged, remove 2 tablespoons)
1½ cups sifted flour
⅛ teaspoon salt
1 egg white

Cream butter and ¼ cup sugar, then add almonds. Add flour and salt and mix thoroughly. Refrigerate overnight.

To make cookies, turn oven to 350° F.

Lightly beat egg white and set near well-greased (or silicone-treated) cookie sheet. Pour several tablespoons sugar on a plate or heavy paper and place nearby. Take off portion of dough, and return remainder to refrigerator. (This is a very soft dough that warms very rapidly.) On a floured pastry cloth, roll out dough with a rolling pin covered with sleeve. Roll as thin as dough can be rolled, but not so thin it will break up. Cut in squares approximately 2″ wide.

Take one square of dough at a time and brush with egg white, then place in sugar and roll up, log-like. (A knife is helpful in the rolling process.) If any wet spots remain, sprinkle with sugar. Place on cookie tin about 1½″ apart. Bake 10 to 15 minutes. Watch carefully last five minutes, as cookies should brown only slightly, on the edges. Cookies can be cooked without rolling up, but are not so delicate.

Yield: 40 or more cookies

Norwegians say there must be a different kind of cookie for each day of the Christmas season, or 14 in all. Serina cookies are one of their best, and very easy.

Norwegian Serina Cookies

1 cup butter, softened
1 cup sifted powdered sugar
1 egg, well beaten
½ teaspoon soda
½ teaspoon cream of tartar
Large pinch salt

2½ cups flour
½ teaspoon vanilla
1 egg white, lightly beaten
½ cup chopped almonds
and/or ¼ cup granulated
sugar

Cream butter and sugar, then add well-beaten egg. Add soda, cream of tartar and salt to flour, then gradually add to egg mixture, mixing well. Add vanilla. Put dough in refrigerator for one hour or longer.

To make cookies, turn oven to 350° F. Shape pieces of dough into small balls and place on cooky sheet. It is not necessary to grease the tin for these rich cookies, but leave well apart. They will spread out to triple size.

Press each cookie with the tines of a fork, then lightly brush with beaten egg white. Sprinkle with sugar and/or nuts. Place in oven and bake about 10 minutes, watching closely. Only the nuts and egg white may brown a bit, not the cookies.

Yield: 85 to 90

Glögg comes from the Swedish verb *glödga* which means to burn or mull, but whether *brannvin* or alcohol should be burned is a moot question these days. One man who appre-

187

ciates the Christmas custom observes that most Swedes of his acquaintance do not ignite their *glögg*. "It seems a shame," he says, "to waste good *brannvin* by burning it!"

Glögg
(*A Potent Recipe*)

1 bottle red Bordeaux wine	24 lumps sugar
1 medium orange, studded with	¼ cup blanched almonds
5 cloves	½ cup raisins
6 whole cardamom seeds	Lemon slices
1 bottle aquavit or vodka	Whole cloves

Put red wine, orange, and cardamom seeds (cracked) in one pan to heat. Heat aquavit in separate pan.

Put sugar in heatproof bowl, pour in one cup hot aquavit, and ignite. As liquor burns, carefully pour in remaining aquavit and red wine. (Latter will put out flame.)

Place a few almonds and raisins in each mug. Fill with hot *glögg*. Top with lemon slice.

Yield: 3 quarts

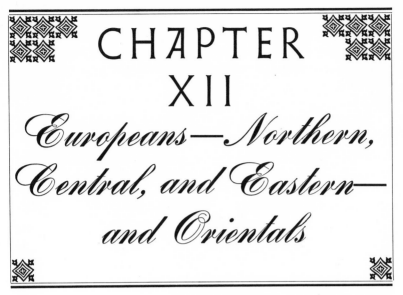

CHAPTER XII

Europeans—Northern, Central, and Eastern— and Orientals

"In Latvian homes we have cooked peas for New Year's Day. Not one should be left, as they symbolize tears, and if all are eaten, there will be no tears, no sorrow in the following year."
—Crown Point, Indiana

"We plant a pot of wheat on St. Lucy's Day. For Christmas it is placed in the center of a ring of kolach with three candles beside it: white for the people, red for livestock, and green for crops, to give thanks to God for all."
—Croatian-American, Portland, Oregon

"Serbians celebrate Christmas on January 6. When the candles are put out, everyone is very still and no one breathes, because the fumes should go straight up. If the smoke turns toward anyone, it means death."
—Washington, D.C.

"Chicago, Jan. 19—a controversy over the proper date for the observance of Epiphany led to violence today in the rectory of St. Nicholas Ukrainian Catholic Cathedral. . . . The church has 9,000 members. . . . Twenty police squads were summoned to restore order as more than 200 parishoners stormed the rectory . . . the disturbance was the latest of several since 1964 when the Most Rev. Jaroslav Gabro, Bishop of the church's Chicago Diocese, . . . ruled that the Gregorian calendar should be followed."
—The New York Times, January 20, 1968

Christmas in many homes of persons originally from Northern, Central, and Eastern Europe—from Syria and Greece to Poland and Scandinavia—remains essentially an agricultural festival related to the cult of the family and commemoration of ancestors.

One of the first indications that Christmas is a harvest festival is to be seen in ornaments made from farm materials— blown-out egg shells, nuts, feathers, wheat, and rye straw. One authority suggests that they are particularly appropriate because such articles "could probably have been gathered near the manger itself."

In Europe, Czech women created Nativity scenes from corn husks dyed in delicate pastels, an art that has been recently revived in the United States. (See illustration, plate 4.) It was in Northern Europe, however, that the art of working with agricultural materials really flourished. The Lithuanians, especially, excelled in the use of supple grain straw. From wheat and rye they wove ornaments of great delicacy: chandeliers, baskets, Christmas bells, chains, and an infinite variety of fanciful forms drawn purely from imagination. In addition, they fashioned some quite literal ornaments related to the harvest, and on their Christmas trees one might see figures of farmers carrying wheat and others holding candles to light the way for baking. Tiny birds were made from walnut shells, with wings and tails of birch bark, metallic paper, or small feathers. They were so lightweight that the slightest air current caused them to twirl and flit about in the evergreen branches.

In the United States the art of making these humble decorations had completely disappeared until 1945, when the Chicago Museum of Science and Industry suggested that Lithuanian residents decorate a tree for the annual museum Christmas show. Mrs. Peter Dauzvardis, wife of the Lithuanian Consul, inquired if anyone remembered making the ornaments as a child in Lithuania, and finally discovered one woman who did. Mrs. Rose Mazelauskas set to work, and in a few days created enough pieces to cover a large tree. Before her death, Mrs. Mazelauskas became known in the Chicago Lithuanian Community as the "Mother of the straw ornaments."

Unfortunately, wheat straw is very hard to obtain in large American cities. A substitution had to be found, and drinking straws seemed to be the answer. They do not have the golden gleam or the airy delicacy of real straw, but they are easier to mold. Today, Lithuanians all over the United States have taken up the custom of working plastic straws into elaborate decorations. Since 1951, the folk art has been stimulated in Chicago by an annual Christmas ornament contest and display at the Lithuanian Youth Center.

CHRISTMAS EVE RITUALS

Throughout the area under discussion Christmas rituals emphasize the necessity of grain to livelihood, and the importance of fertility and crops. From Lebanon to Scandinavia, families plant wheat sometime before Christmas, in time to have a pot of fresh green sprouts for the Holy Day. Serbians ordinarily plant it forty days before Christmas, at the time many begin a pre-Christmas forty-day fast. They believe that the rate of growth of the grain indicates the year's fortune, and pray for particularly tall leaves by Christmas Day.

Christmas Eve in a Serbo-American home begins with a knock at the door at nightfall. "Who is coming?" the children call out, as their father, holding a giant sheaf of wheat straw, opens the door.

"Christ is born!" he announces.

"In truth," members of the family reply.

Beginning an Orthodox carol, "Thy Birth," the father leads a procession through the house. In every room he scatters wheat straw, while the children shower him with wheat grains scooped from a bowl held by their mother. "We used to leave as much straw as possible in every room," a Serbian friend relates, "but now we put out very little because it will go in the rug.

191

"We used especially to stack straw under the dining table," she continued. "But now it is more generally placed on the table underneath the cloth." A similar practice is followed in Lithuanian, Polish, Ukrainian, and Bulgarian homes in America, and sometimes straw is sprinkled under the Christmas tree. In earlier times the straw was gathered from the floor after Christmas and scattered over the land to increase its fertility.

The food for Christmas Eve represents the farmer's land and industry, and consequently there is a wide variety of dishes, with generous examples of all products of the fields, orchards, and gardens. Even in the poorest home, no thought was ever given to economizing because the bounty of the meal was believed to guarantee a good harvest. According to tradition, each person must eat at least a teaspoonful from every dish. For each one left untouched, the saying goes, that many times will he encounter bad luck and unhappiness the following year. Sometime before the Christmas Eve meal, Ukrainians also mix a spoonful of each dish with food of the domestic animals, because animals were the first creatures to look upon the Christ Child.

Perhaps a Christmas Eve ceremony most like that of old days is kept in Ukrainian-American homes, where many in the younger generation try to maintain hallowed tradition. The Ukrainian Christmas period begins officially on December 24 new style, January 8 old style, and ends with Epiphany, January 6 or 17. The matter of dates will be discussed later in this chapter.

The ritual of the Christmas Eve meal, called *Svyata Vechera* or Holy Supper, actually begins in the morning with the lighting of a new fire in the fireplace. All work except preparation of the Holy Supper ceases. Quarreling is absolutely forbidden, but it is acceptable to take magical preventive measures against the evil spells enemies may try to work on this day— doubtless an inheritance from German weihnacht superstition.

A vital part of the Christmas-Eve preparations is the baking of ceremonial bread, *kalach*, for the evening meal. To Ukrainians, bread is more than a necessity; it is one of the most sacred foods. The housewife makes the sign of the cross over it before she places bread in the oven. When any is left over and carelessly handled, older persons consider it so disrespectful that they reverently pick up the pieces and kiss them in apology. Then the mistreated bread is fed to the birds or burned. Poles and Russian Jews inherit a similar attitude.

According to tradition, the fire with which bread is baked is also holy. In old days the housewife lit the oven fires from the Christmas-Eve fire, using twelve pieces of firewood that had been dried for twelve days during the preceding month.

Ukrainian bread for every occasion has its own special ornaments made of dough, as well as a specific name, shape, and symbolic meaning. Kalach, from the word *kolo* or circle, is one of the most important. The circle was an ancient symbol for eternity, prosperity, and good luck that many peoples adopted for year-end rites. Kalach is presented to newly married couples, and is an element in memorial services for the dead.

As Christmas Eve grows dark, a lighted candle is placed in the window as an invitation to any stranger or lost soul that he is welcome to join the family in its celebrations. The youngest child in the family is sent to watch for the first star while the dining table is made ready.

A gaily embroidered cloth is laid over the straw-covered table, and three braided rounds of kalach are placed in a stack in the center. Evergreen is wound around the bottom loaf, and a candle inserted in the top one. Two additional candles, one on each side, complete the centerpiece. Polish-American families often place a plate containing bread and salt between the candles, and a little money underneath the plate. (Traditionally, Europeans take bread and salt as the two essentials of life to any family when it moves into a new home.)

Upon announcement of the first star, the Christmas Eve supper begins. The master of a Ukrainian home brings in a sheaf of wheat, preferably cut at the end of the harvest and carefully stored until this time, and greets all with traditional salutations, expressing gratitude that God has given them good health and well-being for the past year. Then he places the sheaf in a corner of the dining room, where it remains until it is burned on New Year's Day. In urban areas, several wheat stalks may substitute for the sheaf and be placed in a vase as decoration.

All present gather round the table for a recital of the Lord's Prayer and thanksgiving grace. These are followed by "the most important part of Christmas," the *kutya* or *kootia* ritual. *Kutya* is a dish of cooked wheat grains dressed with honey, ground poppy seed, and sometimes nuts. The head of the family takes the first spoonful. Raising it in the air, he invokes God's grace, and extends to all assembled the Christmas greeting, *Khrystos Rodyvsya!* "Christ is Born!"

To which all reply in unison, *Slavim Yoho!* "Let us glorify him!"

Following this exchange, everyone must take at least a spoonful of the *kutya*. In its oldest form, the tradition includes throwing a spoonful on the ceiling, to assure that the bees will swarm the following season, and casting a spoonful through the window upon the ground, inviting the frost to eat it. Sometimes still, a pot of *kutya* with a lighted candle on top is given a place of honor on a high shelf, and a loaf of bread is placed nearby. Folklore scholars believe that originally the *kutya* ceremony represented a spiritual clan unity of all members of the family, living and dead, and that agricultural prosperity was probably secondary in importance.

In old Russia, there were always three *kutyas*, each placed in a separate spot to commemorate the three kings who visited the Christ Child. One was white, made of rice cooked in milk and spiced with almonds, marmalade, and white raisins; another was burnt gold in color, wheat grains flavored with buckwheat honey and dates; the third was black, prepared by soaking rice in dark plum juice and garnishing it with prunes and black currants. The three puddings were made into loaves and served with highly flavored fruit and berry sauce, representing the product of the orchard. The custom is said to be found today in many immigrant communities. In some Russian-American homes, the custom is to take three bites of *kutya* before eating, each person dipping into the same family dish.

A popular legend connects *kutya* with the Holy Family and a miracle that saved the Infant Jesus. A farmer sowing wheat observed Mary and Joseph pass by, it is said, fleeing to Egypt. Later the same day, soldiers stopped and asked if he had seen the couple and child. The farmer replied truthfully that he had seen them, while sowing. Looking to where he had labored earlier, the soldiers saw a field of fully grown wheat and concluded the farmer must have seen some other couple. So they went off in another direction.

Kootia or Kutya

Different nationalities disagree on how kutya should look, and how it should be served. "*Kutya* should not be thick," say the Ukrainians, for whom the dish is mainly ritualistic.

"*Kutya* should be moist, but the liquid should not seep to the bottom," admonish Polish-Americans who serve it as a dessert.

Syrians prepare an almost identical dish called *kilbee* or *ruhmee* for an old rite in the requiem liturgy. Portions of the cooked wheat grains are distributed in memory of the deceased and on the fortieth day after death, as symbol of resurrection. Sugar added to *kilbee* indicates the sweetness of everlasting life.

Sometimes in America cracked wheat is substituted for wheat grains in making *kutya*. The result is more like gröt.

1 cup whole wheat kernels	*2 cups water*
Salt to taste	*¼ cup blanched almonds,*
½ cup poppy seed	*chopped*
1 cup honey (preferably buck-	*3 to 5 tablespoons cream,*
wheat)	*to taste (optional)*

Wash wheat thoroughly. Place in deep bowl, cover well with water (allow for swelling), and soak overnight. Following day, cook in same water, adding more if necessary. Bring to boil, then simmer until tender. This will take at least six hours, perhaps more. Stir from time to time to prevent sticking, and add water as needed. Salt during last hour.

While wheat is cooking, scald poppy seed with boiling water and drain. Do this twice, then soak poppy seed in fresh boiling water for 30 minutes. Drain well, then grind fine.

Heat honey with 2 cups of water to boiling and cook eight minutes. Cool. Stir in cooked wheat with ground poppy seeds. Serve cold topped with chopped nuts.

Polish-Americans mix cream with the poppy seed before combining with honey.

Serves 8 or more

Polish-Americans call their Christmas Eve meal *wigilia* or *wilia*, a vigil supper. When the first star is announced, members of the family gather around the table according to seniority. The place at the head is left vacant for any visitor who might happen by, for "A guest in the home is God in the home." Today, arrangements are sometimes made for an outsider to impersonate the stranger. If a member of the family has died during the year, a place is set for him, because his spirit will join the family on this magical holy night. After the meal, three spoonfuls of each dish are placed on a separate plate with spoons for the souls of dead relatives.

Before sitting at the table, all present take part in a traditional breaking and sharing of the *oplatek*, or "Bread of love," a sacramental wafer blessed by the priest. The act of breaking it is symbolic of brotherly love and peace, and, if any member of the family is not present, a piece is carefully wrapped and sent to him. In this way family ties were preserved between this country and Poland in the old days.

The father breaks the wafer with his wife; then, beginning with the eldest, they both repeat the ceremony with each child, with many kisses and wishes for long life and a happy new year. If any guests or servants are present, they also participate in the ceremony.

When the ritual ends, everyone is seated, but there must be an odd number at the table. Otherwise, someone in the group will surely die before the year ends. The number of courses must also be odd, to insure good luck and good health in the household during the following year. The number of courses varies from five to eleven. The more there are, the greater the good fortune will be.

Polish-Americans eat the Christmas meal in complete silence. If anyone except the wife gets up from the dining table before the meal ends, bad luck will ensue during the year. Perhaps some parent long ago instituted this superstitition to keep restive children quiet, for in the old days the Christmas tree was never seen until the long ritualistic meal ended.

Ukrainians end their meal with *ouzvar*, a compote of dried fruits representing all the bounty of Ukrainian orchards—prunes, apricots, apples, pears, and even cherries, a particular delicacy. To Ukrainians, *kutya* and *ouzvar* represent the sacrament of the Last Supper: *kutya*, bread or flesh, and *ouzvar*, wine or blood. When the Holy Supper ends, Ukrainians place bowls of *kutya* and *ouzvar* beside the icon occupying a corner of every Ukrainian home.

When Ukrainian-Americans finish the Christmas Eve supper, they take dishes of food from the meal to homes where they expect to receive gifts. In each dish is a portion of *kutya*, bread, and elaborately decorated cookies. If there are children in the family, they are sent to carry the dishes, especially to grandparents.

Christmas Eve was a time for predicting the future in all Northern and Central European homes, and in America some of the old superstitions are still honored. Small birthday candles are fastened in walnut shells, for instance, and set in the center of a pan of water. If the shell floats to the rim, it means that its owner will take a trip. If, on the other hand, the shell remains in the center, the owner will stay at home. Another version of this fortunetelling is that the progress of the nutshell predicts whether the owner will have smooth sailing during the coming year. The person whose candle blows out first will be the least fortunate of those testing their luck. In Polish homes, predictions are based on the nutmeat that falls from a shell. If it is fat and light, the year will be healthy and prosperous; but, if it is dark and shrunken, trouble lies ahead.

Some persons melt lead over an open fire, then pour it quickly into a pan of cold water. The resulting shape, called the "New Year's luck," indicates what the year will bring: A ship, travel; a ring, marriage; and so on. Sometimes melted wax is substituted for lead.

SERBIAN VARIATIONS

Serbians burn a Yule log, a custom that came down the Danube to Serbia from Germany. "But where can you find an oak tree in New York City?" a Serbo-American asked recently. "When we lived there, my husband used to go to Central Park on Christmas Eve and take a little piece of oak tree and bring it home in his suitcase. Then we would put the twig carefully on top of the gas stove and watch it burn. Serbians say that you will have as much prosperity during the coming year as the Yule log gives off light while it burns.

"The Christmas Eve meal is a feast of poverty. Usually it is just boiled beans without any oil, and perhaps a few olives or something simple like that. The beans are placed in the center of the table beside a three-pronged candle representing the family—the father, mother, and children. There is also a wheat cake at the right of the father's plate, but it is not cut until New Year's Day."

Serbian Christmas Day begins early in the morning before dawn. Then, a close friend of the family knocks at the door and becomes a guest of the family for three days. "The person who enters the home offers the family good wishes, while the family offers him a chair. But before he can sit down, the chair is snatched away so that he falls to the floor and 'nails' his good wishes to the house! After the first visitor arrives, the Christmas feast begins, and we have three days of Christmas.

"If possible, the first day begins with suckling pig, otherwise, roast pork. Just as the soup is served, the father lights the three-pronged candle. He pours a little red wine over the bread, which is cut in the name of Trinity. When the candle is extinguished, it is done with a few drops of wine.

"We have a sweet cake, something like baklava, made of strudel leaves, honey, butter, and nuts, with a coin hidden in it. Sometimes, red wine is also poured over this to bless it. The wife cuts the cake, and, since she knows where the coin is, she sees that the father always receives it, for the saying is that 'the money goes out of the house' if a stranger gets it. Once my mother had a little too much wine and forgot and gave the coin to a Russian visitor. You should have seen her: she was wild! Our fortune going to someone on the other side of the world!"

On the third day of Serbian Christmas, the straw is removed from the table and house, and taken out as the first visitor departs. Christmas is over.

ORIENTAL-AMERICAN CHRISTMAS

Japanese-Americans exhibit a reverence for holiday customs that are curiously like some of those just described. A handsome young man may wear the delicate insignia of the Freemasons' Scottish Rite, and prefer French wines and food to Oriental; but ask him about Christmas, and he launches into an enthusiastic description of Japanese New Year's customs, for that is his true heritage.

There were never large numbers of Christians in Japan. Indeed, religious scholars have noted that the Chinese and Japanese philosophies had no concepts corresponding to those of Christianity; and since there were no words in their languages for translating Western ideas, the Christian beliefs that developed in the East were different from those we know.

In America, Orientals have added the trappings of Christmas to their own time-honored traditions, and, in the process, brought something uniquely their own to European-American Christmas. Fragile paper lanterns, rice fortune cookies, and traditional Christian hymns and carols sung in Chinese are

199

part of Christmas in Chinatown, along with boned chicken stuffed with sticky rice and flavored with ginger.

Japanese-Americans orientalize Christmas with their gift for decoration. For the holiday table they take whatever is at hand, especially brightly colored vegetables and other foods. Turnips are cut in long ribbons, scalloped, tinted with vegetable dye, and fashioned into roses; tiny, realistic Christmas trees are made with curly green chard and radishes cut like flowers. For the clever Japanese housewife, the variations are endless. Some artisans have adopted the blown-out egg decorations of Europeans, but, again, they have transformed them into something quite different.

While celebrating Christmas, Japanese-Americans prepare for their more important holiday, the New Year, which falls at the same time as ours. During the last days of the old year, housewives prepare *osechi*, or special New Year's food. Everything is cooked in such a way that it will keep for the first three days of the year, so the homemaker can rest from work and enjoy the holidays.

Japanese New Year foods are generally inexpensive. Some are selected for their symbolism. For instance, seaweed means felicity in the coming year; bamboo, long life; langoustes or lobster and red rice, good luck; and so on. Everything is cooked separately in soy sauce and sugar, then placed in a *jubako* or nest of boxes of tiered porcelain or lacquerware, and arranged according to color, texture, and design. At every meal during the New Year, these boxes are brought out, and each person takes whatever he wishes from them.

Better and richer foods than *osechi* are offered at other Japanese festivals and ceremonies. The significance of the New Year food is that everyone can afford it, and that every Japanese—from richest to poorest—eats it on these days.

The first thing a Japanese-American mentions in regard to Christmas is *mochi*, a rice cake the family purchases during the Christmas period. To have to forgo the pleasure of *mochi* because of poverty is the greatest trial a Nisei could have to bear at this time of year.

Mochi, a symbol of happiness essential to all festive occasions, is a flat cake made from pounded cooked rice. For the Japanese, it has the same significance as *kutya* and *gröt* for Europeans. *Mochi* was first offered only at sacred shrines, but sometime around the fifteenth century, Japanese began to use the cakes to make a special soup called *zoni*. Still later, they learned to make New Year decorations by placing a small cake on a larger one.

Zoni made for the new year always has floating on top slivers of lemon rind cut to resemble pine needles. Japanese-Americans inherit a deep respect and love for the pine tree, which symbolizes long life. Naturally, they prefer it for their Christmas tree.

All the important grains were displayed in the North European Christmas Eve meal: rye as a leavening agent in *barshch;* wheat in *kutya* and a wide variety of dumplings; barley with prunes or in another form. Other staples such as lentils, sauerkraut (cabbage), honey, mushrooms, potatoes, and so on were also mandatory.

The Ukrainian meal consists of twelve Lenten dishes, symbolic of the twelve Apostles who gathered for the Last Supper. If the family is poor, they have as many courses as they can afford. Theoretically, the meal is a strict fast, held in memory of the hardships endured by Mary on the way to Bethlehem. All dishes are prepared with vegetable shortening or cooking oil, omitting all animal fat, milk, and milk products. However, ingenuity transformed hardship into a feast long ago, as the following recipes will demonstrate.

In Ukrainian-American homes, the prescribed peas or beans are frequently combined with sauerkraut to produce a remarkable dish. For the Lenten meal only vegetable fat is allowed. Those who are not fasting will enjoy it when made with bacon or pork and served with sour cream.

Ukrainian Sauerkraut and Peas

(*Adapted from* Traditional Ukrainian Cookery
by *Savella Stechishin*)

Dried peas to make 1 cup,	*¼ pound salt pork or bacon,*
cooked	*chopped*
3 cups sauerkraut	*1 medium onion, chopped*
⅔ cup water	*2 tablespoons flour*
¾ cup mushrooms, chopped	*2 tablespoons sour cream*
2 tablespoons butter or fat	*½ clove garlic, crushed*
	(optional)

Salt and pepper

Soak peas overnight, then cook until tender. Set aside. (A "chewy" variety of peas, such as pigeon peas, is especially good because of the contrast offered in textures.) Taste sauerkraut for acidity, rinsing in warm water if necessary. Cook kraut, uncovered, in water for 15 minutes. Sauté mushrooms in butter and set aside. Fry salt pork or bacon until crisp. Remove from fat and reserve. Add onion to fat and cook until tender. Sprinkle flour over onion and brown lightly. Pour in the liquid from cooked sauerkraut and simmer, stirring constantly, until thickened. Combine with other ingredients, including reserved pork, and simmer until well blended, about 20 minutes. Serve as a vegetable with any pork dish, or as luncheon entrée.

If desired, additional sour cream may be added as garnish. Serve with dark bread.

Serves 4 as entrée

One of the most Polish of all dishes, *barszcz* or *barshch*, is seldom made these days, though fondly spoken of by all Poles. The foundation of authentic *barshch* is *kwas*, a sour liquid obtained from fermented beets. The result is so delicious, it is well worth the small effort involved. *Kwas* can be kept in an airtight container in the refrigerator almost indefinitely.

Kwas

(Foundation broth for barshch, *Polish beet soup)*

8 medium red beets, peeled	*3 quarts lukewarm water*
and cut in thick slices	*1 slice sour rye bread*

Place beet slices in a stone jar or other nonmetal covered container (plastic is excellent). Cover with lukewarm water. Drop in slice of rye bread to hasten fermentation. Cover jar and set in warm place if possible. When *kwas* is sour (this will take several weeks or more), pour it off the beets into bottles and refrigerate.

Yield: 3 quarts

Meatless Barshch or Barszcz

2 quarts vegetable stock	*Cooked-beet julienne strips*
(recipe below)	*1 cup sour cream*
1 pint beet kwas	*2 tablespoons flour (optional)*

Mix vegetable stock with beet *kwas*. Bring to boiling point. Taste for seasoning. If a sharper or more sour flavor is desired, add additional *kwas*. Add beet strips.

Traditionally, the sour cream is blended with flour and stirred into soup, which is brought again to a boil. A more attractive and much more delicately flavored soup can be made by placing a large blob of sour cream in the center of each bowl of soup before serving. (Flour is omitted.) Mushroom *uszka* are often included. (Recipe follows.) In this case, add cream last.

Barshch should be beet-red before cream is added. Overboiling or prolonged reheating fades the color. To restore color, grate a beet into a sieve and pour the soup through it into a tureen or soup bowls.

On non-fast days, *barshch* is made by adding good meat stock instead of the vegetable stock. However, it is so delicate when made with vegetable stock that we recommend it. Amount given serves 8 to 10.

Vegetable Stock

4 carrots, peeled and cut
in small chunks
4 stalks celery, cut
in small chunks

1 onion, diced
2 sprigs parsley
2 tablespoons or more butter
Salt and pepper

2 quarts cold water

Sauté chopped vegetables in butter, covered, until they turn yellow. Transfer to deep container and add water. Simmer one half hour. Strain. This stock will keep several days refrigerated.

Uszka

(Polish Stuffed Soup Dumplings)

1 egg
½ cup water
½ teaspoon salt, or more to
taste

2 cups flour
2 tablespoons mashed potatoes
(optional) (dried potatoes
may be used)

Filling (recipe follows)

Beat egg with water and salt. Mound flour on kneading board. Carefully pour egg into flour. Mix and add the mashed potatoes. (Ingredients may be mixed initially in mixing bowl and then turned out on board to complete kneading.) Knead until dough becomes elastic. (This is important. Dumplings will be heavy if dough is not quite springy.)

Break off in chunks. Roll out very thin. Cut into squares or circles. (Uszka are made in 2-inch squares by Poles, but smaller dumplings are more attractive and easier to handle.) Place small amount filling in each square or circle. Fold over. Moisten edges with water and join together firmly. Drop into salted boiling water. Large dumplings will sink to bottom, and are done when they rise to the top. Small dumplings may float, and should be turned. Cook approximately 5 minutes. This dough can be refrigerated overnight satisfactorily.

Uszka can be cooked several days before use, refrigerated or frozen, then warmed in soup. Uncooked *uszka* can be frozen satisfactorily; or cooked *uszka* may be cooled, then frozen. They may be thawed or dropped into boiling water to thaw and cook.

Mushroom Filling

(For Christmas Eve and fast days)

1 tablespoon chopped onion	*2 cups chopped mushrooms*
3 tablespoons butter	*Salt and pepper*

Fry onion in butter until light brown. Add chopped mushrooms and fry very slowy for 10 minutes. Add pepper and salt. Cool before using.

Meat Filling

1 small onion, chopped fine	*Ground cooked beef (about*
3 tablespoons butter	*¾ pound)*
½ cup mushrooms, chopped	*Salt and pepper*

Fry onion in butter until light brown. Add chopped mushrooms and fry very slowly. Add meat and seasoning. Cool before using. Either leftover cooked beef may be ground to make filling or raw ground beef sautéed in butter.

This honey cake is simple and delicious. It can be eaten immediately, but keeps very well in a cool place, and can be frozen. Icing would really be superfluous.

Polish Honey Cake

(Piernik-Miodownik)

8 eggs, separated	*4 cups sifted flour*
2 cups sugar	*1 teaspoon salt (scant)*
1 pound honey (3 cups)	*1 cup chopped almonds*

Turn oven to 325° F.

Beat yolks of eggs until very light in color. Add sugar gradually, stirring constantly. Add honey slowly, then sifted flour and salt, mixing well. Fold in egg whites beaten until stiff, and almonds. Pour in well-greased loaf pan. Place in oven and bake about 40 minutes, or until golden brown. Cut in squares or slices when cool. (½ recipe fills a 13″ x 9″ x 2″ pan.)

In Poland and Russia, beans are often combined with prunes for Christmas Day. This unlikely combination is delightful, and would be a pleasant substitute for baked beans in either a buffet or summer meal.

Russian Prunes and Beans

½ pound prunes   *1 can kidney beans (15½ oz.)*

Cook prunes in one quart water, then cut in quarters or large chunks. (Do not be tempted to increase amount. Too many destroys the balance and contrast.) Drain and rinse kidney beans. Add to cooked prunes and bring to a boil. Chill to serve. Do not drain off juice.

Serves 6 to 8

For Christmas Russian-Americans often make a very white bread that is utterly different from our American breads. In texture and taste it is reminiscent of English muffins. It is wonderful when warmed and spread with butter for breakfast. Small amounts of the uncooked dough can be cooked as English muffins are, by frying in butter.

Russian White Christmas Bread

2 cups lukewarm water   *3 additional cups lukewarm*
1 cake yeast   *water*
2 cups sifted flour   *10½ additional cups sifted*
2 tablespoons salt   *flour*
3 tablespoons sugar   *2 tablespoons salad oil*
Honey to glaze

Note: Allow sufficient time for making this bread. It rises four times, but the first and last do not take long.

Put 2 cups lukewarm water and yeast in a large bowl. When yeast has dissolved, add 2 cups sifted flour and mix well. Let rise one hour. (Bubbles will form.) Add salt, sugar, 3 additional cups lukewarm water, 10½ additional cups flour, and oil. This will make a very soft dough.

Knead by pulling apart with hands, until dough leaves the bowl and hands clean. This will take about 30 to 45 minutes. Sprinkle a little flour on top and cover with towel and allow to rise until double in bulk.

Punch down and let rise again until double in bulk. Divide into two parts. Grease two pans and place dough within. Turn oven to 400° F. Let bread rise on top of stove for one hour. Put in hot oven and bake until golden brown, 40 to 60 minutes. Brush tops with honey immediately after removing from oven.

The Lithuanian-North European way of stuffing duck with sauerkraut is one Americans should learn. As with turkey, sauerkraut makes an ideal foil for the richness of duck. It is also far easier to prepare than many stuffings.

Lithuanian Kepta Antis

(*Duck with Sauerkraut*)

1 duckling, 4½ to 5 pounds

Stuffing

1 large can sauerkraut	*1 small tart apple, peeled and*
1 medium onion, chopped	*chopped*
2 tablespoons butter or	*1 tablespoon caraway seeds*
margarine	

Heat oven to 450° F.

Drain sauerkraut and rinse thoroughly in hot water. Set aside. Sauté chopped onion in butter or margarine until golden brown. Add chopped apple and caraway seeds and mix thoroughly with sauerkraut. Stuff duckling.

Place stuffed duckling breast side down on greased rack in baking pan. Put in hot oven and roast until back is golden brown, about 10 minutes. Turn duck and continue roasting until breast is golden brown, approximately 10 minutes more. Drain off excess fat. Turn heat down to 350° F. and roast until duck is done, about 1½ hours. From time to time, excess fat may be drained off. When done, fat should be well cooked out, and skin crisp and brown (and delicious).

Serves 4

Mushrooms are such an important crop that Lithuanians not only use them freely in the Christmas Eve meals, they imitate them in decorative cookies. The following recipe adapted from *Popular Lithuanian Recipes*, compiled by Josephine J. Dauzvardis, is a particularly good ginger-spice cookie. The dough will keep in a covered container in the refrigerator for several weeks.

Grybai
(*Lithuanian Mushroom Cookies*)

1 cup honey	*1 tablespoon ginger*
⅓ cup granulated sugar	*1 tablespoon nutmeg*
(for burnt sugar)	*1 tablespoon grated lemon*
½ cup granulated sugar	*rind*
¼ cup butter (1 stick)	*1 tablespoon orange rind*
4 cups sifted flour (1 pound)	*2 eggs, lightly beaten*
1½ teaspoons baking soda	*¼ cup sour cream*
Salt to taste	*White Icing (see page 62, or*
1 tablespoon cardamom	*Decorator's Icing, page 156)*
1 tablespoon cinnamon	*Poppy Seed*
1 tablespoon cloves	*Cocoa*

Heat honey in a saucepan. In another pan heat the ⅓ cup of sugar over medium heat until "burnt" or golden brown. Measure ¼ cup of liquid burnt sugar and add to honey. Heat until all is dissolved. Remove from heat. Add the ½ cup sugar, and butter; stir until melted. Stir in grated lemon and orange rinds.

Sift flour with soda, salt, and spices. Add eggs and cream to sugar mixture, alternating with flour and spices. Knead until smooth, adding more flour if needed to make dough firm enough to mold with hands. Chill several hours. Dough may be kept in refrigerator several days before using.

To make cookies: Heat oven to 350° F. Break off very small pieces of dough and pat out in palm of hand to about ¼-inch thickness and 1-inch diameter. (This dough doubles in size in cooking.) On the end of one finger, form rounds into various sizes and shapes of mushroom caps. The indentation in flat side will be used for insertion of stem. Place flat or bottom side down on well-greased cookie sheet and bake 7 to 10 minutes. Cool.

Form stems by making dough rolls of thicknesses to correspond with mushroom caps. (See illustration, plate 9.) Cut into 1- to 1½-inch lengths. Wrap each stem in brown paper, leaving ends open. Fasten paper with cellophane tape or pin; place lapped side down on cookie sheet. Bake 7 to 10 minutes. Cool.

To assemble, enlarge mushroom cap indentation with knife tip. Prepare white decorator's icing. Divide and mix cocoa with one half. Dip one end of stem into white icing, then fit into the indentation of the cap. Allow to set. Ice stems and flat side of caps with white icing. Dip free end of stem in poppy seeds. Ice tops with chocolate icing and sprinkle lightly with poppy seed. For variety, ice some tops with white or a light brown icing made by using less cocoa.

Yield: 6 dozen or more

"In the United States, Latvians have enthusiastically taken up other foods," a friend writes, "but during the holidays there will be more of the foods our parents and grandparents used to like. At a big Latvian party people easily spend five hours at the table—eating, talking, and singing a lot," and periodically replenishing their plates.

For the Christmas Eve feast there are always *piragi*, bacon-filled rolls. Normally, they are rather large and lightly filled. Americans will find them sufficient for a luncheon when accompanied by a green salad and dessert, but double the amount of filling given in the recipe will be needed. Smaller ones make delicious hors d'oeuvres.

Piragi

(Latvian Ham- and Bacon-Filled Rolls)

¾ cup milk	¼ cup lukewarm water
¼ cup butter	1 egg, beaten
2 teaspoons salt	3½ cups sifted flour,
2 tablespoons sugar	approximately
1 package yeast	1 small egg for glaze

First prepare dough. Scald milk. Add butter, salt and sugar, and stir until dissolved. Cool to lukewarm. Meanwhile, dissolve yeast in warm water. Add to milk mixture with beaten egg. Pour in mixing bowl. Gradually add 1½ cups flour, beating on speed for thin batter. Beat until very smooth. Turn speed down to "cream" and continue to add remaining flour until beater can no longer be used. Remove dough and add enough flour to make a soft dough, about 2 cups. Cover dough and let rest 10 minutes. Then knead on floured board until elastic.

Place in a greased bowl, cover with wet cloth and let rise in warm place until doubled in bulk (1½ to 2 hours). Punch down. Piragi can be made immediately, or dough may be stored in refrigerator for several days, until time of use. Dough is somewhat easier to handle after chilling.

To make piragi, break off chunk of dough and roll out to desired thickness. Original directions say ⅓″, which would make good-sized roll. For hors d'oeuvres, very thin may be preferred. Bear in mind that rolls will double before baking. Cut in circles. Place spoonful of filling in center. Dampen edges with water and seal tightly. Shape filled piragi into crescents. Place on greased pan. Beat egg just enough to mix white and yolk. Brush rolls with egg. Set in warm place and let rise until double in bulk. Bake at 400° F. until nicely browned, 10 to 15 minutes for large rolls.

Filling

4–5 slices bacon	*1½ cups baked ham, cut in*
1 medium onion, chopped fine	*small cubes*
	1½ teaspoons nutmeg
¼ teaspoon pepper	

To make filling, cut bacon fine and fry until fat has cooked out but bacon is not yet dry. Remove from fat. Add onions and cook over low heat, stirring often. When golden, add cubed ham, pepper and nutmeg. Heat through. Remove and add to bacon. Add 1½ tablespoons fat from frying pan. Let cool.

Baked piragi may be frozen and reheated quite satisfactorily.

Yield: approximately 2 dozen large rolls

One dish likely to be served at Latvian holiday parties is *Galerts*, cold jellied pork. The spice of horseradish sauce in the following recipe transforms this common Northern European holiday dish into something special.

Galerts

(Latvian Jellied Pork)

2 pounds lean pork	*1 large bay leaf*
2 pounds fresh pork knuckles	*1 or 2 carrots (whole)*
and hocks or 2 pig's feet	*1 stalk celery*
1 large onion, cut in half	*Salt and pepper*
5 whole allspice (optional)	

Sauce

Grated horseradish,	*Sour Cream*
fresh or prepared, to taste	*Pinch salt*

If pork knuckles or pig's feet are not used, gelatin will be necessary. However, the former add flavor.

Place all meat in a large saucepan. Add onion, bay leaf, carrots, and celery. Barely cover with water, bring to boil, skim, then add salt and pepper, and allspice if used. Cover and lower heat. Simmer until meat is just tender. (Do not let boil rapidly.) Remove meat when done. Simmer liquid (uncovered) until reduced to about half. Cool, skimming off fat. (May be chilled for easy removal of fat.) Strain off liquid and set aside. Discard bones, onion, and celery. Cut carrot in fluted rounds for garnish, or cook fresh carrot and cut in rounds. For individual servings, rinse out small bowls with cold water. Put carrot in bowls, then arrange meat on top. Pour cooled liquid over meat slowly. If preferred, meat can be prepared in same manner in one large container.

Refrigerate overnight, or for day or two. Unmold and serve with shredded horseradish mixed with sour cream and seasoned to taste.

Veal or tongue may be used instead of pork, but pork knuckles or feet are necessary for gelatin. Fresh eels are prepared in a similar way in Latvia.

Serves 6–8 as main course

In Latvia every school had a party that was called a "Christmas tree." It began with a religious service and ended with distribution of bags of goodies and gay folk dancing. "Wherever there is a Latvian school in the free world," a friend says, "there is also a 'Christmas tree'" (party). Latvians also observe First, Second, and Third Christmas in America, with many parties and visiting. One Christmas specialty which is universally served at such parties is *piparkukas*, the Latvian version of peppernuts. "Christmas is unthinkable in my country without them," my friend writes. Anyone who makes these cookies will understand why. They are light and sweet, and keep for months. The dough, also, will keep for several weeks if refrigerated.

Piparkukas

(*Pepper Cookies*)

⅓ cup honey
½ cup molasses
1 cup dark brown sugar
½ cup butter
3 tablespoons lard
1 teaspoon cinnamon
1 teaspoon ginger
½ teaspoon ground pepper
½ teaspoon cloves
½ teaspoon nutmeg

½ teaspoon ground cardamom
seed
½ teaspoon ground coriander
seed
2½ cups sifted all-purpose flour
2 eggs slightly beaten
2¼ cups sifted flour
1½ teaspoons double-acting
baking powder
½ teaspoon baking soda
1 egg for glaze

½ cup blanched almonds, halved or chopped

In a saucepan, combine the honey, molasses, brown sugar, butter, and lard. Stir often and bring to a boil. Remove from heat, add at once the spices and the 2½ cups flour. Beat well with wooden spoon.

Let the dough cool gradually, stirring now and then. When it is lukewarm, add the eggs, and beat well. When cooled to room temperature, add gradually the 2¼ cups of flour, sifted with baking powder and soda. With floured hands knead the dough in the mixing bowl until it does not stick. Cover and let dough rest for an hour or longer at room temperature. Roll out as thin as possible on lightly floured board. Cut with star- or heart-shaped cutters. Place on greased cookie sheets. Beat egg with fork just enough to mix white and yolk. It should not foam. Brush cookies with it and garnish with almonds.

Bake a few minutes in preheated 400° F. oven. It will be necessary to experiment to find out what is right for the oven. Cookies must be carefully watched as they burn easily. Let cool on tin momentarily, then remove. They harden as they cool and will keep for months.

Unused dough may be kept unrefrigerated a day or two, if well covered, or several weeks if refrigerated. Bring to room temperature before using.   Yield: a *great* many!

Sarma is prepared in nearly all Yugoslavian homes for Christmas, be they Slovenians, Croatians, or Serbs. If any is left, it is warmed over and served again. "During the holidays, when many friends are likely to be dropping in, a big pot of it is always ready," explained a Yugoslavian who has lived in the United States over twenty years.

"The only problem in this country," she continued, "is tenderizing fresh cabbage leaves, which involves a bit of time. In all the Balkan countries the people salt down cabbage heads to keep them for winter. They put them in big barrels, and the cabbage sours and naturally wilts. The pickled cabbage gives a quite different flavor from the fresh, of course.

"If you want a really red sauce for it, put in plenty of paprika. When the paprika gets hot, the kitchen smells simply gorgeous! Our Yugoslavian paprika is far superior to any other —even the Hungarians admit it! You can't get a really proper red sauce with any other kind."

Sarma is an ideal all-round cold-weather dish. It is especially good for buffet or late suppers because it not only can, but should, be prepared in advance. The flavor improves if the casserole is made several days ahead of time. Boiled potatoes which accompany it can be peeled sometime the day it is to be served and put in water, then cooked just before serving.

Yugoslavian Sarma od Kiselog

(Stuffed Cabbage Leaves with Sauerkraut)

1 smooth head cabbage	½ pound ground lamb
½ large onion, minced	1 heaping tablespoon uncooked
2 tablespoons bacon fat or	rice
lard	1 teaspoon salt
1 clove garlic, minced	1 teaspoon pepper
(optional)	1 large can sauerkraut, drained
½ pound fresh ground pork	6 to 8 smoked sausages or
½ pound ground beef	½ pound bacon (or both)

FOR LATER USE

1 tablespoon bacon fat or lard   *3 tablespoons paprika (or*
2 tablespoons flour   *more)*
                  1½ pints sour cream

Remove any damaged outer leaves from cabbage head and cut out core. Wash and place upright on rack over sink. Pour into cabbage a little boiling water. Gently remove as many whole outer leaves as possible. When no more can be removed, pour over more boiling water. Continue until all except small leaves have been detached. Put all leaves and core in pan of boiling water and let stand 10 to 15 minutes, until wilted.

Sauté chopped onion in 2 tablespoons fat or lard until golden brown. If garlic is used, add it just before removing from heat. Cool and mix well with meats, rice, salt, and pepper.

Stuff softened cabbage leaves as follows: Put spoonful of meat mixture in center of each leaf, near core end. Fold over sides slightly and roll up, tucking in sides of leaf if possible. If necessary toothpicks may be used to secure the rolls, but should not if they can be avoided. A little practice is all that is needed to perfect the method.

In a large fireproof pot or casserole, make bed of sauerkraut. Place stuffed cabbage rolls and any leftover unstuffed small leaves on top of kraut. Put sausages and/or bacon on top, then add water to nearly full. Bring to boil, then turn down heat and cook uncovered very *slowly* for one and a half hours. Dish may be set aside at this point, but should be refrigerated if kept overnight.

To complete preparation, remove cabbage rolls. Taste liquid for salt and flavor. If necessary, boil down further. (It should have boiled down about half.) In a small pan prepare a roux: Melt 1 tablespoon fat or lard (the flavor of butter would be lost in this hearty dish), then stir in flour and cook until well blended. Add juice from casserole slowly, blending in thoroughly. Add paprika. "This is the *pièce de résistance.*" When half a cup of juice has been added to the roux, remove from fire and stir carefully back into casserole liquid. Return cabbage rolls to casserole, cover, and place in 350° F. oven or over fire until whole is well heated, about 15 minutes.

To serve, remove cover. If contents are to be served on platter, dish up *sarma*, and garnish with sour cream as described. If from casserole, let initial steam die down. Then put huge globs of sour cream over all and serve. (Do not put on cream until all heating is completed, as cream will melt.) To make the dish especially festive sprinkle liberally with paprika.

Serbians and Armenians like to add a sauce of yoghurt and mashed garlic. This is spread on top of the *sarma* when it is served.

Serves 8 to 10

"The only thing to have with this dish," says a Yugoslavian, "is boiled potatoes and dark bread. Everyone just loses his mind over it. In our country we always have slivovitz with it. You take a little slug before eating, then a little after! For this ceremony, slivovitz is served in a tiny bottle with a little glass."

Kolacky is served in Bohemian-American homes for any festive occasion, and always for Christmas. It is a very sweet bread, which many Americans would prefer with coffee or as dessert; but in Czech homes it is usually served throughout the Christmas meal.

Kolacky comes in dozens of varieties, more often as individual little rolls or tarts. The following version, rolled like a jelly role, is particularly good. The rich dough is highly versatile and can be used in many other ways. We find the plain marmalade fillings a bit bland, and prefer the nut filling. Poppy-seed filling, however, is quite characteristic.

Czechoslovakian or Bohemian Kolacky

2 cakes yeast	*6 to 7 cups sifted flour*
1½ cups milk	*6 egg yolks, well beaten*
1 pound butter or margarine	*1 teaspoon salt*
1½ cups sugar	*Filling (see recipes p. 217)*

Melt yeast in ½ cup lukewarm milk. Scald remaining cup of milk, and melt butter in it. Add sugar, stirring until dissolved. Set aside until lukewarm. Sift two cups flour in large bowl. Add yeast mixture, milk, and beaten egg yolks. Stir until blended, then beat until smooth. Add remaining flour and mix until well blended, then knead well by lifting up and over with spoon or hands. (This makes a soft dough which cannot be kneaded in the normal manner.) Cover with a warm cloth and place in warm spot to rise, 2 hours or more, until double in bulk.

When dough has risen, do not punch down, but take off portion of dough. Roll on well-floured board. Kolacky can be made in two ways: like a jelly roll which is later sliced, or in individual rolls. For first method, spread large piece of dough with filling, then roll up like jelly roll. Place on well-greased tin and let rise about 15 minutes. Bake at 375° F. until golden brown, 20 to 30 minutes. Dust with confectioner's sugar while still warm. This method makes twelve long rolls using the entire amount of dough. Slices of kolacky roll can be rewarmed very satisfactorily. They can also be frozen.

To make individual kolacky, cut in large circles. Place on large pan, 1½ inches apart. Dent tops in several places and spread with filling, fruit marmalade, or cottage cheese. Or pull edges of dough together and seal, like a pocket. Let rise, then cook in 375° F. oven until golden brown, about 10 minutes. Dust with confectioner's sugar while warm. Individual kolacky can also be satisfactorily frozen and rewarmed.

Poppy-seed Filling

1 cup ground poppy seed (see directions)	¼ teaspoon cloves
⅔ cup milk	¼ teaspoon mace
½ teaspoon cinnamon	⅓ cup raisins
½ cup sugar	⅓ cup chopped walnuts or other nuts

Prune Filling

2 pounds prunes, cooked and
  ground
Sugar to taste
¼ teaspoon cloves
Pinch nutmeg

½ cup stale cookie crumbs
  (optional)
Nuts, coconut (optional)
Lemon juice (optional)
Cream—about ½ cup

Nut Filling

1 pound walnut meats, ground
¾ to 1 cup warm milk

¾ cup granulated sugar
Coconut (optional)

For poppy-seed filling, scald seeds twice with hot water before grinding. For all fillings, put ingredients in saucepan and warm, stirring until sugar is dissolved and ingredients are well blended. Mixture should not be too stiff. Add more milk or cream if needed to thin filling. Cool before using. Fillings may be made a day in advance and stored in refrigerator.

ST. BASIL'S DAY, JANUARY 1—
A GREEK HOLIDAY

In Greece, gifts are exchanged on the name day of St. Basil, who—like St. Nicholas—originally came from Asia Minor. The stories told about St. Basil are remarkably like some attached to his countryman. Basil is remembered as a protector of the poor and indigent, the orphaned and widowed. It is said he used to provide dowries for poverty-stricken young girls by inserting coins in little cakes, then tossing them through the window at night.

On the eve of his name day, or New Year's Eve, Greek-Americans remember St. Basil by ceremoniously cutting a cake in which a coin is hidden. The cake, called *Vasilopitta* or Basil's cake, is sliced according to strict ritual.

The first piece is allotted to St. Basil or the Church; the second, to the poor; and the third to the eldest member of the household. Then pieces go to older members, to the master and mistress, and to guests in line with age or family relationship; and finally pieces are cut for children and servants. For any member of the family not present, a piece is set aside.

The pieces are quickly torn apart in search of the coin, which brings good luck for the year. If it happens to be in St. Basil's portion or in the piece for the poor, the coin is given to the Church or to charity.

Greeks also make a bread called *Christopsomo* or "Christ's bread" for Christmas Day, and the ritual currently attaching to it in some American homes illustrates how traditions change and evolve. Even though December 25 is not the name day of St. Nicholas, some Greek-Americans hide a coin in the Christopsomo and cut it in the name of St. Nicholas on Christmas Day.

In Greece, pork pie is traditional for the new year, but Greek-Americans prefer chicken pie which is more delicate. Often they hide a coin in it, too.

Kotopita

(Greek Chicken Pie)

¾ *pound butter*
2 *small onions, chopped fine*
3 *pounds uncooked chicken,*
    diced
½ *cup water*
½ *teaspoon salt*

5 *eggs, lightly beaten*
1 *tablespoon minute tapioca*
Pepper to taste
8 *oz. filo pastry sheets*
Sterilized coin (for New Year's)

Place ¼ pound butter in pan, and add onions. Cook until golden. Chop chicken meat medium-fine. Simmer with onion and salt in ½ cup water until chicken is just done, about 10 minutes. Set aside to cool.

When ready to assemble pie, turn oven to 350° F.

Add beaten eggs and minute tapioca to meat. Add pepper to taste and adjust seasoning.

Melt remaining butter. With a pastry brush and working *very* carefully and rapidly, butter five filo sheets, one at a time.

Place each carefully in a deep 9" x 13" pan, one on top of the other. These sheets are exceedingly fragile and dry as soon as exposed to air. If they crumble a little, it will not hurt the pie. Fit against bottom and sides of pan.

Cover with half the meat mixture. (A thick layer is not necessary.) Place coin in meat, or between pastry sheets. Place five more well-buttered pastry sheets over meat, then remaining meat mixture. Top with five buttered pastry sheets, and pour over any remaining butter. Roll overlapping edges over and over together, to seal pie and make a pastry border just inside pan. For easy serving, top may be scored in large squares.

Bake 30 minutes, or until top is golden brown.

Best eaten hot, but good cold.

Serves 8 to 9 generously as main course

Note: If using commercially prepared filo leaves, unwrap only as needed. Any leaves remaining may be stored in the refrigerator. They will keep for several months if left in airtight container.

EPIPHANY IN THE EASTERN CHURCH

Epiphany in the Eastern Church is still closely identified with the baptism of Jesus Christ by John the Baptist, and highlighted by a ceremonial blessing of the waters.

On Epiphany Eve, "there is holy water in the refrigerator and the *Prosphora*, holy yeast bread blessed by the priest," explains a Ukrainian-American. The Prosphora is a round loaf with the sign of the Cross stamped on it. In the center of the cross is a square divided into four sections containing two Greek letters each: IC (Jesus), XC (Christ), NIKA (conquers). The center portion is called the Lamb, in memory of Christ and His triumph over evil.

Ukrainians use the holy water to mix with flour and make crosses of baked bread to place above the doors of their houses, a fact that seems to reinforce the theory that blessing the waters began as a pre-Christian rite. Often parishioners preserve the water throughout the year for good fortune or as a means of seeking divine help when needed. Some girls wash their faces in the holy water for greater beauty.

Ukrainians have a feast very similar to that for Christmas featuring smoked jellied pork similar to Latvian Galerts. Syrian-Americans, however, gather in the church hall for a feast on two kinds of raised doughnuts, *zalabee* and *awam*. The latter are served with a sweet, lemon-flavored syrup. Sugar sprinkled on the doughnuts represents ever-lasting life.

In old days, Syrian cooks "baptized" the doughnut dough for Epiphany: The dough was tied in a white cloth, carried to a fountain, and immersed in the name of the Holy Trinity as the baptismal chant was repeated. Then it was hung in a tree for three days. During that time the dough would ferment and rise without yeast. Small crosses made from the dough were placed wherever food was stored, and the miraculous new leaven furnished yeast for the year.

Wherever there is a sizable Greek community near a body of water, a ceremony of blessing of the waters is held at the water's edge at high noon on Epiphany. In New York City, it takes place in the icy Hudson River; but the most colorful and complete enactment is in Tarpon Springs, Florida. After blessing the water in the marble kiosk in the church, the Bishop leads a colorful, chanting parade through the flag- and bunting-draped streets. His resplendent robes are decorated with bells similar to those of the High Priest Aaron. In one hand he carries a serpent-twined crosier or crook, symbolizing the serpent Moses lifted up in the wilderness, and in the other a crucifix. Gorgeously robed acolytes and lesser clergy follow, and behind trail a Byzantine Choir, a dove carrier, and special guests.

Upon reaching Spring Bayou, the Bishop blesses the sponge-fishing fleet, then dips his gold Cross into the water three times while delivering prayers of divine blessing. The third time, a white dove is released as symbol of the Holy Spirit that descended from Heaven at the time of Christ's baptism.

Eager young men dive in after the Cross, for whoever retrieves it will enjoy good luck throughout the year.

Banquets in the Greek Community Hall and in private homes follow the ceremony in Tarpon Springs, as in other Greek-American communities. The holiday ends with an annual Epiphany Ball.

DIFFICULTIES WITH THE CALENDAR

Ever since Pope Gregory modified the Julian calendar there has been disagreement about the dates for Christmas and Epiphany. Even before, the Armenians had refused to accept December 25 for celebration of Christ's birthday, and they have never yielded on their stand. Today the Julian or old calendar is thirteen days behind the Gregorian calendar. The discrepancy causes confusion on the part of the general public, and, at Christmas, great distress with children who have to wait thirteen days longer than their friends to receive gifts.

Difficulties over the calendar appear to be in part the differences between the younger and older generation, and in part a reflection of how completely assimilated a national group is. Ukrainians, for instance, who have so vigorously opposed any change, still live in virtually closed communities in which Ukrainian is the first language spoken, and the only one used by older members.

In New York City there are two Ukrainian churches, and each uses a different calendar. "It is a joke," observed a young woman who has lived most of her life away from her homeland and appears not to revere ancient tradition as highly as her parents. "In one part of the city, the Ukrainians go by one calendar, and in the other they keep the old one. So, if a man who should be fasting for Christmas in January wants to play cards and have a good time, he goes across town and visits his friends who have already celebrated Christmas." (The very strict fast in this case forbids card-playing and entertainment in general.)

On the other hand, national ties exert great pressure, even on the third and fourth generations. "We have a Christmas tree in December," commented a young third-generation Russian-American. "With children there is no choice. But we try to go to church on January 7." The tone of his voice indicated clearly that he would personally prefer to hold all celebrations on the later date.

In recent years, certain branches of the Eastern Orthodox Church have reconsidered the matter of the calendar, and modified their position on this issue. Except in the Holy Land, the Greek and the Syrian Orthodox Churches now accept the Gregorian calendar; the Slavic Church and the Church of Jerusalem keep the Julian calendar; and the Russian Church allows local parishes to choose their calendar. (The calendar does not affect Easter, which always follows Passover in the Eastern Orthodox Church.) Some priests see the option as leading toward eventual adoption of the new calendar by all branches, and have led a fight for compromise.

But no matter what adjustments members of the Orthodox Church make, it seems unlikely Armenian-Americans will ever accept December 25 for celebration of Christ's Birthday. They do not quarrel over the calendar, but the date itself.

Armenia was a large country at the beginning of the second century, when Christians began to commemorate Christ's Birthday on January 6. It extended from the Caspian Sea on the east almost to the Black Sea on the west, with Cappadocia, Assyria, and Mesopotamia bordering it on the south.

When the Eastern and Western bodies of the Catholic Church began to argue and hold councils to reach agreement, the Armenians withdrew and sent no delegates. They believed that both sides would be governed by political considerations and feared being caught between the two. Armenia did not make an open break with Rome as the Eastern Orthodox Church did; but, on the other hand, they did not accept all of Rome's rulings—a stand that occasionally brings criticism today from both groups.

In regard to Christmas, Armenians base their refusal to

yield to December 25 on a literal reading of particulars of the Annunciation found in the Gospel of Luke. An Angel of the Lord, Luke records, appeared to Zacharias to announce that his wife Elizabeth would bear a child (John the Baptist). According to the Scriptures, Zacharias was in the temple at the time, burning incense. It could only have been the Jewish Day of Atonement, Yom Kippur, the Armenians say, a date that is definitely known.

With this date in mind, they turn to the time of the Annunciation to Mary, six months later. Calculating how long it was before Zacharias returned home and saw his wife, the date of April 7 was established as the annual unmovable date for celebration of the Annunciation in the Armenian Church. To them, it "appears reasonable and logical" that calculations of the Annunciation should begin from the time Zacharias reached his wife.

The celebration of *Sǒurp Dznount* or the Holy Birth, begins on the eve of the feast, January 5, with the *Jrakaloutz Badarak*, "The Eucharist of the Lighting of the Lamps," in honor of the actual birth of Christ. The Liturgy the following morning is that of Epiphany, in honor of the manifestation of Jesus as the Son of God. Following the Liturgy, the mystery of Christ's Baptism is commemorated by the blessings of water, as previously described.

In Armenia, most people observed a week's fast in preparation for Epiphany, which they referred to simply as The Feast, or *Don*.

In the United States, no set period of fasting is prescribed. "We were not so religious in our family," says one Armenian-American, "but on the day before Christmas Eve my mother never let us touch a bite of food. Not until after the Vesper Vigil were we allowed to eat." The days preceding are often semi-fast days.

The Christmas Eve meal begins with wine and a sacramental wafer. At the vesper service, Armenians are given "Holy Butter," which they mix with other shortening in the preparation of the meal and when eating. Economic circumstances have more or less abolished the tradition of twelve courses. The traditional Christmas Eve fast meal permits fish, spinach, and eggs, as foods believed to have comprised the first meal eaten by the Virgin after Christ's birth.

A special round bread called *dari* is baked for New Year's Eve feasting, and a good luck coin is inserted in it. Gift exchange was formerly also on this date, but, like Greek-Americans, Armenian-Americans have gradually adopted the custom of gift exchange in December. However, in recent years, some members have begun to exchange presents on January 6, to consolidate American folk custom with Armenian religious tradition. It is a move that many devout Armenian-Americans deplore.

In Armenia, *kutya* was transformed into something special called *anoush abour*, which translates literally as "sweet soup." One Armenian-American says he "would walk a mile for *anoush abour!*"

Armenian Anoush Abour

(Sweet Soup)

1 cup wheat grains	¼ cup walnuts, chopped
2 cups water (approximately)	¼ cup almonds, chopped
Salt to taste	½ teaspoon cinnamon
½ cup sugar	⅛ teaspoon nutmeg
1 cup raisins, white and dark	2 teaspoons cornstarch

Wash wheat thoroughly and pick out any unhulled grains. Place in pan and cover with water. Soak for six hours, then drain.

Place soaked wheat in heavy saucepan and add 2 cups water. Bring to boil, cover and simmer six hours, or until wheat is tender. Stir from time to time, and add more water if necessary. Add salt to taste, about ¼ teaspoon, during latter part of cooking.

When wheat grains are well done and split, remove from fire and let stand one hour. Then add sugar, raisins, nutmeats,

225

cinnamon, and nutmeg. Dissolve cornstarch in a little luke-warm water and stir into grain mixture. Add more water as needed and cook for about five minutes. Pour into individual dishes. Serve cold. Will keep in refrigerator overnight, but no longer.

Serves 4 to 6

CHAPTER XIII

Hawaii

"The big Hawaiian man sat barefoot and serene on the cemetery lawn, carefully hanging ornaments on a tiny Christmas tree placed in a decorated container beside the grave of his child. Around him, as at other ceremonies here now, was a sea of scarlet poinsettia and other flowers.

"In a big store a barefoot little boy crawled up on Santa's lap and shyly offered him some cracked seed. . . ."

—Editorial in the Honolulu *Advertiser*, December 24, 1964, reminiscing about Christmas in Hawaii

Although Christmas never really caught on in Hawaii until the mid-nineteenth century, the first celebration held there in 1786, aboard British ships lying in the Harbor of Waimea Bay, would be considered today as typically Hawaiian, since it featured coconut punch and roast pig. (It remained for restaurateurs to discover the salability of coconut-mixed drinks. Captain Dixon noted in his journal that "perhaps it pleased more on account of its novelty than from any other circumstance.")

The night before, on Christmas Eve, Captain Portlock had gone ashore and distributed a pocketful of trifles to Hawaiian women and children who surrounded him wherever he went. The following morning, a regal Hawaiian arrived in a long double canoe with some hogs and vegetables for the ship. Captain Portlock gave the Hawaiian something in return (his journal does not specify what, but it seems likely that it was of less value), and thus were Christmas gifts exchanged for the first time in the Islands.

It was also the last time for many years. When the New England missionaries came, they would have no part of Christmas celebrations. However, they did bring with them the proud American customs of Independence Day and Thanksgiving. Curiously, the latter was held in Hawaii on the last day of the year. The way it was celebrated—with gifts, social calls, and a groaning board—would seem to indicate that the missionaries had plastered their Thanksgiving over a year-end tribal ritual in the same way the early Church superimposed Christmas over pagan festivals.

All the Hawaiian settlers were not New Englanders and many Europeans kept the holiday in their own homes. At Christmas, 1843, while King Kamehameha IV was a young boy in the missionaries' Chiefs' Children's School, someone sent the school a cake. The nine-year-old boy had heard about Christmas, and somehow assumed this was a Christmas cake. He assumed also that the day was a holiday, so all the Hawaiian boys took the day off from classes! "The children," the Puritan schoolmaster later noted in his diary, "thought it would be doing God service to devote this day to merriment."

The schoolmaster could not cope with a King's son, though, and the Christmas cake became established as part of the school ritual, in spite of all missionary misgivings. Three years later the royal pupils themselves made Christmas preparations. In the school's kitchen the girls baked cakes, and the boys poured candles. Within three years, the habit of giving gifts was established, even though by that time the prince was away studying in England.

In Britain, King Kamehameha learned more of Christmas celebrations, and took the holiday to heart. His school adventures, perhaps, as well as changing times, prepared the missionary teachers for the royal proclamation issued in 1856: Both

Christmas and Thanksgiving were to be legal holidays, and both were to be celebrated on the same date, December 25. Thus did the whole history of the Christmas celebration come full circle, back to its origin as a harvest-thanksgiving-fertility ritual.

According to an old-timer who observed the reactions of all concerned—Europeans and Americans, Episcopalians, Catholics, and Puritans—everyone was pleased. "Each celebrated according to his own idea," he reported in later years, "either as Thanksgiving à la Yankee, or with Christmas cheer in British fashion."

This joint Christmas-Thanksgiving observance was a one-year arrangement, but it firmly established the observance of Christmas in the Hawaiian Islands. Two years later, in 1858, Santa Claus was introduced at a party. In front of a tree illuminated with candles and loaded with gifts, he held court, passing out presents and handfuls of candy.

Finally, in 1862, Christmas was proclaimed a national holiday by King Kamehameha IV, seventy-six years after the first celebration held in the harbor. It was a gala occasion. The King sent to the mountains for cypress, and offered myrtle, orange boughs, and flowers from his own gardens, for decorating the temporary Episcopalian Cathedral. The Fort Street Calvinist Church gave in to the irresistible force. In front of the building, a huge Christmas tree was decorated with some two hundred small lights and hung with gifts for over seventy students. No two gifts were the same.

On Christmas Eve all were ready. From the top of its dome to the street below, the Roman Catholic Cathedral blazed with lights. When the midnight service began in the Anglican Church, the altar was lit with the King's own candelabra. When the service ended around 1 A.M., guns were fired from a battery on a peak nearby, and flaming tar barrels were sent rolling down from the crest. Then the King and the bishop led a slow procession from the church to the palace, followed by a choir of twenty islanders singing Christmas hymns and twenty bearing native Kukui-nut torches. From time to time the assembly stopped along the way to light innumerable green candles.

At the palace gates everyone came to a halt in front of a circular pond ringed with torches and blue lights. "The fountains played grandly," Archdeacon Mason recorded later, "and the reflection of the torch lights, together with the clear brilliant moonlight of these latitudes on the water, and on the dark excited faces of the people, was very remarkable.

"At this moment, some really good fireworks were let off, and rockets shot up into the air amidst deafening shouts from a thousand voices for the King and Queen.

"Then we sang the grand old carol 'Good King Wenceslas,' and after a glass of champagne punch we made the air ring with the National Anthem. Another round of protracted hurrahs, and so to bed."

There has probably never been another Christmas like it since, in Hawaii or elsewhere.

In the years between King Kamehameha's legalization of Christmas and the present, many peoples settled in Hawaii. A large number came from the Far East, bringing with them a variety of religions, most notably, Buddhism, Confucianism, and Muslimism. It could have made a difficult situation. But in Hawaii, an amicable arrangement evolved. Perhaps it was fostered by Oriental children, who soon learned what it meant not to celebrate Christmas and receive gifts from Santa Claus.

Or, perhaps, even more, the climate of Hawaii prevailed, both literally and figuratively. Christmas comes to the Islands at the most delicious time of the year, when a profusion of colorful flowers blossom everywhere. As trade winds blow softly, the balmy weather calls to one and all to put away all worry and care, and come out of doors. It is no time for theological or philosophical argument.

The Pacific Commercial Advertiser pointed the way differences would be resolved in the Islands in a description of the Honolulu Christmas Eve crowds in 1909. Getting out and mingling in the crowd had become the thing to do, the paper reported, and Oriental Hawaiians joined in the scene as enthusiastically as Europeans and Americans. Chinese women appeared, dressed in their best raw-silk trousers, and Japanese wore the highly prized silk obis they usually saved for New Year's Day celebrations.

Today, non-Christian islanders do very much as their Christian neighbors at Christmastime. Oriental and Christian holidays fuse into one long period of festivity, which begins with *Bodhi*, an important Buddhist holiday when Japanese dances and cultural programs are featured, and ends with Chinese New Year. For Christmas, some popular Christmas carols have been refitted with words from Buddhist *sutras*, Oriental sacred writings.

Soon after *Bodhi* comes the annual Festival of Trees on Waikiki Beach, a fund-raising exhibit of rare and elaborate Christmas trees and decorations Hawaiian style. Native materials such as coconut husks and pandanus leaves are employed in unusual and beautiful ways. A few years ago, the three kings in a much-admired native crèche wore leis of fresh orchids and bore gem-sprinkled pineapples and talking mynah birds as gifts for the Christ Child.

Along the streets and highways, palm trees strung with colored lights are a common sight. Even the sacred Indian Banyan tree is so arrayed. The mainland Christmas flower, the poinsettia, grows so luxuriantly everywhere that it is not considered special enough for decorations. Rather, exotic flowers like orchids and bird of paradise are preferred. Sometimes, a Christmas tree in a private home is festooned with leis of red carnations, which add a heady fragrance to the smell of Christmas.

Downtown, store window displays are likely to portray Santa's helpers as *menehunes*, the legendary little people who are supposed to have been the first inhabitants of Hawaii, before the Polynesians seized it. "*Mele Kalikimaka!*" signs proclaim, "Merry Christmas!" in Hawaiian.

Explanations of how Santa gets to the Islands for his annual visits are changing. It used to be that he came in by outrigger canoe, riding a huge wave. But legend is keeping up with the times. In the outer islands, it is told that Santa comes by helicopter.

In the old days, preparations for the Christmas feast began many days in advance on the island plantations. The Portuguese baked huge rounds of *pao doce*, a sweet bread, sometimes a yard in diameter, containing whole hard-boiled eggs; the Japanese made *mochi* (see Chapter XII); Hawaiians made *kulolo*, a dish something like a stiff sweet-potato pudding, and *haupia*, a bland sweet prepared from coconut milk and a starchy root. The English, quite naturally, had plum puddings and Christmas simnel cake, prepared by Chinese cooks from old and treasured recipes brought from the British homeland.

The greatest change in today's Christmas feast is the main course. In former times, it was always a roast pig. At high noon, an elder Polynesian would intone an ancient Hawaiian prayer to the ocean gods, and another in English to the newer Christian God. Then the rock oven was opened to reveal a succulent pig, surrounded by little bundles of choice foods wrapped in ti and coconut-palm leaves. In those days pig was common. Turkey was a status dish that only the rich could afford. Today the situation is just the opposite. Everyone can buy frozen turkey, which is brought over from the mainland, but land in Hawaii has become too valuable for raising pigs, and their price has skyrocketed.

Since so much of life is spent outdoors at Christmastime, turkey cooked Japanese style, *teriyaki*, over a pit or barbecue, has become a leading favorite. "It is very good sliced and served in buns," reports the wife of a Hawaiian Senator. "Often women slice the turkey while it is still frozen, because it is easier to manage that way. Then they put the slices in the marinade to soak and thaw out. You cannot really cook *teriyaki* in an oven," she warns. "The *shoyu* [soy sauce] will smoke and burn."

Turkey Teriyaki

*10–14 pound turkey, sliced or
cut in chunks*

Marinade

*2 cups soy sauce
1¼ cups brown sugar
2 cloves garlic, minced*

*1 tablespoon fresh ginger,
grated
4 tablespoons vegetable oil*
¼ cup sake or sherry, optional

Mix marinade ingredients in large container. Add turkey, turning to make sure it is well coated. Leave in marinade 20 minutes or longer. Cook over open fire.

The first thing any Mainlander notices about Hawaiian social events is the variety of national foods presented. "For a Christmas party," one Islander says, "you may be served both Oriental and European food, with Hawaiian poi, and have eggnog to drink." Poi is a gelatinous mass derived from taro root. Everyone who grows up in Hawaii adores it. Others find it tasteless. In his 1786 Christmas journal, Captain Portlock noted that he had taro root with pig as part of his Christmas Eve meal ashore.

One Oriental specialty which finds universal favor at holiday parties is Korean barbecued or broiled beef.

Korean Broiled Beef

(*Pul Koggi* or *Bul Kogi*)

*4 tablespoons sesame seed
1 pound lean beefsteak
 (round, sirloin, rib, or flank)
2 to 3 tablespoons sugar
1 tablespoon sesame or
 vegetable oil
2 tablespoons soy sauce*

*1 green onion, including top,
 chopped
1 large clove garlic,
 chopped fine
1 tablespoon flour
Pinch black pepper
1 tablespoon sherry or beef
 broth*

Place sesame seeds in a pan and brown slowly over low heat. Then grind them in a mortar.

Combine the ground sesame seeds and remaining ingredients except meat, and mix well.

Slice steak very thin, diagonally across the grain from top to bottom in slices approximately 1½″ wide. Add the meat to the marinade and stir until well coated. Let stand at least 20 minutes.

Grill, preferably over charcoal, or under an oven broiler. Cook approximately ½ minute per side. Turn with spatula. Serve hot.

This would make a delicious, lean hors d'oeuvre. Cut meat about 1½ x 2½ inches. When broiling, turn with a spatula.

The Portuguese settled early in Hawaii as they did throughout the Pacific. Today *Pao Doce*, a sweet bread, is a great favorite for the holidays in Honolulu. It has become popular because many groups make it and sell it for fund-raising events. As in olden days, whole eggs or charms are sometimes hidden inside. There are many ways of making *Pao Doce*. The following recipe produces a particularly light, delicate bread, almost cakelike.

Pao Doce

(Portuguese Sweet Bread)

1 cup milk, scalded
½ cup shortening
½ cup butter
2 pkgs. yeast
1 cup lukewarm water
8½ cups sifted flour
2½ cups sugar

2½ tsp. salt
1 tsp. lemon extract
8 small or 7 large eggs
Dark raisins (optional)
Caraway seeds (optional)
1 egg for glaze

Add shortening and butter to scalded milk. Set aside to cool. Dissolve yeast in 1 cup warm water and add to milk.

Sift flour, sugar, and salt into a large mixing bowl. Stir in yeast-milk mixture, add lemon extract and eggs, one at a time, beating well after each addition. This makes a very soft dough that cannot be kneaded in the usual manner. Knead as follows: Dip hands into dough and lift up into air and let fall back into bowl repeatedly for about 20 minutes until dough tends to form a sponge and not flatten out like a batter. It should also develop a gloss. With floured hands, continue to knead 30 minutes, until dough begins to pull away from bowl.

Cover with a wet towel and put in warm place to rise until double (about two hours). Punch down dough, shaping into circular tube pans. Add raisins or caraway seeds if desired. The dough will not only double before baking, it will double once more in baking, so be careful not to overfill pans. Cover pans with wet cloth and let rise once more until double. Brush with beaten egg. Bake for 30 to 60 minutes (depending on size of loaves), in oven preheated to 350° F.

This should make 2 rings of bread in an 8½-inch torte pan with tube or one angel-food tube pan and one small loaf.

CHAPTER XIV

Chanukah or Hannukah, the Jewish "Festival of Lights"

"My daughter said the rabbi had an interesting discussion this morning. He told the group there are three important holidays at this time of year—secular Christmas, religious Christmas, and Chanukah."
—Conversation with a Jewish mother, 1967

The pattern of American secular Christmas celebrations was so firmly established in the United States by the end of the nineteenth century that immigrants came to identify the ideas of Santa Claus, the Christmas tree, and gift exchange with being "American." Those who did not take part felt painfully and conspicuously different.

The increasing emphasis on children and gifts presented a peculiar dilemma for parents. For most newcomers the solution was to adopt the American Christmas whole and to abandon many of the old ways. Jewish immigrants, however, could not easily accept this compromise. Some families argued that it was harmful for their children to feel different, and introduced the Christmas tree, a little embarrassedly, as a "Chanukah bush," merely a pleasant seasonal ornament with no religious content. For others, Christmas became a time of bitter frustration, of feeling rejected and left out of the most important party of the year, one to which everyone else was invited.

Instinctively, thoughtful Jews turned to a legitimate holy day of their own which fell at approximately the same time of the year. Chanukah, which commemorated a victory of the Maccabees, was a season lasting eight days, with an added advantage that, like Christmas, it was also a Festival of Lights.

The history of the Maccabean War is related in the Apocrypha. In the fourth century B.C., Syria and Egypt began a fight for control of Palestine, until finally the Syrian ruler, Antiochus, won temporary control. Rivalry continued, however, and to prevent subversion at home, he instituted a program of systematic Hellenization, attempting to integrate the Jews, who continued their distinctive manner of life and exasperatingly claimed the land to be rightfully theirs. In 168 B.C. all subjects were ordered to worship the Greek gods. The Jewish Temple was stripped of its magnificent accouterments, and an idol placed in the Holy of Holies.

An aged, conservative Jewish priest named Mattathias, of the Maccabee family, resisted the desecration, and killed a Syrian officer in the struggle. Mattathias and his sons fled and began a kind of guerrilla war that culminated in a succession of singular victories. In 165 B.C. the partisans stormed the Temple hill, drove out the Syrian police garrison, cleansed the sanctuary, relit the Temple fire, and re-established the traditional order of service.

To celebrate their victory, the Maccabees held an eight-day celebration of reconsecration of the Temple, and obtained permission from ecclesiastical authorities to perpetuate it by the lighting of lamps or lights on eight successive days, the only religiously ordained feature of Chanukah.

At the time it originated, Chanukah was essentially the celebration of a successful rebellion against ruling power, and inherently dangerous because of its implied militancy. Perhaps to divert attention from this fact, a lovely legend that accentuated the lighting of the lamps in a ceremony of dedication developed. Scholars believe it may be a Jewish version of the Roman year-end festivals, or that it may have even earlier antecedents.

After the Maccabees cleansed the Temple, it was said, they could find only one small flask of unadulterated oil for relighting the Temple fire. Since it would require a week to prepare new oil, they proceeded anyway, hoping the flame would last the night. Instead, it miraculously burned for eight days, until fresh oil was ready.

For Chanukah, eight candles are placed in a Menorah or candelabrum. Usually, one is lighted on the first night, and an additional one on each successive night, the flames being lit from right to left by a ninth candle or *shammas*, which is often placed in an additional branch of the candelabrum. Some ancient authorities, however, insist that all eight candles should burn each night.

Lighting of the candles is accompanied by an appropriate blessing and a brief statement that the ceremony commemorates God's "miracles, deliverance, deeds of power and acts of salvation at this season," and that the lights are symbolic, not utilitarian.

In America, and wherever Christianity is dominant, the Christmas influence has led to increasing secularization of Chanukah in the form of gifts and parties. In New York City it is a time for great fund-raising events for Israel. The giving of gifts began in relatively recent times with "Chanukah gelt," a gold coin given children on the first night of the festival. Gradually, presents increased in number and value. Now, gifts are given each night, a practice which succeeds in making many Christian children as discontented as Jewish youngsters once were.

A popular pastime at Chanukah parties is a form of an ancient gambling game, the spinning of a four-sided top called a *trendel* or *draidel*. Playing it is justified by the admonition that there should be no "use" made of the Chanukah candles, that is, no work should be done by their light. The top has letters on each of the four sides, indicating winnings and losses. In a piquant example of pagan custom made kosher, the letters have been given new Hebrew words having nothing to do with the game of chance. Instead, it is said that they stand for the words, "A great miracle occurred there," referring to the ever-burning oil.

In the United States many schools honor Chanukah along with Christmas, and there has been a growing trend toward joint Christmas-Chanukah celebrations for adults. Some scholars believe that the dates for both Christmas and Chanukah were based on the same pagan holiday; but for those celebrating Christ's birthday there is an even more appropriate reason for the combination: The Maccabean victory saved the Jewish faith from oblivion a century and a half before the birth of Jesus. The Feast of the Nativity, therefore, can be said to be directly dependent upon it.

For the first night of Chanukah, *latkes* or potato pancakes are traditional. According to legend, Jewish Maccabean wives prepared *latkes* behind the battle line as the quickest possible nourishment for their fighting men. The Maccabean *latkes* would have been quite different from those made from the following recipe because potatoes were not introduced to Palestine until after the discovery of America.

Latkes are served with a variety of garnishes—applesauce, dried-apricot purée, or powdered sugar, with cream cheese or sour cream.

Potato Latkes

Peel 6 large potatoes and soak in cold water several hours. Grate and drain off excess juice. Measure the pulp and for each 2 cups add:

2 well-beaten eggs	*Pinch of pepper*
1 tablespoon flour	*1 tablespoon onion juice*
½ teaspoon salt	*or ½ grated onion (optional)*

Vegetable oil or chicken fat for frying

Mix all ingredients except oil together and beat well. Heat oil or fat in a skillet and drop in batter by tablespoonfuls. Fry to deep brown on each side. Serve hot with chosen garnish.

Yield: 30 or more large pancakes

Jewish folkways are by and large general folk customs which the Jews found wherever they lived and ingeniously adapted to their own traditional teachings. The same is true of food. Jews have added to their cuisine specialties from every country where they have lived, so that it is multifarious as a whole.

In America, the Chanukah feast, held either on the first night or for the Chanukah Sabbath Eve, tends to be very much like the Christmas feast, featuring goose, duck, chicken, or turkey.

Cookies, breads, and cake are also popular for the holidays, and may well include the following typically "American" fruit cake. Since it is so light, it is delicious for any time of year, and perfect for weddings.

White Fruit Cake

½ cup white raisins
½ cup grape or apple juice, or brandy or sherry
1½ cups flour, sifted
½ teaspoon soda
⅛ teaspoon salt
1¾ cups sifted confectioner's sugar
⅔ cup soft butter
6 egg whites

2 tablespoons lemon juice
½ teaspoon vanilla extract
⅔ cup candied cherries, red and green
½ cup candied pineapple, cut in chunks
⅓ cup blanched pistachio nuts
¼ cup blanched, slivered almonds
¼ cup flour

Glaze (optional)

3 tablespoons water
6 tablespoons white corn syrup

Candied fruit and whole nuts

Soak white raisins overnight or longer in fruit juice or liquor. When ready to make cake, drain and discard liquid.

Turn oven to 325° F.

Sift together 1½ cups flour, soda, salt, and sugar. Cream in butter, then add egg whites one at a time, beating vigorously after each addition. Add lemon juice and vanilla.

Dredge fruits and nuts in cup of flour, then fold into cake mixture. Pour into lined tube or large loaf pan. Bake 40 minutes, or until just done (very lightly browned only).

Combine water and corn syrup and heat to boiling. Cool until warm. Spoon over cold fruit cake. Decorate as desired by placing candied fruit and nuts on while syrup is sticky. This glaze is ideal for any fruit cake and will help to keep it moist.

The cake itself needs no aging, but keeps very well.

CHAPTER XV

A New American Christmas Tradition Evolves

DECORATIVE CHRISTMAS COOKING, OLD AND NEW

Until sometime this century the Pennsylvania Dutch decorated Christmas trees almost entirely with edible ornaments, and it was customary to "eat the tree" throughout the Christmas season, so that it was virtually dismantled by Twelfth Night. In Europe, the custom still continues.

American women began to give up decorating cookies elaborately because it did not seem worthwhile to spend a great deal of time working on something soon to vanish. However, a nationwide revival of interest in decorative baking was sparked in the winter of 1965–66 by a show, "The Baker's Art," sponsored by the Museum of Contemporary Crafts in New York City, and shown later in many other cities.

Especially exciting were creations from the Hussian School of Art in Philadelphia. These can be traced directly back to

242

German tradition through one of the teachers, Mae Gerhard, who learned the pleasure of elaborate Christmas baking from her Pennsylvania Dutch mother. Recently Miss Gerhard created a fantastically beautiful gingerbread crèche of more than two dozen pieces varying in height from five to six inches, all trimmed in brilliant Byzantine colors. One gingerbread recipe she uses is the following. She says that the secret of obtaining particularly effective colors is to make a very dark dough by using dark brown sugar. Some figures from her crèche are pictured in plate 8.

Mae Gerhard's Gingerbread Angels

½ cup shortening	1 teaspoon soda
½ cup brown sugar,	1 teaspoon ginger
firmly packed	2 teaspoons cinnamon
½ cup molasses	½ cup buttermilk
3½ cups flour, sifted	½ teaspoon vinegar
½ teaspoon salt	

Cream together shortening, sugar, and molasses. Sift together flour, salt, soda, and spices. Blend into first mixture alternately with buttermilk and vinegar. Chill thoroughly. For freeform designs, draw patterns and cut from waxed paper. Turn oven 350° to 375° F. Roll dough out to about ¼" thickness. Lay waxed paper patterns on dough and cut around them with sharp knife. Holding pattern with fingers, transfer dough to greased baking sheet. The dough will cling to the waxed paper, making the transfer quite easy. Lift pattern from dough. Bake 10 to 15 minutes. Cool. Best results in frostings can be obtained with decorator icing (p. 156).

This dough can be used in molds, but reduce shortening to ¼ cup; additional flour may be necessary to obtain firm dough. To use wooden mold, roll dough out to ¼-inch thickness, or more if mold is cut very deeply. Lay dough on mold and press firmly into design with fingers, making sure no outline is overlooked. Trim off excess dough. Lift dough from mold carefully and transfer to greased baking sheet. With sharp knife cut away open spaces and any excess dough.

For a darker dough, substitute dark brown sugar and black-strap molasses.

CHRISTMAS COOKIE TREE

Wooden-frame Christmas trees hung with enticing home-made cookies have become increasingly common in American homes. Sold in dismantled pieces, they can be assembled, then taken down after use for easy storage. They stem from Sweden's *pepparkakor* trees, similar to the old German pyramid tree. Wooden rods are inserted horizontally through a central vertical pole set on a platform of wood.

Cookies of various shapes and sizes are hung from the rods by colored twine or yarn. To be completely authentic, dark cookies with fancy cutouts and decorations of pale icing would be used, but any very simple sugar-type cookies may be substituted. Also, as in Sweden, a cluster of wheat may be tied to the top with a ribbon and lady apples or other small red apples thrust on the ends of each branch rod. A contemporary *pepparkakor* tree, topped with the traditional sheaf of wheat as a true Swedish tree would be, is pictured in plate 10.

In Eugene, Oregon, Mrs. Leopold Pospisil has perpetuated an old Czech tradition of preparing edible Christmas-tree ornaments from meringue. Her creations—pigs, ducklings, snow-men, Santas, lambs, Madonnas, Christmas bells, and so on—require some artistic skill. However, anyone with the patience to experiment can master the basic technique and use it to create delightful freeform ornaments of spidery swirls vaguely resembling snowflakes, icicles, wreaths, and whatever comes to mind. Vegetable dyes offer a wondrous range of colors.

Making meringue ornaments is an excellent way to use up leftover egg whites. Stored in an airtight container in the refrigerator for a month, egg whites may still be converted to decorations, or they can be frozen and thawed for use. Leftover decorator icing made from egg white may also be converted to ornament meringue, by adding sufficient confectioner's sugar to make the stiff paste required. Decorator icing may be kept overnight at room temperature if well covered, and additional sugar may be added the following day. The *Redbook* test kitchen experimented with Mrs. Pospisil's recipe, and they found that a softer meringue, using approximately one cup of confectioner's sugar per egg white gave very satisfactory results in a 250° F. oven.

CZECHOSLOVAKIAN BAKED MERINGUED DECORATIONS

1 egg white (at room temperature)	*Food coloring (vegetable)*
2 to 3 cups sifted confectioner's sugar	*Waxed-paper cornucopias (see directions)*

Heavy green string

Draw designs actual size and place near working area as a guide and for comparison with actual figure of meringue.

Beat egg white until stiff, then slowly add 1½ cups sugar, beating constantly. When quite smooth, remove from beater; stir in additional sugar very carefully, a little at a time, until the mixture is thick and heavy, with a texture something like cookie dough. Take a small portion to work with and put in smaller container. Cover remaining meringue so that no air can get to it. Stir down from time to time to prevent hardening or sugaring. This meringue will not keep overnight.

To work with meringue use waxed-paper funnels or cornucopias. To make: Fold a paper square into a triangle; the diagonal will be the pointed end of funnel. Take one end of diagonal, wind it firmly around center, keeping point sharp. Fill no more than ⅔ full, then fold one top side and fold the other side over it to close top and prevent meringue coming out. To use, grasp top edges with fingers, press icing down to funnel. Cut off bottom point with sharp scissors to allow flow of icing. For small figures, fine detail, cut only a small opening. For fat bodies of chicks, et cetera, opening can be large. Work cornucopia funnel from time to time with the free hand to soften meringue and force it to the bottom.

Put sheets of waxed paper on table or counter. Mix colors one at a time and keep any unused portion completely covered. Apply blobs of colored meringue to waxed paper in shape desired, making main body first. Then add details—facial features, neckties, buttons, et cetera—one color at a time. With a toothpick insert twine or other string in top of figure. Done properly, this will bake into it and allow the ornament to be hung on the tree.

Set figures aside to dry completely for five hours or longer, depending on humidity. If not completely dry, decorations will swell and bubble in baking.

Carefully transfer dried meringues to well-greased tins. (Do not use silicone-treated tins—they get too hot.) Preheat oven to low heat, then place tins in top of oven. Watch carefully after 15 minutes; if figures begin to change color, remove immediately. Perfectly executed, whites will be virginal, colors elsewhere pure and bright. Mrs. Pospisil bakes hers for about ½ hour, but oven heats vary, so they must be carefully watched.

The art of meringue decorations has been passed on from generation to generation by word of mouth and demonstration. So far as we know, no one has ever written instructions. We have tried to make the directions clear, but suggest experimentation.

Some of the breads prepared for European Christmas Eve feasts have always been inedible, playing a symbolic role to foster fertility in the soil and honor the spirits of the dead. "The Baker's Art" show fostered new developments with such bread, which is spoken of as "baker's clay." The variety this medium allows in artistic expression can be seen in plates 17 and 18.

From inedible dough has evolved still another art form which utilizes uncooked dough or "clay" mixtures of flour and water. In some instances the dough is worked like papier-maché. The artist forms the object by hand, decorates it according to fancy, then allows it to dry.

In yet another variation on this theme, one artist in Oregon works with dough almost as with paint, squirting it from a tube. (His method seems to be somewhat similar to that of making meringue Christmas-tree decorations, previously described, and it may be there is a direct influence.) His creations, which run to the snowflake-like ornament variety, are fired.

"I find it all very exciting," comments a Eugene, Oregon, gallery owner whose 1967 show "The Nativity" last winter featured works from both cooked and uncooked dough. One entry was an elaborate, very lifelike crèche of gingerbread dough. "It is appropriate and Christmasy, yet it gets away from the commercialization we all deplore."

Working with Inedible Dough, or Baker's Clay

Even a child can make simple sculptures with baker's clay. The possibilities would seem to be unlimited, depending only on imagination, ingenuity, and willingness to experiment. In Philadelphia, Edward Huber and Bill Crawford have built up a collection of "instruments" for cutting out odd sizes and shapes of dough, and for pricking designs into it. Odd-shaped bottle tops are carefully saved; in addition to obvious tools for scratching the dough surface—awls, belt buckles, forks, screwdrivers—they look constantly for unusual configurations and graduated sizes of the same design-motif. On one sun face, for instance, Crawford used the writing end of a ball-point pen to prick the tiny holes, and the other end to make larger ones.

The dough is baked as long as necessary to attain the right shade of cream or brown. The artists have found that it is better to apply color after baking and cooling. They use Dr. Martin's artist's dyes obtainable from art-supply shops. Vegetable dyes do not work well for this type of dough; heat changes them radically, although experimentation with vegetable dyes might result in exotic effects, they indicate.

The important thing, they say, is "You have to play with the dough a lot until you find what it will do." Working both from sketches and from mental images, their animal creations tend to be stubby-legged creatures like rhinos because spindly-legged creations are more difficult to make satisfactorily. To achieve difference in tones of light and dark, daub dough with water while baking. The watered parts will remain light. If a design is to be in a light patch of dough, wait until the damp dries, then attack it.

Just as no two cooks agree on the exact same ingredients for special recipes, so these artists do not agree on their recipe! One prefers a ratio of 3 to 1 for flour, the other of 4 to 1. New experimenters may achieve a still different proportion.

Inedible Dough or Baker's Clay

1 cup uniodized salt   *3 to 4 cups flour (unsifted)*
1¼ to 1½ cups water

Inexpensive salt is best for baker's clay—"The cheaper, the better," say the artists.

Combine ingredients in a bowl, working and kneading well with hands until a malleable dough is obtained. Knead dough as for regular bread, until it has a "fleshy" quality. Add more water if needed, but do so very gingerly. Dough sculpture may be formed directly on a well-greased cookie tin, or on a board from which it can be transferred. (The grease makes it much easier to slide baked sculpture off tin.) Keep hands well floured while working with dough sculpture. To build up sculpture where depth or layer effect is required, coat bottom layer with water and add another to it. The water acts as glue. If any section is thin and might break, reinforce it with a twine outline between layers of dough. If sculpture is to be hung, be sure to leave a hole for later insertion of twine. Place cookie tin

248

on a high rack in a slow oven. Huber and Crawford bake their creations 2–4 hours, depending on shade of darkness desired. The resulting bread, they say, "Is almost as hard as a rock—very difficult to damage." If a piece should break off, it can be repaired with Elmer's glue. It will then be stronger than ever.

After they cool, sculptures can be touched up with color. A piece will seldom bake uniformly, even with the most loving attention—that is, it will vary from light to very dark—so it will probably be necessary to even up browned or burned spots. For additional color, earth tones are most effective.

Bill Crawford once experimented with cookie dough sculpture, using pieces colored with vegetable dye. They came out fine, he said, but he finds bread dough a much more interesting medium.

Acknowledgments

This book could never have been written without the interest and assistance of a great number of people and organizations. In particular, I am grateful for the encouragement and editorial assistance of the man who became my husband, Jacob Kainen. Invaluable aid was also offered by Thyrssa Anderson, Grace W. Buscher and the Coco Palm Resort Hotel, Henry P. Chapman, Colonial Williamsburg, Anna Maria Gacek, Dzidra Damerel, Josephine J. Dauzvardis, Mrs. William D. Elkins, Mae Gerhard and members of the Hussian School of Art, Frances Griffin and Old Salem, Inc., John Hawkins, Mrs. Sten Johanson, Nina Kuydych, Paul Kendall and Pan American World Airways, Mrs. Francis Knouss, Vernon Nelson and the Central Moravian Church of Bethlehem, Frederick J. Ashley and the Museum of Science and Industry in Chicago, Betty B. Ross, James Rouse, Jr., and the Jamestown Foundation, and Paul J. Taylor.

Additional Christmas recipes were given by Maria Bilecky, Mrs. Beurfod Cole, the Department of Tourism of the Commonwealth of Puerto Rico, Sonja Dragamanovic, Hedy Giusti-Lanham, Mrs. Santiago, Dorothy F. Hutcheson and the Rice Council, Mrs. Daniel Inouye, Mrs. Ragnor Johnson, Ruth C. Lawler, Les Vingt Quatre Club, Mrs. Lee Loevinger, Doris Luhrs, Aphrodite Pappas, Mrs. Cornelius J. Rassa, Dr. Michael Semanitzky, Mrs. Katherine Thiberg and Santa Claus Land in Santa Claus, Indiana, and Mary Thompson and the Public Service Company of New Mexico.

In addition, the following contributed valuable information regarding Christmas customs and food: Phyllis A. Anderson and the *New Glarus Post*, Dean Thomas J. Arceneaus, Prelacy

251

of the Armenian Apostolic Church of America, Gourgen Assaturian, Margaret Benston and the Eugene *Register Guard*, the Bethlehem Living Nativity in Kentucky, the Bethlehem Star Parade Association in Van Nuys, James F. Bezou, Bonnie Borelli and the Berks County Pennsylvania Dutch Association, Phil A. Brady and the Greater New Orleans Tourist and Convention Committee, Anita Brenner and *Mexico This Month*, Corinne Cockburn, the Rev. Spyridon Coutos, the Dole Company, Bertha P. Dutton and the Museum of Navaho Ceremonial Art in Santa Fe, Vaughn Hammond, James J. Heslin and the New York Historical Society, Jalmar Johnson, Deacon H. Kasparian, Scoop Kennedy, Joseph Krupinski and the New York Convention and Visitors Bureau, the Maine Historical Society, Brigadier Andrew S. Miller of the Salvation Army, Mike Miller, the New Mexico Department of Development, Jose Ocasio and the Puerto Rican Community Development Project of New York City, the Ogema Lions Club, Padua Hills Theatre, Mrs. Jack S. Peterson and the San Antonio Conservation Society, the Pineapple Growers Association of Hawaii, the Polish National Alliance of Brooklyn, Miss L. M. Prince and the Bangor Historical Society, Santa's Workshop, Omar Sawyer, Terrebonne Parish Library, Marion R. B. Sweet, Robert G. Wheeler and Sleepy Hollow Restorations, the Texas Institute of Cultures, the Torrington Park and Recreation Commission, Gertrude Carraway and the Tryon Palace Restoration, A. M. Villareal, Frank Zapolis, Joseph M. Zurawski and the Polish Museum of America, and many Chambers of Commerce, especially those of Taos, New Mexico; San Antonio, Texas; Rockford, Illinois; Minneapolis, Minnesota; and El Paso, Texas.

The Embassies of Austria, Belgium, Bulgaria, Denmark, Great Britain, Czechoslovakia, Denmark, Ireland, Italy, Finland, France, Germany, Greece, The Netherlands, Norway, The Philippines, Poland, Spain, Sweden, and Switzerland furnished important background materials. The National Travel Offices and Information Services of Austria, Denmark, Germany, Ireland, Italy, The Netherlands, and Scandinavia were also helpful, as was the Instituto Italiano di Cultura.

General Index

Recipe Index